UNDER THE WILD SKIES
An Anthology of Modern Malayalam Short Stories

UNDER THE WILD SKIES
An Anthology of Modern Malayalam Short Stories

Edited with an introduction by
K. SATCHIDANANDAN

NATIONAL BOOK TRUST, INDIA

Cover photograph: Colour Library International Ltd.

The stories included in the anthology are reprinted with the permission of the copyright holders.

ISBN 81-237-2198-6

First Edition 1997
First Reprint 2002 (*Saka* 1923)
© K. Satchidanandan, 1997
Rs 65.00
Published by the Director, National Book Trust, India
A-5, Green Park, New Delhi - 110 016

*Dedicated to the memory of
Vaikom Mohammed Basheer
(1908-1994)
The Master Craftsman*

CONTENTS

Introduction : A Century of
   Malayalam Short Story   1

THE PIONEERS

The World-Renowned Nose	Vaikom Mohammed Basheer	17
In the Floods	Thakazhi Sivasankara Pillai	25
The Whispering Plough	Ponkunnam Varkey	31
Rooms for Rent	Uroob	41
Cool Drink	P. Kesavadev	56
Poovanpazham	Karoor Nilakanta Pillai	61
Night Queen	S.K. Pottekatt	69
A Good Omen	Kovilan	75

THE MODERNISERS

The Death of Makhan Singh	T. Padmanabhan	85
Little Earthquakes	M.T. Vasudevan Nair	98
The Court of King George the Sixth	M.P. Narayana Pillai	116
The Rocks	O.V. Vijayan	126
The Blue Eclipse	Kakkanadan	132
Delhi, 1981	M. Mukundan	138
The Infantry Arrives	Punathil Kunhabdulla	143
The Messenger	Sethu	150
Memory	P. Padmarajan	158
A Christmas Story	Zachariah	168

THE PARALLEL STREAM

The Sixth Finger	Anand	175
The Razor's Edge	C.V. Sriraman	186
Akbar's Upanishad	Pattathuvila Karunakaran	195
Broken Glasses	M. Sukumaran	203
Before the Cock Crew	N.P. Mohammad	209

Unichiram Veettil Unniatha Had Five Brave Sons	U.A. Khader	218
The Colonel	V.K.N.	229

THE SECOND TRADITION

Come Back	Lalitambika Antarjanam	235
Trees for Shade	K. Saraswati Amma	244
Marine Drive	Madhavikkutty (Kamala Das)	257
Inside Every Woman Writer	Sarah Joseph	265
Serpents of the Holy Mound	Manasi	271
Chamundi's Pit	P. Vatsala	283
The Rock	Gracy	288

BEYOND MODERNISM

Guadalajara : A Thottekkadan Memoir	K.P. Nirmal Kumar	295
The Twelfth Hour	V.P. Sivakumar	303
Blue Pencil	N.S. Madhavan	311
We, the Sons	C.V. Balakrishnan	317
The Postman of Kalleri	V.R. Sudheesh	322
A Path in the Moonshine	N. Prabhakaran	329
The Cry of the Earth	P. Surendran	335
The Psychology of Lean Men and Women	Methil Radhakrishnan	340

Notes on Authors   348

INTRODUCTION
A Century of Malayalam Short Story

The Malayalam short story celebrated its centenary in 1991. During these hundred years of its dynamic and even turbulent existence, it has passed through several phases in terms of theme and idiom, structure and ideology; a history in which periods of gradual evolution alternate with periods of rupture, and syntheses are preceded by major aesthetic shifts and philosophic revolts.

Like other Indian languages Malayalam too has had a long tradition of oral narration before the modern short story came into being. Most of them were imaginative retellings of tales from Indian mythology and epics or legends from Kerala's own life and history, first recorded by Kottarattil Sankunni in his *Aitihyamala* (A Garland of Legends). The first printed stories in Malayalam were translations of stories from English or parables from the Holy Bible, both of a moralising kind. The Malayalam text books of the second half of the nineteenth century designed didactic tales from *Aesop's Fables*, *Panchatantra* or the Old and New Testaments of the Bible. All these helped the maturing of Malayalam prose that soon became a perfect tool for the realistic narration of contemporary life and for imaginative self-expression, bringing into being the modern institution of the 'author'.

The first 'short story' proper in Malayalam, most scholars believe, is *Vasanavikriti* (The Mischief of Instinct) published in the *Vidyavinodini* monthly in 1891. A dramatic first person narrative, the story lays bare the tensions and regrets of a man who has just come out of jail after serving a long term of imprisonment and has made up his mind to go to Benares to expiate his sin. *Vasanavikriti* declares its identity as a short story through its close-knit narrative structure and the psychological drama it plays out. The story was published anonymously; but most researchers agree that it was authored by Vengayil Kunhiraman Nayanar who used to assist C.P. Achyuta Menon in editing *Vidyavinodini*.

It is possible on the basis of major shifts in sensibility to divide the history and the genre in Malayalam into five phases, admittedly with the risk of some simplification, since each aesthetic transition in the discourse is the product of an overdetermined conjuncture, and since several levels of sensibility co-exist and fight for hegemony at each moment of literary evolution.

The first phase during which the short story as a genre began to make its presence felt in Malayalam may be said to have lasted for four decades, from 1891 to 1930. The writers of these stories thought of storytelling as no more than a pastime: they never considered it a proper medium for the criticism of life. The writers belonged to the same leisured class to which their readers belonged. The stories were wordy and descriptive; the structure was one-dimensional and the narration, direct. The stories dealt with hunting, romance or recent history. There were also detective stories after the model of Sherlock Holmes tales. Rarely the stories also took up for criticism social evils like drinking, love of gold, and child marriage as in the works of Moorkoth Kumaran. Love portrayed in these stories was always idealised, platonic. Some of them were so eventful that they could easily have evolved into novels while others, like those of K.Sukumaran were humorous stories almost verging on the ribald. Entertainment was the chief if not the sole aim of short-story writing in this early phase.

But the scenario changed radically towards the end of the 1920s when Kerala was passing through a social renaissance in the fullest sense of the term. Kerala's public sphere began to be formed as part of this Renaissance that began with a self-criticism of the feudal caste society. In its early stages the social reformers were constrained to operate within the structures of caste in order to abolish sub-castes, purge the caste of evil and outmoded beliefs and practices and initiate their people into modern knowledge and useful crafts. All castes were involved in this process of auto-critique and re-orientation though the chief thrust—that really shook the whole society up from its complacency and stupor by a shock treatment—was subaltern since only the lower castes were capable of dreaming of a casteless society which naturally meant depriving the upper castes of their special privileges. The success of the Sree Narayana Movement that spearheaded the restructuring of the society lay in its subtle reversal of the significance of the oppressors' legitimating discourse through a secular reading of their sacred texts and a subversive use of their signs, symbols and images: a typical Indian reformist strategy employed by Vivekananda and Gandhi in their broader struggles against orthodoxy including the caste system itself. The second stage of the Renaissance that came with the formation of the Congress with its total disavowal of colonialism produced the first line of truly secular intellectuals in Kerala while the third stage, a natural outgrowth of the earlier phases, consisted of a reorientation of the Renaissance towards a resurgence of the marginalised brought together on the basis of class. Communism in Kerala, unlike in most other parts of the world, is our indigenous democratic phenomenon rooted in Kerala's social reform and nationalist movements of the earlier decades, though its identification with the backward castes and its democratic complexion are yet to be adequately theorised. What concerns us here, however, is the impact that the three-tier movement had on literature. Literature had established itself as a social sub-system in Kerala by the sixteenth century A.D., but it began to be recognised and assessed as literature only when Kerala's public sphere began to be formed as part of this general democratic movement that we have already qualified as Kerala's Renaissance. The translation of classics from Sanskrit and English providing a norm for the critical appreciation of literature and the original composition of long verse narratives, epics, novels, short stories and essays led to the establishment of the 'aesthetic' as a specific realm of life and culture and transformed literature from the sacral to the secular. The codification of grammar helped the growth of a prose style. Literary criticism consolidated the specificity of the 'aesthetic' while literary journals like *Vidyavinodini, Kesari, Kerala Patrika, Swadesabhimani, Bhashaposhini* and *Mangalodayam* and organisations like 'Sahitya Parishad' and 'Bhashaposhini Sabha' provided ample scope for expression and dialogue. The spread of modern education and printing technology further activated the growth and expansion of the public sphere. Literature was released from its ritual use with the undermining of traditional word pictures by the basic ideology of fair exchange.

The short story—along with the novel—became the principal medium for the expression of the new social awakening spurred on by the reform, anti-feudal and anti-colonial movements. The first products of the reform movement were a bit too propagandistic and suffered from an antinomy of emotion and idiom as is the case with the stories of M.R.B., V.T Bhattatirippad, M. Bhavatratan Nambudiri and others. It was the great scholar-critic Kesari Balakrishna Pillai who persuaded fiction-writers to handle contemporary reality with a positive vision and to thematize the darker areas of life considered taboo by conservative imagination. Life in the raw, with its basic intincts of hunger and lust, was perceived to be the primary source of creative literature. Kesari translated European short stories of different themes, forms and narrative techniques by authors as varied as Chekhov, Pirandello, Maupassant, Isaac Babel, Kafka and D'Annunzio besides a host of East European, Spanish, Norwegian, Hebrew and Dutch authors. Through his elaborate introductions to books and articles published in his journal *Kesari* and other literary magazines, Kesari also acquainted the writers and readers of Kerala with the various trends and movements in European literature. He also published a study of genres and forms titled *Roopamanjari* besides directly influencing writers through his comments as an editor. M.P. Paul, another influential critic, also published a book on the short story *Khandakathaprastanam* (later the title was changed to *Cherukathaprastanam*) in 1932 that acknowledges Kesari's contribution to the growth of the Malayalam short story. The progressive literary movement—first known as *Jeevatsahitya* and later as *Purogamanasahitya*—was another major influence that shaped the short story in this period into a powerful medium of social criticism. The impact of the movement on fiction was far greater than its impact on poetry in Malayalam; the short stories of the '30s were 'pages torn from life with blood on their tips' to imitate a phrase that M.P. Paul used to qualify Basheer's early novel, *Balyakalasakhi* (Childhood Friend).

The pioneers of this new age in fiction were Thakazhi Sivasankara Pillai, Vaikom Mohammad Basheer, S. K. Pottekkat, P. Kesava Dev and Ponkunnam Varkey. Thakazhi is a keen observer of social transformation, acutely aware of its objective as well as subjective implications. His psychological insights are as strong as his ideological convictions. He is acutely aware of problems like poverty and unemployment that maraud the underprivileged while equally conscious of the basic libidinal drive that is as central as hunger to human existence. This synthesis of Marxist social analysis and Freudian psychoanalysis was characteristic of the early progressive literature in Malayalam that shocked conservative sensibilities through its uninhibited portrayal of life with its basic impulses. Kesava Dev was a social realist fired, however, by romantic idealism like most communists of the period. If Thakazhi was essentially the narrator of the tales of the peasants, Kesava Dev turned to the workers, and the jobseekers. His dramatic stories constantly implied the urgent need for a radical restructuring of the social order. Ponkunnam Varkey is a rebel and a heretic, who continues to fight the Church that he finds to be in a macabre alliance with feudal and capitalist forces. It was not easy to battle against orthodoxy and ostracism, and meet opposition from the leaders of his own community of Christians in Central Tranvancore. But the victims of economic and religious oppression celebrated him as their champion.

S.K. Pottekkat who was committed to leftist ideology in his personal life was seldom political in his world of action. He was an irrepressible globetrotter and a great writer of travelogues; he infused his stories too with something of his experience, his encounters with men and women from every part of the world. He had an eye for the odd and the different in character and a penchant for the romantic mode in vision and the lyrical mode in idiom. Unforgettably distinct characters, humorous dialogues, strange situations and a reassuring optimism that asserts the ultimate unity of the human species : all these made his stories of love and travel particularly enchanting and readable. Vaikom Mohammed Basheer was a great stylist. All his stories have an undercurrent of gentle humour that springs from a recognition of the paradoxes of life; he combines a cartoonist's eye with a philosopher's vision in portraying his characters in semi-fictional narratives. Basheer does not strain after effects; his idiom is easy, natural and deceptively simple. He is an optimist, and his optimism comes not from an evasion of reality but from a confident confrontation with life and a robust acceptance of tragedy. Basheer was in fact a modernist who never knew he was one. He broke new grounds quite unselfconsciously just by narrating his varied experiences within and outside the borders of Kerala. He understood and sympathised with the whole of suffering humanity; his heaven was open even to cheats and villains. Though he came from a generation that worshipped rigid ideologies and arid experiences, he picked up his tales from the throbbing warmth of life's poetry. It is difficult to pin Basheer down to a specific period since his stories talk to all generations of readers.

The forties of this century witnessed the emergence of some significant new voices. Karoor Neelakanta Pillai was the spokesman of the lower middle class. His stories about the day-to-day struggles of low-paid schoolteachers have attracted special attention for their poignancy as also for their craftsmanship. P.C. Kuttikrishnan (pseudonym, 'Uroob') was a humanist by conviction; he shared Basheer's faith in man and life. A rustic sense of humour, poetic delineation of scenes and events, and taut narration make his stories lively pieces of admirable art. Joseph Mundasseri, the literary critic, M. Govindan, the poet and editor, Ponjikkara Rafi, Nagavalli R.S. Kurup, Vettoor Raman Nair, Pullimana Parameswaran Pillai, I.K.K.M, Tatapuram Sukumaran, B. Madhava Menon and Vaikom Chandrasekharan Nair were also among the new practitioners of short fiction. T.K.C. Vadutala specialised in stories about the Dalits, inspired by the Communist ideal, and wrote stories with sincere ideological commitment, mostly about peasants, workers and lower-middle-class families. Malayattoor Ramakrishnan, E.M. Kovoor, N.P. Chellappan Nair, M.N.Govindan Nair and P.K.Rajarajavarma wrote stories in a lighter vein that carried on the tradition of the first-generation writers while also improving on it.

During this phase, the short story ceased to be the mere entertainer that it had been during the years of its emergence as a genre. It dealt with primary instincts like hunger and lust and with man's ruthless struggle for survival. It placed man in concrete social contexts that lent credibility to its characters and boldly took up political, economic and moral questions impelled by ideals of social justice. It was realistic in narration and utopian in its vision of a fuller life and a more egalitarian community. It also began to show a new awareness of form. Unlike the earlier stories which were crammed with events enough to make a novel, here it began to concentrate on a single episode that illuminated a whole life, a whole society. The omniscient author still held sway; many tales were first person narratives or were narrated by one of the characters, often the protagonist himself/herself. Time was mostly linear, and the logic of events chronological in spite of reveries and flashbacks. Language was mostly native and strong; dialects were often used to denote specific regions and communities.

II

The influence of the Progressive Movement began to wane by the middle of the century. The movement became divided chiefly due to the narrow sectarian and dogmatic attitude upheld by some of its leaders who, in the typical Zhadanovist fashion, insisted on literature serving the changing strategic interests of the communist organisation. Most of the writers who believed, in spite of their commitment to social justice, in the relative autonomy of literature naturally refused to fall in line. They preferred to follow the models set by Uroob and Basheer rather than those who dwelt on the surface of reality: their reading of Henry James, Joyce, Virginia Woolf and the more introspective writers of Europe like Dostoevsky, Thomas Mann and Proust, besides the profound impact of Freud as understood in those days (an understanding that has radically changed in the recent years with the publication of his complete works and the interpretations of Lacan) also pushed them deeper into an exploration of the inner rather than the outer realities of life. Politically, the left was still hegemonic; but literature had declared its autonomy, in poetry as well as in fiction. Kerala has never suffered from that confusion between cultural heroes/heroines and the political ones, characteristic of some other South Indian states. The accent of the short story too changed with the times; writers like T. Padmanabhan and M.T.Vasudevan Nair turned their attention from the outer drama of events to the inner drama of minds. The post-Independence atmosphere of despair and disillusionment also compelled the new writers to concentrate more on the effects than the events, on the subjective dimensions of experience rather than the objective social factors that constitute it. T. Padmanabhan's stories, for example, are the pained reactions of a solitary mind to the erosion of love and tenderness from human relationships. His stories are not eventful nor are they noted for their suspense.

They are subtle, suggestive and lyrical delineations of certain moods, mostly a kind of interior monologue. M.T.Vasudevan Nair explored the inner world of the men and women of his village, a world of discontent, repression, desire for revenge and impotent anger. He was also intrigued by the contradictions of the city and the country, in economic, behavioural and moral terms. Many of his characters are uprooted young men who are forced to come to the infernal city in search of employment or fortune and suffer from disgust, self-contempt, nausea and nostalgia. The angry young men burning with resentment, indignation and despair that often turn them into social outcasts and hated anti-socials, in a way foreshadowed the solitary, disillusioned protagonists of the 'modern' short stories of the sixties and the seventies, in search of an identity. Kovilan, another important writer of the same generation, continues to address himself to the basic questions of existence, man's physical struggle for survival, though he does this much more subtly than the earlier writers. The intensity of his narration makes him a predecessor of the modernists who came after him. N.P. Mohammed's stories, on the other hand, are more intellectual, restrained and experimental. N. Mohanan, C. Radhakrishnan, Thulasi, Vijayan, Sreevaraham Balakrishnan, G. N. Panikker and Jaya Devan also belong to this pre-modernist generation. Nantanar and Parappurath, along with Kovilan, are supposed to have inaugurated a genre of short stories known in Malayalam as *Pattalakkathakal* ('Soldiers' tales') as they often narrated tales from the armed forces—tales of hardship, nostalgia, sexual adventure, brotherhood and humour. The Malayalam short story acquired a pan-Indian character in their stories: this was to become a major characteristic that differentiated Malayalam short stories from those in other languages later as the modernists, most of whom lived outside Kerala, also began to bring in characters from different regions. This is symptomatic, since the people from Kerala are scattered all over the world, compelled as they have been to seek their livelihood elsewhere since the still largely unindustrialised state cannot afford to feed its dense population whose educated members prefer a modest white-collar job to gainful self-employment.

During this phase, the short story became a vehicle for the articulation of individual sorrows, tensions and desires. Society had not disappeared, yet it was pushed into the background; it was only a milieu that produced the varied individuals who dominated the story. The dominant paradigm had changed, shifting the focus from the social to the individual, from the event to the character, from behaviour to the psyche, from action to contemplation. Short stories were no more tales of external events told by an author; they were revelations of an inner drama, often soliloquies, streams of consciousness. The 'story' element now became secondary, what mattered was the exploration into the character, into the mind, even the unconscious. In this sense, the short story may be said to have moved closer to poetry in this phase. Time was no more the historical time but the internal, psychological one. Space too was more internal; the story was enacted in the inner space, the de-populated inner courtyard of the mind.

In the next 'modernist' phase, ontological questions came to the fore. The general theme was the human condition; time and place were unimportant. Sartre, Kafka, Camus, Beckett, Borges and Salinger were the most popular models, to be joined later by Marquez and his ilk. The thematic shift to solitude, alienation and the loss of identity was rather smooth since the introspective fiction of the earlier phase had already investigated these possibilities. Death now became one of the dominant themes of short fiction. This was also a period of format experimentation and structural innovation. The content became secondary, the short story became primarily a linguistic artefact. Naturalism was discarded; fantasy, surrealism, black humour and irony became the chief vehicles of expression. The short story ceased to be the description of an event; it was a metaphor that captured a state of mind. The younger readers of literature, who were disgusted with the useless education they had received and the amoral society they found around, could easily identify themselves with the characters in these stories who were tormented with self-doubt, existential angst and a depressing sense of futility. The modernists became immediately popular among these young, often unemployed, intellectuals who had already befriended the anti-heroes of Western modernism, despite stiff resistance from the progressives who condemned these stories as decadent exercises in futility. Most of the pioneers of modernism, in Malayalam, lived in the metropolises outside the state, like

Bombay and Delhi, that lent authenticity to their nausea and desolation. Kakkanadan, M. P. Narayana Pillai, O. V. Vijayan, Anand, M. Mukundan, Zachariah, Sethu, Punathil Kunhabdulla, V.K.N., all of them wrote under the impact of the cities with their anonymous crowds, labyrinthine streets, squalor and sin. If some like Kakkanadan and O.V Vijayan attempted to develop an oriental modernism that combined a sense of the metaphysical with existential despair, some others like M. P. Narayana Pillai and Paul Zachariah used humour and fantasy to reveal the hollowness at the heart of modern life. Writers like O. V. Vijayan and Anand also shared a moral-political concern as they were disgusted with the macabre real-politik pursued by political parties of various hues. Some of the modernists, like Kakkanadan and Vijayan, who had embraced communism in their early years were sad about the dissensions within the movement, and angry with the Stalinism that they found not only in the Soviet Union but in the daily practice of the Indian communists too. M. Mukundan's anarchy in his early stories also comes from a similar frustration. The social renaissance in Kerala was by now exhausted; the very forces that had led the reforms had compromised their principles for temporary material gains. The caste-reformist organisation had turned rapidly communal; the Congress had become mostly corrupt, the communists had taken to the politics of bargaining and conciliation. No alternative had emerged; there was little to look forward to. Sethu's nightmarish tales, Kunhabdulla's anti-romanticism, Zachariah's cynicism, V. K. N's sarcasm, Anand's intellectual rebellion, Vijayan's sense of the absurd, Narayana Pillai's irrationalism, K. P. Nirmalkumar's sense of solitariness, T. R.'s spiritual questioning and Mukundan's introspection have their roots in the post-Independence social scenario of India, even though some of them are admittedly Western in their sense of form and technique. This saves their stories from being mere specimens of 'cultural pastiche' that some critics find much of modernism to be.

III

The modernism of anguish and despair, however, did not remain unchallenged. The seventies produced its own variety of political modernism, indirectly inspired by the radical political movement that began from Naxalbari. M. Sukumaran's allegories and monologues were powerful, if oblique, critiques of the status-quo that drove home the urgent need for its radical transformation into a more democratic and egalitarian order. Sukumaran, however, was far from being a passive admirer of 'existing socialism'; he was sincerely critical of its totalitarian and imperialist aberrations. Pattattuvila Karunakaran's stories were sharply intellectual; they were either imitating political satires or intense revolutionary debates held with extreme sensitivity to the textures of language. If Sukumaran dealt with the destiny of the proletariat, Karunakaran was more preoccupied with the analysis of the radicalised middle classes. U. P. Jayaraj, P. K. Nanu and C. R. Parameswaran also contributed to this political awareness in the modern short story.

There was, too, a whole section of short-story writers who refused to follow the modernist paradigm and kept up a meaningful relationship with the land and its people, C.V. Sreeraman and Vaisakhan being the chief among them. They were committed writers but not in any narrow ideological sense: they continued to explore the meaning of relationships among real men and women. Vaisakhan dealt with the material and moral dilemmas of the lower-middle class while Sreeraman went to the fundamental passions from lust to devotion; his stories often had a spiritual dimension to them. E. Harikumar, Satrughnan, Gautaman, Mundur Krishnan Kutty, M. R. Manohara Varma and S.V. Venugopan Nair also belong to this group of writers who were never swept off their feet by modernist trends while understanding them. Their stories often lacked the consummate artistry of those of say, O.V. Vijayan and the reflective profundity of say, Anand, and still they too have their place in the history of the genre as tellers of human tales.

Short fiction in Malayalam has a strong tradition of women's writing. Kerala's Renaissance had taken up the women's question earnestly, and laid great emphasis on women's education. A lot of women's magazines were published during those early decades of the century, all of which carried powerful articles and stories of the kind now termed 'feminist'. Lalitambika Antarjanam was a product of this awakening against patriarchy and phallocracy in society and literature. She had her predecessors in early women writers like J. Bhagavati Amma, T. C. Kalyani Amma, M. Saraswatibai, V. Parvati Amma and others who, however, were pushed into oblivion by the 'mainstream' that has always remained the 'male stream' in literature. Lalitambika Antarjanam quarrelled with the inhuman patriarchal customs and practices she found among the Nambudiris that silenced women and pushed them into the darkness of the ante-chambers. K. Saraswati Amma was more open and aggressive in her attack of the dominant male values. The sharpness of her satire came from a tragic sense of the woman's status in society. She had found from her own experience that even education and employment would not emancipate women from their patriarchal prisons; even her refusal to marry was a sign of her protest against male domination. Rajalakshmi, who ended her life at the age of thirty-five, wrote some intensely tragic stories that drew their situations from her immediate surroundings. Madhavikkutty (Kamala Das) explores the innermost recesses of the female psyche in her unihibited portrayals of man-woman and woman-woman relationships. Her stories, while not ignoring the body, also often go beyond the libidinal, attempting a sort of metaphysical transcendence through idealistic love. She is, however, not consciously feminist like Sarah Joseph or Gracy of the generation that succeeded her: Sarah Joseph's highly poetic stories are truly subversive in their questioning of patriarchal myths as well as hegemonic values. Her stories often have a radical political edge, while Gracy is a narrator of Desire, challenging the male world through a robust assertion of female sexuality. P. Vatsala, (the late) P.R. Shyamala, Sarah Thomas, Nalini Bakel, Manasi, Ashita, Shobha Variyar, Mariyamma, Sumitra Varma, B. Saraswaty, K.B. Sreedevi and M.D. Ratnamma are also among the women fiction writers who have written some powerful stories that expose the hypocrisy of most human relationships and observe the society from a subaltern point of view, or probe the solitary world of the woman with her suppressed dreams and longings for freedom.

The present phase of the short story in Malayalam has been called 'anti-modernist' and 'post-modernist' by writers and critics, though both the terms appear inadequate to qualify the range and variety of the genre. Some of the writers often listed together with modernists were in fact quite different from them : Anand, for example while sharing some of the tensions and anxieties of the modernists has been more concerned with the physical realities of existence and the ravages of real history than the metaphysical truths that the modernists appeared to be after. V. P. Sivakumar was another transitional writer who strove, almost alone, to go beyond the established canons of modernism by attempting a mock-serious commentary on contemporary life that mixed quaint humour with a tragic awareness of existence. N. S. Madhavan's deeply committed stories that strive to create a dense new idiom for the short story in Malayalam also move beyond the ideology of high modernism by being intelligent and meaningful analyses of reality. C. V. Balakrishnan, N. Prabhakaran, Thomas Joseph, George Joseph, K. V. R. Sudheesh, P. Surendran, T.V. Kochubava, Babu Kuzhimattom, Akbar Kakkattil, E.V. Sreedharan, Ashtamurthy, U. K. Kumaran, Shihabuddeen, M. Sudhakaran, Asokan Cheruvil, V. S. Anil Kumar, K. Raghunathan, M.A. Rahman, N. P. Hafiz Muhammed and other short-story writers of the present generation who have just published their first or second collections, also refuse to share the themes and attitudes of modernism though they are stylistically indebted to the modernists. They do not subscribe to any fixed ideology; instead, they like to observe life as it is and try to create a new kind of realism, though it is yet too early to judge the nature of their contribution.

The present anthology is no more than an attempt to reflect the various trends that constitute the recent history of the genre in Malayalam through translated specimens from its different phases. It does not claim to be comprehensive, yet, is so designed as to give the readers some insight into the thematic diversity and the formal richness of the short story in the language. I thank the writers and copyright holders for their kind permission to include their stories in the anthology and the translators for having competently handled the task assigned to them. I am grateful to National Book Trust, India, for having made the book possible in the first place, and all those who were involved in the various stages of its production

K. Satchidanandan

THE PIONEERS

THE WORLD-RENOWNED NOSE

Vaikom Mohammed Basheer

It was a stunner of a news. A nose became the subject of heated debates and hair-splitting arguments among intellectuals and philosophers. It soon became universally acclaimed.

I record here the true history of that nose.

The history of the nose begins at the point where our hero entered the twenty-fourth year of his life. I wonder whether there is anything special about the age of twenty-four. One thing is certain anyway: if you would care to look into the annals of history, I am sure you would find something remarkable about the twenty-fourth year of the great men who adorn them. Students of history may resent my reminding them of this most obvious fact.

Our hero was a poor cook, not particularly remarkable for his intelligence. He knew neither to read nor write. His world was his kitchen. He was not bothered by anything that happened outside it. And why should he be? His routine consisted of cooking, eating heartily, taking a good pinch of snuff, sleeping, waking up, and busying himself with his cooking again.

Mookken[1] did not know the names of the days or the months. His wages were paid to his mother when they were due. The old woman bought him his snuff. Thus, he lived in peace and happiness till the twenty-fourth year of his life. And then, hey presto! It happened.

Perhaps there was nothing unusual about it. But Mookken's nose started growing longer all of a sudden, crossing his mouth and going down to his jaw in no time!

The nose went on growing day by day. Within a month, its tip was level with his navel. It was not something you could keep

---

[1] Mookken - The name, not uncommon in Kerala, also means ' one who is all nose (Mookku)'!

under wraps for long. But did it make Mookken uncomfortable in any way? Not a bit. It discharged its functions like any other nose: breathing, taking in snuff, distinguishing one smell from another. Perfectly normal.

Of course, the occurrence of such noses have been recorded in history—rare cases of nasal aberrations. But do you think this was just another of those kinky noses? You bet it wasn't. Our poor hero was dismissed from his job on account of his nose.

But why?

There was no union to fight for his reinstatement. All political parties turned a blind eye to the gross injustice perpetrated on him.

Why did they dismiss Mookken? Nobody who called himself a humanist or a philanthropist asked the question. Where were our masters of culture when Mookken was thrown out into the street?

Poor Mookken!

Mookken knew very well why he was dismissed. The family that employed him did not have a moment's peace after his nose started growing. Large crowds assembled before the house to take a peek at his nose. Photographers, reporters, TV crews . . . it was a roaring sea of humanity that laid siege. The house was burgled several times. There was even an attempt to kidnap a girl from the house.

But as he languished in his humble hut, the poor retrenched cook became convinced that his nose had acquired everlasting fame!

People continued to arrive from far and near to have a look at his nose. They were amazed at the sight of it. Some of them ventured to touch it. But nobody, not a soul, bothered to ask him the questions that would have fallen on his ears like music: Why do you look so weak? Have you had any lunch? There was not a paisa at home even to buy snuff. How long could he live like a starved animal at the zoo? He too was a human being, though not a very bright one. At last, he called his mother and gave her strict instructions. "Tell them to beat it, and shut the door on their faces."

His old mother tactfully persuaded the curious visitors to disperse and closed the front door. This proved to be a turning point in Mookken's life. Fortune smiled on the old mother and her young, illustrious son. Thousands of visitors, their curiosity unsatiated, offered to pay for a *darshan* of Mookken's nose. What more could you expect from an asinine people? Of course, a group of conscientious intellectuals and philosophers raised their voice against this open swindle. But their protests fell on deaf ears. The government initiated no action against Mookken. Enraged at this criminal abdication of responsibility on the part of the government, the intellectuals and philosophers joined hands with subversives and saboteurs of various shades.

Mookken's income from his nose swelled. To cut a long story short, in six years' time, the poor cook who could not get a square meal a day, became a millionaire.

Mookken acted in three films. *The Human Submarine*, a technicolour extravaganza, attracted millions of viewers. Six renowned poets wrote encomiums on Mookken. A dozen biographies of Mookken were published, earning fame and money for the biographers.

Mookken's mansion kept open house. Anybody could get a free meal for the asking—and a pinch of snuff.

At this time, Mookken had two secretaries. Both were beautiful and well educated.

Both loved and worshipped Mookken. It may be mentioned here that some beautiful women can always be relied upon to love even a highway robber or a homicidal maniac.

If you turn the pages of the history of the world, you will find that there was always trouble when two women loved the same man. It happened in Mookken's life too.

Like his two beautiful secretaries, the people gave their wholehearted love and admiration to Mookken. If a universally acclaimed nose, long and charming, reaching down to the navel, is not a sign of greatness, what is?

Mookken gave statements on all events of international importance and the reporters lapped them up eagerly:

"Reacting to the introduction of the new generation of jets capable of flying at speeds upto 10,000 k.p.h., Mr Mookken remarked that . . . "

"Talking to newsmen after Dr Furasi Baros announced his miraculous success in bringing a dead patient back to life, Mr Mookken, relaxing into a gentle smile which broke through his inscrutable expression, quipped . . . "

When news came about the conquest of the highest peak in the world, people asked each other: Well, what did Mookken say about it?

If Mookken did not say anything about it . . . tcha! It was not worth talking about.

Soon Mookken's views were solicited on a variety of subjects: the origin of the universe, garbage disposal, impressionistic painting, stream-of-consciousness in fiction, toilet soaps, life after death, sewage treatment plants, global warming . . . There was nothing under the sun or beyond it that Mookken was not aware of.

At this juncture, a series of conspiracies were initiated, and plots hatched, to appropriate Mookken. If you have read enough of history, you will know that there is nothing very original about appropriation. In fact, the history of human society is the history of appropriations.

What do we mean by appropriation? Let me illustrate.

You plant a few coconut saplings on a plot of land and water it every day. Years pass. The saplings become tall coconut trees, heavy with bunches of large coconuts. One fine morning, a neighbour of yours who hasn't done an honest day's work for years, grabs your coconut grove by hook or crook. This is appropriation.

Appropriate Mookken! The idea occurred to many at the same time.

The first attempt to appropriate Mookken was made by the government in an operation resembling a bloodless coup. It was one of the most shrewd decisions the government had ever taken. It conferred on Mookken the title, 'Knight Commander of the Long Nose (KCLN)' and awarded him a gold medal. The medal was given away by the President at a special ceremony. Instead of shaking Mookken's hand, the President shook his long nose. The newsreels of the function were shown on television and in cinemas across the length and breadth of the country.

It was the turn of the political parties next. Comrade Mookken should lead the historic struggle of the people! Comrade Mookken?!! Poor Mookken! They were bent on dragging him into politics.

But which party should Mookken join?

There were many. The prime objective of all of them was

people's revolution. But Mookken could not give his allegiance to all the people's revolutionary parties at the same time.

Mookken said to himself:

"Me join them parties? Oh, bother!"

One of his comely secretaries seized the opportunity:

"Comrade Mookken, you must join my party if you really love me."

Mookken said nothing.

"Should I join any of them parties?" he asked the other damsel.

She was quickly on to what was in Mookken's mind.

"Oh, why should you?" she said with a shrug of her shoulders.

But the workers of one of the people's revolutionary parties were convinced that Mookken was their man.

"Comrade Mookken zindabad! People's Revolutionary Party zindabad!" their slogans resounded.

This did not go down well with the other people's revolutionary party. They made one of Mookken's secretaries give a damaging statement to the press.

"I regret the fact that Mookken, the worst bourgeois reactionary of our times, made me a party to the appalling fraud he devised. I apologize to the people. Let me reveal, though belatedly, the truth about Mookken's nose: it is only a piece of rubber!"

Wow! All the newspapers in the world splashed the news on their front pages. Long-nose miracle exposed—a clever conman, a political opportunist preying on the gullible public—the connivance of the powers that be . . . Original nose, my foot!

It was only natural that the news should send shockwaves through the centers of power. The President was bombarded with telegrams, phone calls and letters.

"Death to the Knight Commander of the Rubber Nose! Down with Mookken's reactionary clique! Inquilab zindabad!" shouted the workers of the People's Revolutionary Party (Anti-Mookken). But the People's Revolutionary Party (Pro-Mookken) got into the act soon enough. The result was a press statement by the other secretary of Mookken:

"Comrades and friends, the statement of my colleague, who has distinguished herself with her convincingly fabricated lies, is merely a piece of malicious propaganda. She is jealous of Comrade

Mookken for having spurned her opportunistic advances. As everybody knows, she was after Comrade Mookken's money and the glamour she got from being his secretary. Besides, her brother is a member of that party of opportunists who shamelessly call themselves 'people's revolutionary party'. I use this opportunity to expose them for the scoundrels and bloodsuckers they are. As the trusted and loyal secretary of Comrade Mookken, I know his nose is original—as true as my heart. I salute the people who have rallied behind the leadership of Comrade Mookken in this hour of crisis. Comrade Mookken zindabad! People's Revolutionary Party zindabad! Inquilab zindabad!"

What were the people to make of all this? There was utter confusion everywhere. The People's Revolutionary Party (Anti-Mookken) hurled a volley of accusations against the government.

"It is transparent to all except the most gullible, why Mookken was made the 'Knight Commander of the Long Nose' and awarded the gold medal encrusted with diamonds. The President and the Prime Minister are directly involved in this gross deception of the people. It is no doubt part of a wider conspiracy. The President has to go—and the Prime Minister too. The best thing under the circumstances would be for the whole cabinet to resign. The rubber-nose swindler must be brought to book at the earliest."

The President was provoked. So was the Prime Minister. Tanks rolled towards Mookken's mansion. Mookken was arrested.

There was no news about Mookken for several days after that. People began to forget Mookken and his nose. Everything was calm and peaceful. And then the President dropped a bombshell! When Mookken had nearly faded out of everybody's memory, there was this communique from the President's office:

"There will be a public trial of Mr Mookken, Knight Commander of the Long Nose on the 9th of March. Mr Mookken is now under detention facing charges of fabricating a rubber nose of extraordinary dimensions and extorting money from the people by exhibiting it as an original nose. Medical experts from forty-eight countries will examine Mr Mookken's nose to determine whether it is original or artificial. Reporters representing all the major dailies of the world, and radio and TV crews, will be present on the occasion. The people are requested to remain calm."

But the people were an asinine lot. They didn't remain calm. They flocked to the Capital, raided restaurants, ransacked newspaper offices, burned down movie theatres, looted liquor shops and destroyed police stations and government installations. There were several communal clashes. Several men and women became martyrs in the cause of Mookken's nose.

9 March. Hundreds of thousands of people packed the lawns and roads surrounding the Presidential Palace. When the clock struck eleven, the loudspeakers positioned around the Palace roared: People are requested to maintain self-restraint. Silence! The examination has begun.

The medical experts converged on the Knight Commander of the Long Nose in the presence of the President and the Prime Minister. The multitudes gathered outside the Presidential Palace waited with bated breath!

One of the medical experts blocked Mookken's nose. Mookken opened his mouth. Another expert pricked the tip of Mookken's long nose with a pin. And ... wonder of wonders! A drop of blood appeared at the tip of the celebrated and controversial nose.

The nose is flesh and blood, original—the verdict of the medical experts was unanimous.

Mookken's trusted and loyal secretary, who had stood by him through thick and thin, rushed towards Mookken, breaking the cordon of security men and medical experts, and kissed him fervently on the tip of his long, original nose.

"Comrade Mookken zindabad! People's Revolutionary Party zindabad! Hands off Comrade Mookken's original nose!" The slogans shook the walls of the Presidential Palace.

When the slogans died down, the President came up with another of his shrewd manoeuvres. It was announced over the loudspeakers that Mr Mookken would soon be honoured with a *Mookkashri* and nominated to the Parliament.

Mookkashri Mookken, MP!

A prestigious university honoured Mookken with an M.Litt, while another went a step further and conferred a D.Litt on him.

Mookkashri Mookken, Master of Literature!

But the People's Revolutionary Party (Anti-Mookken) formed a united front to fight the government. Undeterred by the verdict of the medical experts, they cried: "Down with the President!

Down with the Prime Minister! Death to Mookken and his rubber-nose! Death to the abetters of the colossal fraud on the people!"

The course of people's revolution never runs smooth!

As for the intellectuals and philosophers—what were they to make of all the din and confusion? They had to reckon with a universally acclaimed nose.

Exit the historian.

(Translated by K. M. Sherrif)

IN THE FLOODS
Thakazhi Sivasankara Pillai

The temple stood on the highest spot in the village. But the god who resided in it was now neck-deep in water. Water had become the all-pervading reality. The villagers had mostly left for the distant villages and towns, which were out of reach of the floodwaters. The better-off families had left behind a young son or a servant to look after the house, or what was left of it. The guard was lucky if the family owned a row-boat. On the first floor of the temple, in three rooms were huddled three hundred and fifty-six humans—sixty-seven of them children—and a large number of dogs, cats, goats and hens. They displayed a rare unity of purpose. No bickering, no fights.

Chennapparayan had spent a whole night and a day in his hut surrounded by water. He had no boat. His master had fled for dear life three days before. When the water first entered the hut, he had piled up twigs and *madal*[1] to make a crude loft, out of reach of the intruding water. He sat tight for two days waiting for the water to recede. Besides, there was the haystack and the five bunches of bananas in the yard to think about. It would be a windfall for the thieves stalking deserted houses.

Now Chennan stood in knee-deep water on the loft. The last two rows of thatched palm-leaves which made up the slanting roof were under water. Intermittently Chennan hollered for help, hoping against hope that somebody passing by in a boat would hear him. So far, only his wife, their four children, a cat and a dog, all huddled up in the tiny room in the hut, had heard his cries for help. Chennan calculated that it wouldn't take more than twenty-four hours for the floodwaters to submerge the hut completely and for him and his family to meet their watery death. It was three days since the terrible rains had stopped. Chennan tore at the thatched wall of the hut with all his strength. He succeeded

---
[1] Madal—The leaves of a coconut tree.

in making a hole just big enough for a man to squeeze through. Emerging into the open through the hole, he surveyed the endless expanse of water, dotted by the heads of trees and the roofs of houses. A small boat was rowing away towards the north. Chennan cupped his hands and hooted. Fortunately the men in the boat heard him. As they rowed up to the hut, Chennan pulled out his wife, children, the cat and the dog in quick succession through the hole he had made in the wall.

As the kids were getting into the boat, Chennan heard a shout from the west. "Chenna-*acho*, ahoy there!" Chennan turned to look. It was Madayithara Kunheppan. "Bring the boat here!" Chennan hurriedly pulled his wife into the boat. The cat followed her with a leap. Chennan was too frantic to notice the absence of the dog. It was still sniffing about in the hut.

The boat rowed away. Soon it became a speck in the distance.

The dog came back to the roof. The boat had disappeared from view. The dog howled pathetically. But who was there to listen to its helpless cries? It ran round the hut, sniffed in nooks and corners, and whined.

A frog perched leisurely on the roof was startled by the din the dog made. It dived into the water with a splash. The splash scared the dog which leaped a step backwards and stared at the ripples in the water.

As the dog resumed its desperate hunt for food, another frog urinated on his nose and jumped into the water. Stung by the foul smell, the dog sneezed, shook its head vigorously and wiped its nose with its paw.

It started raining heavily again. The dog lay curled up on the roof and bore the fury of the rain stoically. Its master and his family had reached Ambalapuzha safely.

Night fell. A monstrous crocodile slithered through the water, its body rubbing against the half-submerged hut. The dog tucked its tail between its hind legs and barked. Unruffled, the crocodile continued on its journey.

Sitting on the roof, the dog, stung by hunger, stared wrathfully at the dark, cloudy sky and whined. Its pathetic cries travelled through the air in the desolate countryside. *Vayu Bhagavan*, the god of the air, taking pity on the dog, bore its cry far on its wings. The men who had stayed back to guard their houses heard the cry and said to themselves: Poor creature! God knows how long it has been up there on the roof. At the seaside in Ambalapuzha, his master would be having his supper. Perhaps, out of force of habit, he would roll a ball of rice for the dog too.

The dog moaned loudly for a long time. One of the lone men guarding their houses began reciting the *Ramayana*. It was a melodious rendering and the dog stopped moaning to listen. Deriving no solace from it, it moaned again. The voice trailed off and faded into a cool, gentle breeze. Soon everything was quiet, except for the rustle of the wind and the gluk-gluk of ripples lapping against the submerged huts.

The dog now lay quietly on the roof. It breathed heavily. Intermittently, it gave vent to what sounded like dejected muttering. Suddenly a fish tripped on the surface of the water. The dog jumped up and barked. A frog made a sudden leap into the water. The dog growled.

Another day dawned. The frogs in the water stared at the dog as it moaned pathetically. It gazed wistfully at the frogs as they leaped into the air, skimmed the surface, and dived into the depths.

It looked hopefully at the thatched roofs visible above the water. They were all deserted. Nowhere could it see a curl of smoke, the sign of food being cooked. It caught some of the flies which sat on its forelegs, with its tongue, and munched them. Others which sat on its hind legs were driven away with its muzzle.

The sun came out of the clouds. Its warmth sent the dog to sleep. When it woke up, it saw the long shadows of banana leaves swaying on the roof as the wind blew. It leaped up and barked at the shadows.

The clouds blacked out the sun again. The wind raised up waves in the water. Carcasses appeared on the vast sheet of water, floating downstream with the current.

In the distance, a small boat was rowing away swiftly. The dog got up and wagged its tail. The boat disappeared into a grove of young coconut trees.

A thin drizzle made patterns on the surface of the water. Seated on its forelegs, the dog stared all around in vain. The despair that filled its eyes would have melted a stone.

The drizzle petered out. A boat skirting the house on the

right stopped under a coconuttree. The dog wagged its tail enthusiastically and gave a low grunt. The boatman climbed the coconut tree and plucked a tender coconut. He cut open the coconut and drank the milk. Throwing away the shell, he got into the boat and rowed away.

A crow flew up and perched on the carcass of a huge buffalo. The dog barked longingly. The crow tore pieces of the rotting flesh with its beak and swallowed them. Having had its fill, it flew away.

A parrot flew up. Perching on a banana leaf, it squeaked. The dog barked. The parrot flew away.

An ants' nest swept down by the welling waters ran aground on the roof. The ants had escaped death. The dog, taking it to be a piece of food, sniffed at it. It was seized by a paroxysm of sneezing.

In the afternoon, a boat with two men in it approached the hut. The dog barked gratefully and wagged its tail. It tried to speak to them in a language which they did not understand. It put its forelegs into the water and prepared to jump into the boat. "Hey, there is a dog here," one of the men said to the other. "Don't bother," the other said. The dog tried to leap into the boat again.

The boat was moving away. The dog whined. One of the men in the boat turned to look.

"Oooon!"

It was not the boatman's expression of sympathy, but the dog's pathetic moan. But the wind broke it up. Only the lapping of the waves could be heard now. The dog gazed at the boat till it disappeared from view. It climbed onto the roof again with a growl. Perhaps it had taken a resolution never to trust human beings again.

Lapping up a few mouthfuls of water from the pool collected in a depression on the roof, it looked up sadly at the birds in the sky. A water snake, moving its body with a writhing motion through the water, looked into the hut. It entered the hut through the hole through which Chennan and his family had made their escape. The dog looked into the hut through the hole. Its expression was fierce and cruel as it barked. But it was fighting a losing battle against fear and hunger. It was trying to communicate what it felt, in a universal language—a language Martians would have understood as perfectly as earthlings.

Night fell. The rain arrived to the accompaniment of a terrifying gust of wind. The roof swayed dangerously. Twice, the dog nearly fell into the water. The long, terrifying shape of a crocodile rose to the surface of the water. The dog howled with the pain of death. Suddenly a chorus of cocks crowed somewhere in the neighbourhood.

"Where is the dog barking from? Aren't all these houses deserted?" A boat overloaded with hay, coconuts and bunches of bananas rowed up and stopped under a tree three-fourths below water.

The dog raised its tail stiffly in the air. It barked at the two men in the boat. One of them started climbing up the banana tree.

"Hey, watch the dog!"

The dog leapt at him. He slid and fell headlong into the water with a splash. His companion dragged him up into the boat. The dog swam back to the roof and started barking again. The thieves cut all the bunches of bananas in the yard. "Wait till I get my hands on you," one of them shouted at the dog, shaking his fist at it. They loaded the whole of the hay from the haystack into the boat. Then one of them rashly climbed onto the roof. The dog pounced on him and bit into his leg. It got a mouthful of flesh for its pains. The man kicked with the other foot and dived into the water with a howl. The man in the boat struck the dog a vicious blow on the underside of its belly with the rowing pole. The dog's yelps sounded like a cat's 'miaow'. Soon it died down. The bitten man lay in the boat howling with pain. "Keep quiet! We've had it if some busybody rows up to investigate," his companion warned him. They rowed away.

It was a long time before the dog could get up. It barked in the direction in which the boat had disappeared.

At around midnight, the carcass of a cow floated up and settled momentarily among the submerged trees in front of the house. The dog eyed it longingly, but did not venture out into the water. The carcass moved slightly. It was getting ready to resume its journey downstream with the current. The dog growled and scratched at the thatched walls of the hut. As the carcass was just about to get out of reach, the dog went down and pulled it up with its teeth. Soon it was biting off large chunks of the carcass and devouring them. What a well-deserved feast it was!

Crack! The dog disappeared into the depths of the water. The carcass took a dip and floated away.

For a long time the howling of the wind, the croaking of the frogs and the lapping of the waves ruled the darkness. Nobody heard the dog barking any more. More carcasses came down with the current. When the day broke, crows pecked at them. There was nobody to shoo them away. Neither were the marauding thieves balked in their plunders in broad daylight.

The water-level rose steadily. The roof tumbled into the water. Soon there was nothing visible above the surface of the vast expanse of water. The resistance of the roof to the ravaging floodwaters was a tribute to the dog's loyalty to its master, and its heroic efforts to protect his property from thieves. The roof had held out till the crocodile snapped up the dog in its jaws. Now it had no business staying above water. It resigned itself to the inevitable.

The floodwaters were receding. Chennan swam towards the ruins of the hut in search of his dog. He found its mangled body under a coconut tree. The waves rocked it gently. Chennan turned it over. He could not make out whether it was really his dog's body. One of the ears had been bitten off. The skin had rotted. There was no way to identify its colour.

(Translated by K. M. Sherrif)

THE WHISPERING PLOUGH

Ponkunnam Varkey

Ousepp was crazy about his bullocks. It was not for nothing that the farmers of the village called him a 'bull-buff'. His Kannan was the showpiece of the whole village, the apple of his master's eye. Stout and thick-set, his skin a pleasing grey, his horns short and cute like the stem of a mushroom, the depression on his back trailing away towards his haunches, it was a spectacle to watch when Kannan, yoked to the plough, trotted towards the fields. Kannan was smart enough to figure out what was in Ousepp's mind even before he was given any instruction, whether it was to break up the clods, or to level a patch with a plank. Ousepp never hit him with a switch as other ploughmen did, though he often brandished it for form's sake. Neither did he ever have to holler his lungs out to make Kannan work. Ousepp treated Kannan like a trusted friend. Kannan was the unchallenged leader of all the bullocks who worked with him in the fields. When one patch was done, Kannan didn't wait for Ousepp's directions to move on to the next. He knew perfectly well how to go about it smoothly and unobtrusively. Often, it was Ousepp who pleaded for a break.

"Half a second, mate. Let me have a chew of betel. It's ages since I had one."

Kannan would stand rooted to the ground till Ousepp was through with his chew. When Ousepp signalled to him with a nod and a hum, Kannan would quickly move on to the next patch. It was a sight to watch Kannan stepping from one patch to another without ever treading on a hedge. He knew that it required no more than a light tap with his hoof for the wafer-thin hedge to collapse.

Ousepp never found any need to tie up Kannan after the work was over. He was free to go to the pond for a drink of water, or to wander at will over the meadows and along the narrow mud tracks. Ousepp merely gave him a perfunctory warning when he untied him from the plough.

"Fill your belly with whatever you get. But don't go anywhere near that banana." Kannan never touched the bananas or coconut saplings which Ousepp grew so diligently. He might as well gore his master to death with his horns.

Ousepp was very particular about giving Kannan a proper scrub and a bath after the ploughing was done. "The right leg, you idiot, not the left! What are you shaking your head for? I'll skin you if you rub those horns of yours anywhere on my body . . ." Kannan understood every word of Ousepp's affection and care. Those farmers who had never known the magic a kind word could work with animals, would admit grudgingly that the most incorrigible rogue among the bulls would become putty in Ousepp's hands. They said Ousepp flirted with his bulls! They were amused at the way he searched high and low for their fodder. But the 'Save the Cattle' campaign did not impress Ousepp.

"They shoot their mouths off about protecting our cattle wealth. But does the government ever give us an inch of land to grow grass? I suppose they want us to feed them with promises!"

Ousepp could not eat a hearty meal till he was satisfied that his bullocks had had their fill. He believed that to let cattle go hungry even for a day was to invite the curse of God on the household. He also insisted on them getting clean and wholesome fodder. If it was tapioca stems, he chopped them into small pieces and crushed them. If it was pine leaves, he carefully removed each thorn before slicing them into pieces.

The first thing Ousepp did on coming home was to call Kannan. Kannan would respond to his master's call instantly by lowing loudly. He would wait patiently for Ousepp to go up to him. Ousepp always brought some gift for him; a small bundle of green grass or a couple of banana peels. As Ousepp rubbed his back gently, Kannan would express his love for his master by licking him. He liked the taste of the salt in Ousepp's sweat.

Kannan could easily distinguish his master's voice from any babel of voices. It thrilled him like thunder in summer thrills a peacock. Kannan always wanted Ousepp to hold the plough when he pulled it. If it was somebody else, Kannan wasn't averse to playing a trick or two. Often Ousepp had to intervene to make things all right for his hapless substitute. "Now, now, don't you try to be cheeky. It is our Kuttappan. Don't you know him?" Ousepp's mediation always worked.

There is a tune which ploughmen hum when they work. It is not set to any score or pattern. "Heeeeeeh-oh-oh-oooh . . . ", it went. Ousepp's voice sent the tune sailing far and high through the air. It stretched loud and clear for two minutes. It is the prototype of the humming in love songs and choral chants. As Ousepp's humming rose into the air, Kannan lost himself in it. Everything faded away—the burden, the pain and the suffering. The tinkling of the bell around his neck and the splash made by his hoofs as they cut into the soft mud, beat time to the tune.

One day there was an amusing incident. It was Pachan, Kelan's son, who held the plough. Ousepp was laid up in bed with a troublesome fever. The ploughing on Kelan's plot would have been unnecessarily held up if Kannan was not available. So Ousepp decided to send Kannan to team up with his 'ploughmate', come what may. The first furrow was done without any untoward incident. When they moved on to the second, Pachan got it into his head to give a rendering of the ploughmen's tune. Unfortunately, a good voice was not one of his assets. But Pachan thought otherwise. Kannan could not stand it. He shook his head vigorously to register his protest. But Pachan did not notice it. As for Pachan's companions on the field, their knowledge of music was not deep enough to tell one tune from another. Kannan could not hope to get justice from them. Exasperated, he gave Pachan a vicious kick on his shin. The budding singer had to call it a day and spend the next three days at home nursing his foot.

II

Kannan served Ousepp faithfully for twelve years. The tall trees that lined the pathways of the village watched the passage of time impassively. The scepters and crowns of the monarchs who gambled with the lives of men ended up in the dustbins of history. Miraculous changes swept the world. There was talk of the coming of a new age in which no man could exploit another. But Ousepp was forced to sell his bullocks. His land, his goddess of prosperity, was already mortgaged. Not that Ousepp liked to do it. He had to. He was the father of a girl of marriageable age.

The monster of dowry sunk its teeth into the flesh of yet another family. The mortgage fetched him fifteen hundred rupees. The amount would barely make up the dowry. He still had to find money for the expenses of the wedding. There was no way out, except to sell the bullocks, however much he loved them.

Ousepp had invested all his youth and energy on the good earth. There were few who possessed his knowledge and skill in cultivation. But what did he gain? His hair had turned completely white. He had lost much of his eyesight. His skin was wrinkled all over and rheumatism never left him alone. The skin on the inside of his palms was so thick that even a knife could not cut through. But what was his balance sheet after a life of sweat and toil? The tools he used were much the same as his ancestors had used five thousand years ago. His lips mumbled the same prayers the peasants in Rig Vedic times chanted—prayers to the gods of rain, wind and the sun! His state was in no way better than that of the Rig Vedic peasant. But the new markets and the sophisticated methods of exploitation, intent on squeezing out the last drop of his dignity and self-respect, had already begun to stalk him.

When the end of the rope tied to Kannan's neck was handed over to the buyer, Ousepp did not have the fortitude to watch it. He forfeited the 'rope money' of one rupee that was due to the seller when a cow or a bull changed hands. But nobody had estimated the worth of the tears that streamed down his cheeks as he leaned against a tree in the backyard and wept. Kannan had sensed something amiss. He turned his head in all directions to look for his master. Not finding him, Kannan lowed pathetically. His master had reached that stage in his life when his words held no meaning.

Words never touch the soul of love. If you can call the communion of two minds laden with sorrow love, there was, perhaps, no love as fervent as the love between Ousepp and Kannan. They never complained about their hardships to each other. That was why their hearts refused to be torn from each other.

Some of the farmers, groaning under the burden of debts, their dignity and self-respect torn to shreds, headed for the hills of Wayanad.

"It is a god-forsaken place. One's folks can never reach there in time if anything happens. And the whole place is infested with malaria. How can I let you go when I know all this?' Kittussar, Ousepp's neighbour, wondered as they discussed the exodus to Wayanad.

"What else can I do, Kittussar? Can you give me a piece of fertile land? The good earth beckons me. I will die a dog's death if I have no land to till."

Ousepp's life drifted aimlessly like a boat without oars. The journey to Malabar was postponed indefinitely. He had not been able to find a buyer who would pay a reasonable price for the small plot of land on which his house stood. There was another reason too. His daughter, Kathrikkutty, was expecting. Ousepp was reluctant to leave for Wayanad before his first grandchild was born.

It was Easter. Even for the poorest among the Christians, it was an occasion for gaiety and rejoicing. The aroma of meat curry rose from kitchens. The intoxicating smell of *vellappam*[1] cooking in chinese pans spread in the air. *Vellappam* and meat-curry, spiced with curry leaves and coconut shavings, with a couple of bottles of pure toddy made up a feast. There were few homes which went without these on Easter. But the tidings of Easter brought no cheer to Ousepp. The ploughmen's tune which rose from a field where ploughing was in progress reached his ears like a mocking laugh. He stared at his plough, now covered with cobwebs, which lay on the roof of the cowshed. Would he have the good fortune to possess a team of bullocks and a piece of land to till, in his life again?

Ousepp's wife, Mariya, shared her husband's worries. They had to send Kathrikkutty the next day to her in-laws in the traditional manner. She had delivered a boy. That was fortunate. There would be no row over gold ornaments. But they had to have a waist-chain of silver made for the baby. And, of course, a new dress had to be stitched for it.

They had not been able to give anything much by way of clothes to Kathrikkutty for her wedding. Poor Kathrikkutty! Her in-laws had taunted her quite a bit for 'walking about in rags'. Now she had to have at least a couple of dresses, even if they had to beg for it. Strictly speaking, the occasion called for gifts too:

---

[1] Vellappam - A delicacy made of rice flour.

sweets, furniture, a milch cow ... That could be dispensed with, considering the dire straits they were in. But there was no getting away from what were considered the bare necessities. As they fretted over it, they had an unexpected piece of luck. Mariya won a draw in a *chitty*[2] she had been running. She had had to use all her resourcefulness to run it, scraping up everything she had and skipping meals occasionally to make up for the deficit. Now she had forty rupees in hand. Ousepp had not yet learned about his wife's good luck. Mariya shook him out of his brooding.

"Look, what do you think you are doing, moping like this? We have to send away the girl tomorrow. Thank God, I got forty rupees from the *chitty* I have been running. You must go to Kottayam and get the things we need.

Ousepp brightened. "Smart girl!" he thought. It was his responsibility to look after such things. He had failed. But his wife had managed to avert the crisis. Pulling out the small box in which they kept betel, arecanuts and tobacco, he cheerfully mixed the ingredients for a good chew before he set out for Kottayam. "Fine! I'll be off in a minute."

"Appa, don't buy any of that paper-thin clothing for my *chatta*[3]," Kathrikkutty warned her father.

"You can pay the tax as well. It's long overdue," Mariya reminded him.

"All that for forty rupees?" Ousepp was sceptical.

"That is your problem. I want a couple of *chatta* too," Mariya made another addition to the list.

"A *mundu*[4] and *chatta* for Kathrikkutty, two *chatta* for you, and the tax to be paid. All these with the colossal sum of forty rupees! Why don't you make the trip to Kottayam yourself? I don't work miracles."

"I see. I was under the impression that women cooked and washed and looked after the house while the men brought in the daily bread. I suppose my father had the same idea when he married me off to a stout young man, moustache and all. All right, you can wash those dishes and start cooking something while I go up to Kottayam!"

---

[2] Chitty - A kind of people's bank, usually run by womens, very popular in the countryside
[3] Chatta - A kind of blouse
[4] Mundu - A cloth wrapped round the waist

Kathrikkutty suppressed a laugh.

Ousepp started for Kottayam with an umbrella under his arm, a shawl over his shoulders and a cloth-bag in hand.

Kottayam did not lag behind in Easter festivities. The shops owned by Christians were all closed. But there were quite a few cloth stores owned by merchants of other communities. He went into a couple of them to have a look.

"Oh God!" Ousepp could not help clutching his brow at the fancy prices quoted by the salesmen. Why did clothes have to be so dear? He decided to look in a few more stores before making a purchase. He had to save every single paisa he could. His wanderings took him to the Municipality Office. He saw a number of bullocks tied to stakes in the yard. They were all old and emaciated, just bundles of skin and bones, some with the mark of the plough deeply embedded on the backs of their necks. Ousepp was appalled at man's cruelty towards his fellow-beings. The Municipality had stamped its black seal of death on their bodies. The butchers would be prosecuted if they slaughtered animals which were not inspected by the Municipal Health Officer. The Municipality, whose prime concern was the health of the citizens, could not afford to be slaughtered. If it relaxed its vigil, there was no guessing what kind of rotten flesh the butchers would pass on to their unsuspecting customers. As for the branded cattle, death could only be a blessing to them, for it would redeem them from their lives of misery. They had worked tirelessly for their masters when they had the strength to. When they became too old and weak to work, only cruel indifference awaited them. Death was a hundred times better than the tortures of life. There were about forty bulls. More were being brought in. Ousepp stared at the condemned animals for a long time—like a man bidding farewell to his friends on the death row in a prison.

Ousepp walked towards the shop at the end of the street. Suddenly he stopped dead, startled. He wondered whether his eyes, which he could no longer trust, were playing tricks on him. Ousepp stared at the bull which was no better than a walking skeleton. He felt dizzy. Kannan!

"Kannan!" Ousepp called from the depths of his heart. He rushed at the poor animal. The bull looked up when he heard the voice that was music to his ears. The joy and contentment of his life, which had been snatched away from him, returned momentarily. "Son, don't you recognize me? How sad that I have to set my eyes on you in this condition!" Ousepp rubbed the back of Kannan's neck affectionately. He pulled Kannan's head to his chest, so that the poor animal could hear his heart weeping for the strongest bond of friendship ever forged between man and beast. Kannan was too weak even to low. But his eyes said it all. Suddenly Ousepp let go of Kannan's head. He ran his eyes over Kannan's body. Yes, the seal of the Municipality was there, stamped clearly on one of his forelegs. Ousepp rubbed it vigorously. But the Municipality's seal could not be so easily erased.

There was an open wound on the underside of Kannan's belly. Flies hovered around it.

"Did he belong to you?" one of the butchers asked Ousepp.

"Did you bring him here?" Ousepp asked the butcher in reply.

"Yes."

Kannan licked his master's chest, savouring the now forgotten taste of his sweat. His whole life had been devoted to lightening the burden of his master's life. Now the old ploughman was repaying his debt with his tears as the bull awaited its death at the butcher's hands.

"Come on, let me take him away. I have to supply the meat to the shops before noon." The butcher was annoyed at the reunion which threatened to waste his time. He herded three other bulls and started walking away with them, gesturing to Ousepp to send Kannan after them. Kannan too was to reach the tables laid for the Easter feast in a couple of hours.

III

The day was burning itself out. "Sweep the parapet clean before you light the lamps," Mariya, who had been staring into the distance, her eyes scanning the mud-track for a sign of Ousepp, told her daughters.

"Why is *Appan*[5] so late?"

---

[5] Appan - Father

"It takes some time to reach here from Kottayam, doesn't it? He will be coming any minute now."

"But he always comes back long before dusk when he goes to Kottayam." Kathri was impatient to see the clothes her father would be bringing from Kottayam. But there was no sign of Ousepp. Kathri lighted the lamps.

Suddenly they saw something white moving in the distance. "It's *Appan!*" Kathri said gleefully. Mother and daughter fixed their eyes on the approaching figure.

"Is it Ousepp *chettan*[6]?" their neighbour Mathu asked them. Mathu was a tailor. He had been summoned to stitch the three *chattas*—two of Kathri's and one of Mariya's—during the night. Kathri had to leave early in the morning.

But Ousepp had brought no clothing for his wife and daughter who were eagerly looking forward to wearing their new dresses. Behind him, Kannan trotted wearily into the yard.

"Oh, Kannan!" Mariya cried.

"Where is the clothing?" Kathri demanded.

Kannan lowed joyfully on stepping into the yard he knew so well.

A volley of questions were fired at Ousepp. Clutching his jaw, Ousepp sat like a man gone dumb. Mariya raved at him. Kathri whimpered. But Ousepp neither heard nor said anything.

"Appa, I never thought you would do this to me," Kathri burst into tears.

"Kathri, you are my daughter and Kannan is my son. The butcher . . . " The rest of his utterances dissolved into a sob.

It was a cruel night. None of them got a wink of sleep.

At dawn he went into the cowshed with an ointment he had made of herbs to apply on Kannan's wounds. Ousepp had a ready stock of remedies for most of the diseases which cattle fall prey to. Kannan was lying on his back with his legs spread out.

"Kannan," Ousepp called gently. But Kannan's soul had already bid farewell to the world. Perhaps he had willingly given himself to death to forestall any more trouble he would have caused to his master.

As the poor farmer's tears fell on the body of his most loyal

---

[6] Chettan - Literally a brother, generally an elder.

friend, a lizard clinging to the plough on the roof of the cowshed, now covered by a maze of cobwebs, squeaked. Ousepp could not understand what it said.

(Translated by K. M. Sherrif)

ROOMS FOR RENT
Uroob

I was seething with rage as I entered the building. I hadn't foreseen such an abrupt shifting of residence. I owed only three months' rent. Not that the old misanthrope had starved because I didn't cough up. He was merely obsessed with fattening his bank balance by a certain amount every month. No allowance for the fact that I had been his tenant for the whole of four months. "Take out your things, sir. No, I don't want to confiscate them for the rent you owe me. I will be delighted if you just vacate the room." So calm and nonchalant! Why didn't he say,"Get out, you son-of-a-bitch," instead? That would have meant he was just giving vent to his annoyance. But no, he was a cool customer. What did the old screwball think I would do next? Did he think I owned a palatial bungalow somewhere under a false name, that I had rented his dungeon for a lark?

Where in this wicked world would he ever get another tenant like me? What a quiet, decent gentleman!—the neighbours would surely have remarked about me. My predecessor was a real-estate broker, who had had to vacate the room in the face of sustained and vociferous protests from the neighbours. During his occupancy, the room was a second home to the vast majority of street-whores who did business in the city. If you think the landlord had objected to his room being used for such a charitable purpose, you have got another think coming. The broker paid his rent promptly on the first of every month and the landlord had no brief for defending public morality.

No member of the fair sex had as much as stepped into the room after I occupied it. "Is he dumb?" I had heard the old woman who lived in the next room asking a young woman in the neighbourhood. Meditation, writing, sleep—the three processes made up the whole of the time I spent in the room. The only time I had indulged myself was when I read a poem of mine rather loudly. The old woman looked in through the window and smiled at me. "It's a poem, isn't it?" That settled it. I clamped my mouth shut. Not a sound did anybody hear from me after that.

Unfortunately, being a gentleman doesn't pay these days. Take the broker. Smart chap. Got his money's worth for the rent he paid. Of course, he earned the neighbours' wrath. But that didn't do him any harm. When the joint became too hot for him, he just left it. There were a thousand landlords who would welcome him with open arms for the money he was willing to pay. The upshot was that the room remained unoccupied for more than a month. It had to wait for me to move in to redeem its lost respectability. The old miser had spared me the humiliation of confiscating my things. What a human gesture! I would have cracked his thick skull if he had laid his hands on my things. I would have thoroughly enjoyed the lamentations of his bereaved family, consisting of his loud-mouthed wife, the fatso of a son and the three skinny daughters.

The son was a more unbearable character than the father. I couldn't stand that freckled face of his. There was nothing outrageous about his wife having left him. Would any woman in her right senses live with him? I couldn't stand the way he hovered in the background when his father spoke to me. And that ridiculous, shrill voice of his! I was under the impression that donkeys were credited with the worst voice in the animal kingdom. What beats me is how his wife managed to live with him for some time before calling it quits. I think she ought to be canonized for putting up with her father-in-law's stinginess and her husband's stupidity at the same time. I haven't been able to see her. She left a month before I came. Neither the father nor the son had anticipated her leaving in a huff like that. Her father was rich too. He owned several buildings which were rented out, and had quite a large amount stashed away in bank deposits. There was absolutely no need for his daughter to put up with the churlishness of the father and son. Of course, they had left no stone unturned in their efforts to bring her back. But she was no fool, not she.

She must really be an angel. "Only a ratsnake can live with you," she had told her husband when she left him. The fact is that such a feat is beyond the capacity of even ratsnakes. No sooner did the father ask me to remove my things, than the son fell rapturously on my bedding and dragged it out of the room. For a moment I thought of digging in and making a fight of it. "Go to hell!" I could have told them. But I would have cut a sorry figure before my neighbours for whom I was no less than a minor saint. So I decided to move out without making a fuss. The buggers must be under the impression that they had intimidated me into writing a promissory note for the three months' rent I owed them. The poor fish! I would have given them a piece of my mind if the neighbours hadn't been around. Thank goodness the episode ended without violence.

But I was still seething with rage. I shudder to think what would have happened if a friend of mine—bless his heart—had not fixed up this room for me. Spending the night on the footpath was out of the question—not in this horrible rain, anyway. The dirty old man and his monster of a son were least bothered about their social obligations towards their lesser brethren.

I was still cursing them as I walked towards the staircase. I must have been too distracted by the bitter memories of my exodus to notice the woman who stood gazing at me on the veranda. When I did, I stopped dead, startled.

"Are you the man who has taken room number seven?" she asked in a soft, pleasant voice.

"Yes. Why do you ask?"

"Don't you want the key?" her voice became softer.

"Yes. Why did you ask?"

"Here is the key. Keep it carefully with you. There is no duplicate." She extended the key to me.

"Are you the landlady?"

"Yes, I am."

"I am sorry. I confess I didn't have the faintest notion about who owned the building."

"I can see that. It is all right."

"Well, thanks a lot. I will move in right away." I was in a hurry to get away. But she said suddenly, "Come, I will show you the room. I think it has to be cleaned up."

"Oh, don't bother. I will take care of everything."

"I suppose you don't have a broom, do you?" she asked matter-of-factly.

I didn't have one. So I said nothing. The coolie who had already gone up with my bedding and suitcase came back. "Sir, the room is locked."

"Come, I'll open it for you,' said my landlady and ascended the stairs with firm steps. The coolie and I followed. She had long, curly hair which swung to and fro like a pendulum as she walked. It seemed she had just had a bath, for her hair was wet and the smell of oil and perfumed soap emanated from it. It was a pleasurable experience following her up the stairs.

She stopped before room number seven. "Give me the key, will you?"

I gave her the key. She opened the door. As she surveyed the room, I was running my eyes over her. She must be about twenty-four years old. She had the complexion of a *champaka*[1] flower. Her studded ear-rings flashed as she turned her head.

"I think I'll give the room a once-over. Leave the suitcase in the veranda for a minute, will you?"

I paid the coolie and surveyed the room. There were two windows which brought in plenty of light and air. Unlike the dungeon I had been living in, this was certainly fit for human habitation. And the landlady had impeccable manners too. Look at the way she offered to clean up the room like a maid. And the veranda was terrific. You could feast your eyes on the lush foliage that surrounded the building.

"I have kept you waiting, haven't I?" She had come back with a broom. "It won't take a minute." She swept and mopped the floor. She then helped me carry the suitcase and the bedding into the room. It was then that I got a good look at her. Her eyes were not beautiful, but sharp and flashing. They were capable of asking a thousand questions which would cut right through you like a knife. But let them ask a million. I wouldn't be bothered.

"You were living in Mr Sankaran's house before you came here, weren't you?"

"Yes."

"How did you manage to stay alive?"

"Well, it was a tough job. Proper rat-hole it was."

"And that old bulldog breathing down your neck all the time."

"You seem to know them quite intimately."

---

[1] Champaka - An Indian tree (*Michelia Champaca*) of the magnolia family, of great beauty, with oppressively scented flowers.

"Sure I know them," she giggled. "Who do you think is the lesser of the two devils, father or son?"

"They tie for the first place."

She giggled again. "Yes, the son is a fiend in humam shape."

I laughed. I liked the way she said it. Here was a kindred soul.

"He tried to throw you out, didn't he?"

I said nothing. I didn't know she was aware of what had happened. My friend had no business divulging the unsavoury details to her.

"Thought you would have to sleep on the pavement, did he?" she went on.

"That, I think, was his assumption."

"Would you call him a human being?"

"Certainly not."

"I can't stand the sight of him."

"Neither can I," I said gleefully. A fiery glow lit up her face as she released her pent-up fury against father and son. "If you would excuse me, I think I should learn the name of my landlady."

"Pankajam."

"Is your father at home?"

"He is not in. We live in the building next to this. If you need anything, just let me know."

"Sure Thank you."

After Pankajam left, I mused about her. A smart and cheerful woman. Very efficient too. And she hadn't tried to make a pass at me, young though she was. I wished all women would be like Pankajam.

"Care for tomatoes, anybody?" It was the vegetable vendor. Without replying, I went into the bathroom to take a bath.

I dried my body with a towel, put on my clothes and went downstairs. Pankajam was pacing the veranda on the ground floor.

"Going out for supper?"

"Yes."

Pankajam appeared in my room the next morning. She had visited all the tenants on her way. In the room next to mine lived a clerk who worked in a timber depot, a stand-offish chap who kept his own counsel. The room next to him was occupied by an able-bodied gentleman with a curled-up moustache. I learned later that he was the husband of a headmistress and had left his wife after a tiff with her. He looked so mournful that I thought he would cry if you engaged him in conversation. And last, but not least, was the old man in khadi, with unkempt hair and a grotesque face. I noticed him when I heard his voice, turned on in high volume. He was airing his views—very strong views from what I could gather—on politicians and ministers. Pankajam smiled at him and passed on with a nod. She came into the room and stood with her back to the door. "Is everything all right?"

"Oh, yes."

"I am honoured to have a poet as my tenant."

Oh, she had learned about my profession too. I had been under the impression that she held me in some esteem. But now... I grinned sheepishly and changed the subject. "Who is that old man? I mean the one who was lambasting the powers that be." She gave me a brief life-sketch of the old man. "Poor old man! Tottering on the brink!"

"Off his rocker?"

"Well, not exactly."

He had been imprisoned four times in the days of the nationalist movement. Got knocked about by the cops quite a bit. Now, to preserve his right to free speech, he kept his distance from political parties of all hues. His only son, who was working in Bombay, sent some money regularly to the old man. That was what sustained him—and the self-righteous tirades against politicians which occupied most of his waking hours.

"The things men do out of disillusionment! Terrible, isn't it?"

"Well, I've seen folks do some terrible things."

I invited Pankajam to take a chair. She declined the offer. But she was not in a hurry to go either. She preferred to talk standing. The conversation soon veered round to Sankaran. Pankajam gave a blow-by-blow account of the beast's cruel deeds. "It seems you have a very intimate knowledge about him."

"That was the one mistake I made in my life."

"I beg your pardon?" I realized later that I shouldn't have asked the question.

"I lived with that brute for a year."

"So you are his. . .?" I jumped out of the chair.

"Yes, you guessed right. I am his wife."

I was speechless with amazement. Realizing that I was struck dumb, Pankajam continued, "Can any human being live with him?"

I refrained from stating the obvious. She rambled on as I gave her a patient hearing.

"The way he treated me! I suffered everything in silence. I didn't want to make a scene for the busybodies of the neighbourhood to feast on, or for my poor father to worry his head off. But there is a limit to what one can put up with."

"There certainly is."

"But that moron did not seem to realize it."

"I pity you, Pankajam."

"Anybody with a heart will pity me. And you are a poet—a man who can see deep into the human soul."

I flashed that sheepish grin again and took the compliment in my stride.

"Oh, I am wasting your time, aren't I?" She turned and walked away.

She came to my room every morning after that. After a brief round-up of world news, she would launch into a full-blooded attack on Sankaran, using the choicest epithets for the purpose.

Soon the old man in khadi joined us for the morning session. "Everything has gone to the dogs. Can you show me a single one of them who is not crooked?" he asked me. "No leader trusts his followers. Thinks they are plotting behind his back to overthrow him. They want to lie back leisurely while a thousand worker-bees bring them honey. Wishful thinking, isn't it, sir?"

I didn't tell him that it wasn't just wishful thinking.

"Husbands don't trust their wives," Pankajam said, joining the discussion.

"Wives don't trust their husbands either." We turned to look at the source of the voice. The estranged husband of the headmistress was also out in the veranda. I saw his eyes discharging a couple of tear-drops onto his thick, voluminous moustache. The atmosphere suddenly became melancholy. Nobody said a word after that. We dispersed and Pankajam disappeared down the stairs. "Scoundrels!" the old man muttered as he went back to his room. He didn't mean us. The estranged husband of the headmistress too retired. What a sad world! I was inspired to throw a poem on its face. But I felt sleepy. I stretched myself on the bed and dozed off.

The following evening found me sitting alone in the veranda. There was perfect peace and tranquillity in the surroundings. The headmistress's husband had gone out. He would be waiting behind the broad trunk of a *kanjiram*[2] on the side of the road, to gaze fondly at the headmistress as she returned home from school. When she disappeared from his sight, he would wipe the tears off his moustache and slink away. He must be wallowing in his martyrdom, wearing his cross with all solemnity. The old man in khadi was sleeping. He slept from four to eight in the evening. The rest of the day, morning and afternoon, barely sufficed to loose off invectives against politicians. He would be busy writing letters most of the night. Every day in the morning he carried a thick bunch of letters to the post box. This was the most peaceful hour in the building. I looked out of the window at the yard. The golden hue of the departing sun was splashed over everything. The trees and bushes had a bright, cheerful look about them. Not a bad world, this, I thought. Was there an echoing ring in the air—what you hear when you take away your hand from the strings of the veena, after strumming a high note? Was it mingling with an echo in my heart? Something was happening!

"Tomatoes, anybody?" I usually ignored the vegetable vendor. But now I said pleasantly, "Pass on, brother."

"Who is passing on?" I turned to find Pankajam smiling at me. I got up. "Sit down," I offered her my chair.

"No, don't bother, I'll take this chair." She sat on the rickety chair in the corner. She wore a yellow blouse and a red sari. Her ear-rings flashed intermittently. The departing sun drew a halo around her face. But in the middle of the halo were eyes that glinted like a razor's edge.

"Who were you speaking to?"

"The vegetable vendor."

"Oh," she pulled the chair closer. Today, for a change, the conversation *opened* with a reference to Sankaran. "He wants me to patch up everything."

"What happened?"

"He sent an emissary—an aunt of his."

"What was the outcome?"

---

[2] Kanjiram - A tree belonging to the Loganiacea family.

"I gave her a piece of my mind. She wanted me to go back to that lout. Only a ratsnake can live with him—if it is prepared to make some sacrifices, that is!"

I gazed at her without a word.

"Poor father! Listened to everything patiently. But not me." She went on with her account of the encounter.

"What made you leave him?" I interrupted her with a question and added hastily, "Forgive me if I am being too inquistive."

"Not a bit. I am piqued at you for not asking me anything all these days. Let the whole world know. I don't give a damn."

"What made you leave him?" I asked again before she could digress into side issues.

"He is a slave—a serf."

"Slave? To whom?"

"To his father, to his mother, to anybody who can push him around. Do you know what he does? Whenever I suggest anything, he goes into a deep meditation. Would his father approve? Would his mother like it? Finally, I would have to give it up. I needed the good-will of his sagacious parents to go for a movie! It was hell. But I suffered everything in silence. The breaking point came when I asked him to register a ten-room block, rented out to traders, in my name. It had just been retrieved from the old tenants. The block was in *his* name, mind you. The old man had no rights on it. Not that I was gold-digging. I just wanted to test him, to find out whether he really cared for me."

"And he didn't budge?"

"No. There was a tussle between his saucy mother and me. I didn't give in an inch. She even tried to lay her dirty hands on me. I told her to stuff it and walked out of the house."

"Oh!"

"Why didn't he turn over the block to me? Couldn't he trust his own wife?"

"There was no reason why he couldn't."

"Why should I live with that scoundrel? And now, he has the audacity to go around breathing fire and brimstone against me for giving you a room here."

"Oh, does he?"

"I know whom to rent my rooms to. It is none of his business."

She looked intently at my face for my reaction. I looked out of the window. The world was clad in the russet mantle of dusk.

Pankajam rambled on. It was a long time before she finished. My contribution to the conversation consisted of a few monosyllables, most of them expressing agreement with her views. That was all that was required of me.

"Oh, you haven't gone out for supper," she said as she got up to leave. "I am sorry if I have made you too hungry."

"Oh, no," I blanched. "The fact is that I have an upset stomach."

"Is it bad? I will send you a tablet. It's good for digestion."

I let out a groan as she went down the stairs. The only thing my stomach would get upset over was that it had been empty for a considerable period of time now. But there was nothing to worry about. My editor friend had promised me a bonanza of ten rupees. Pankajam's tablet for digestion would certainly come in handy—after I had had a plate of the best biriyani the restaurant could offer.

When I returned, I saw a boisterous gathering in the room of the old man in khadi. There were about half-a-dozen men in the room. Their arguments and discussions were punctuated by loud, ringing laughs. Such a thing had never happened before. I took a good look at the gathering before going to my room. I soon fell asleep and dreamt of Pankajam's studded ear-rings.

The next morning as I stood at the door, lost in sweet reveries, the old man in khadi appeared with—for a change—a beaming smile on his lips.

"They are adamant, sir. How can I say no? They are all old friends of mine after all."

I didn't get the hand of it. I looked quizzically at him.

"They have zeroed in on me."

"I beg your pardon?"

"They want me to be their candidate. How times change! Ha, ha, ha!"

"Are you talking about the elections?"

"Yes. They say I am the people's choice. I have never spurned an opportunity to serve the people—ha, ha, ha!"

"Did you agree to the proposal?"

"How can I disagree? Ha, ha, ha!"

"Ha, ha, ha!" I too laughed.

The old man was busy the whole day. Writing letters, packing, shouting to the coolie he had hired...

"I am shifting," he said to me as he vacated the room in the evening. "See you sometime."

"See you." I accompanied him down the stairs to the veranda. The headmistress's husband accompanied him as far as the gate. There was a tear-drop on his moustache as he returned.

Without the old man's invectives against politicians, the atmosphere wore a sombre silence which suffocated me. "Poor old man!" Pankajam said to me later. "It will be quite some time before he takes another shot at politicians. It is human nature."

"It sure is."

"But if I were in his place, I would have thrown out those scheming friends of his and shut the door on their faces. What would you have done?"

The unexpected question threw me into confusion. But I couldn't let it pass. "I would have locked myself up for a week."

Pankajam looked at me with a knowing smile. "You look quite run down. You should take some nutritious food."

"I suppose I should."

"You are a little hard up, aren't you?"

"No, not anything to worry about."

"I know how hard it is for a poet to pull on. Don't worry. I have fixed up everything. From today your meals will be brought to you here at the proper times."

"Oh, you shouldn't have bothered."

"We are all human beings, aren't we," was her explanation. "Don't think all landlords and landladies are like that old miser who threw you out."

"No, no. I have never thought of you that way."

"By the way, he sent another messenger today."

"Did he?"

"He is prepared to give me half of the block—five rooms, that is."

"He is improving."

"Idiot! I told the messenger to tell him he should have started the offer with one of the walls of a room! The whole block fetches a mere two hundred and fifty rupees as rent. He wants me to split it with his father—a hundred and twenty-five each! Thought he could buy me so cheap. Do you think my reaction was too mild?"

"Good thing you were not provoked."

"I suppose so. By the way, I wonder whether you will like our food."

"I'm sure it will melt in my mouth. But really, you shouldn't have bothered."

"It is no trouble at all."

Another month passed. I had not paid any rent yet. There is no hurry, I thought. Pankajam too seemed to be in no hurry to collect the rent. But I was becoming uneasy.

"I am sorry I haven't been able to pay. . . " I began one day.

But she cut me short. "Don't fret over it. Remember, I am not like your former landlord. Poverty and plenty are twin sides of the same coin, aren't they?"

I stared at her as she walked away. What an angel she was!

Three days later I was gazing idly at the street through the window. It was early in the morning. But the peak-hour rush had already begun. Students and office-goers on foot, on bicycles and in cars, jostled for space on the road in front of the market. Suddenly I saw Sankaran. It was not difficult to distinguish his grotesque face in any crowd. He pushed open the gates and entered the compound. What! Right into the lion's den! He must have gone out of his head.

I drew back from the window. A couple of minutes later Sankaran walked down the veranda and stopped before my room.

"I wanted to see you."

"Well?"

"What about the rent you owe me?"

"I don't have any money now."

"When do you propose to pay up?"

"I will send it to you as soon as I get some cash."

"Don't you think you are just being evasive?"

"Look here, are you trying to teach me manners?"

"Don't think you can fool around with me for long."

A heated discussion followed. I did not give an inch.

"You don't own the place." Sankaran was startled by Pankajam's voice. Red-faced, her hands on her hips, Pankajam was ready to confront him. Sankaran was dumbfounded. It seemed he would drop dead on the floor any moment.

"Did you think you could haunt me here too?" Pankajam glared at him.

"I . . . I wanted to have a talk with you—alone. That is why I came here."

"But would you condescend to visit me here?" Pankajam was unmoved.

"But that is what I came for. Please . . . " They moved towards the stairs. I pricked up my ears.

"I have brought it. I have had the whole block—all the ten rooms—registered in your name. Here are the papers."

"But how can you afford to trust me?"

"Pankajam, I can't live without you . . ."

I didn't hear the rest. They were descending the stairs and going out of earshot.

I wondered about the outcome of the discussion. Pankajam was not likely to be coaxed into going with him. It was more probable that she would leave him reeling under a volley of the choicest invectives she had invoked for the occasion. Not even a ratsnake could live with him.

The lunch was brought in as usual. I was relieved. But I was curious to know what had happened. Pankajam had not turned up yet. She would certainly come in the evening. The pink of her cheeks, her long, lush hair and the flash of her ear-rings played hide-and-seek in my mind. She was like a rainbow!

I came out into the veranda earlier than usual that evening. I counted the minutes as they passed by. I pricked up my ears at every sound. The hues of dusk, not she, came in through the grills. I turned my gaze into my heart. There was a riot of colours there!

Would she come? Why shouldn't she? But the pink of the sky turned a dull grey. The grey thickened into the oblivion of the night. She didn't come.

Why did I expect her to come? I went back to my room and opened a volume of poems. I thought of meditating seriously on poetry and the emotional ferments a poet is capable of creating. But when you do it deliberately, your thoughts have a way of going round and round in circles, instead of taking you where you want to go. Let me hum a poem. It will clear my mind.

> *O, bird of life, confined in your cage of flesh,*
> *How long will you pine for your liberty?*

The bird of life is imprisoned. . . and. . . tchah! It was no good. I shut the book. I felt drowsy. My heart brimmed with gratitude for God who granted the boon of sleep to his creations.

Something hummed like a beetle in my ears. O, bird of life. . . I turned and tossed in bed, tried out a tune, jerked my feet . . . Minutes, or hours later, I dozed off. When I woke up, I saw my supper gone cold in the plates. Who had brought it? It could only be one of the servants.

I sat up in bed and lit a beedi. I heard footsteps in the veranda. It was Sankaran. Before I could ask him what he wanted, he said: "The rent."

"I have told you what I am going to do about it. I haven't changed my mind since yesterday."

"Not that. I meant the rent for this room."

You can give it to him," said a sweet, enchanting voice behind him. I took my eyes off Sankaran to look at Pankajam for a moment. Then, without a word, I rolled up my bed and started stuffing my things into a suitcase. "I am vacating the room today," I said when I was through.

"And the rent?" Sankaran insisted.

I said nothing.

"You can take away your things when you come to pay the rent," Pankajam's voice was as sweet as ever.

When I put on my shirt and came out into the veranda, Pankajam asked me, "Where is the key? There is no duplicate."

I pointed to the key on the window-ledge, turned and walked away. As I descended the stairs, the headmistress's husband joined me. "Are you leaving too?" he asked me as we reached the gate.

"Yes."

He sighed. There were tears in his eyes. We looked at each other in silence. I thought I was looking at my reflection in a mirror. What was he thinking?

"Tomatoes, tomatoes anybody?"

"Give me some." I fished in my pocket for change. There were about nine *annas*[3]. I bought two large, ripe tomatoes and handed one to the headmistress's husband. "Have one. It is vitamin-rich."

---

[3] Anna - A former monetary unit. The sixteenth part of a rupee.

I munched on the tomato and walked down the road. How comfortable it was to walk with empty hands! The bedding and the suitcase would have been a nuisance. I humed the lines: *O, bird of life...* The tomato was good. The poem too.

(Translated by K. M. Sherrif)

COOL DRINK

P. Kesavadev

"Cool drink! Cool drink!" The cry from the corner of the street attracted Janu, who was plodding along in the blazing sun, thirsty and exhausted. Standing behind a table, on which were arrayed bottles of *sherbet* with a lemon each on their open mouths, and half-a-dozen glasses, Ahmed was giving a proper speech: "Haai....Haai...cool drink, first class cool drink, first class..." Janu walked up to the corner and stood on the patch of wet mud before Ahmed and his wares, a brass pitcher clutched under her arm. She stared longingly at the bottles, the lemons and the pot of drinking water under the table. The little girl could not express the urge to wet her parched throat with the water(she did not know what 'cool drink' meant) that Ahmed was selling.

Ahmed was still at his speech. "Cool drink, cool drink. Take a sip and feel it cool you from head to feet." A head-load worker with a load on his head and a large basket in his hand stopped before Ahmed's stall. "Gimme some," he ordered. Without stopping his speech, Ahmed started preparing a glass of cool drink. When he took a pen-knife from the folds of his dress and cut a lemon, Janu's eyes entered the insides of the lemon. When Ahmed squeezed the lemon-juice into the glass, Janu's eyes stuck to it. When he poured two spoons of *sherbet*[1] into the glass, Janu moved a step forward and pressed her body against the table. When Ahmed took some water in a tin tumbler from the pot under the table and poured it into the glass, she could not hold back her desire any longer: "Will you give me some of that?"

Ahmed glanced at her with a mocking smile on his lips. He handed the glass of cool drink to the head-load worker and grinned at Janu again. Watching the worker's adam's apple moving up and down as he gulped down the 'cool drink', Janu

---

[1] Sherbet - An artificially flavoured drink.

asked Ahmed: "How much is one glass?"

Ahmed felt pity for her. "What do you have on you?"

Clutching the folds of her dress at her waist, Janu said, "I have ten *annas*—what I got from selling milk."

Taking the empty glass from the worker, Ahmed said, "Give me six *kasu*[2] and I'll give you a glass of cool drink."

"Bapa will beat me up if I give you a cool drink free," Ahmed said.

"But how can your Bapa see it?"

"How can your Amma see you giving me the money?"

"She'll count the money when I give it to her."

"What if Bapa counts the money when he comes here?"

"Give me just a little, please, I am thirsty."

"You can have some water then."

"Add a little of that too," Janu pleaded, pointing at the bottles of *sherbet*.

Ahmed took pity on her. He mixed some cool drink in a glass and handed it to Janu. Janu beamed at him as she took the glass from his hand. "I will give you your six *kasu* some time— when I get some money from Amma."

"Oh, you needn't give me anything for this," Ahmed said sympathetically. "Where do you live?"

"It's a long way from here."

"Do you come to town every day to sell milk?"

"Yes, every day. We get five litres of milk from our cow. It is dusk by the time I reach home every day."

"Push off then. You will be late."

Janu gave Ahmed a long look of gratitude before walking away.

Janu was only thirteen years old. She was the only daughter of a farm labourer. Her family belonged to a small village outside the city limits. She set out for the town early in the morning every day after drinking some *pazhankanji*[3] and returned late in the evening. She did not dare spend any of the money she got from selling milk. Her mother would thrash her if a single *kasu* was missing. When she finished selling milk in the afternoon, the sun would still be scorching hot. She would walk home then,

---

[2] Kasu—A Monetary unit, old coin.
[3] Pazhankanji - Rice gruel of the previous day.

drinking only a glass of water from some shop or house on the way.

Ahmed's cool drink was nothing less than a feast to her. She had never drunk such a thing before. Its taste lingered on her tongue when she reached home. She immediately told her mother about the delicacy she had tasted. When she woke up the next morning, she felt its taste still on her tongue. She drank her *pazhankanji*, took up the pitcher of milk and walked hurriedly towards the town.

After selling her milk, Janu wandered into that narrow street. "Cool drink! Cool drink! Come on! For a refreshing glass!" She heard Ahmed's voice as she turned the corner. Janu walked up and smiled at Ahmed. Ahmed went on with his speech, showing no sign of their acquaintance of the previous day.

After failing to attract his attention for some time, Janu asked him loudly: "Will you give me a glass of that for three *kasu*?"

Ahmed did not reply. After waiting for a few more moments, she took six *kasu* and extended it towards Ahmed. "Here, give me a whole glassfull."

Suppressing a smile, Ahmed took the money from her. "*Edee*[4], where is the six *kasu* you owe me for yesterday's cool drink?" he asked her as he mixed the drink.

"I'll give it to you tomorrow. Fill up the glass to the brim, will you?"

Ahmed filled the glass to the brim with cool drink and handed it to Janu. She drank it, put down the glass on the table and turned to go without a word to Ahmed. But something held her back. Her mother would thrash her for spending six *kasu*—that was for sure. Was there any convincing lie she could resort to? Janu stood indecisively for a few seconds. She was not so bold as to ask for the six *kasu* back from Ahmed. She should not have bought the cool drink. But what was the use of regretting it now? She had drunk it and paid for it as well.

Janu's eyes filled with tears. Tears streamed down her cheeks. Ahmed's attempts at containing his mirth failed. He burst out laughing. "What are you crying for?"

"Amma will give me a hiding," Janu whimpered.

---

[4] Edee - A way of addressing familiar women.

Ahmed took six *kasu* from the small pile of coins on the table and handed it to Janu. "Here, take it. You needn't give me any money. Come here every day after you finish selling milk. I'll give you some cool drink."

Janu wiped her tears, smiled at Ahmed and walked away, turning once to give him a look of gratitude.

From the next day, she appeared every day in the afternoon at Ahmed's open-air cool drink stall. He would promptly give her a glass of cool drink. After drinking it, Janu would sit on a wooden crate and relax for some time. Sometimes she swept the stall clean for Ahmed. She bought beedis for him too.

One day she presented Ahmed with a small packet of jackfruit. She had stowed them away from her share of the jackfruit she had got for supper the previous night. She had managed to bring them with her in the morning without her mother noticing it. Ahmed gladly accepted her present. Soon she began bringing something for him every day. She was sad when she didn't get anything to bring with her.

Days and weeks passed. Summer came to an end. The rains began. Nobody bought Ahmed's cool drink any more. He decided to wind up his business and return to his village.

Ahmed lived in a remote hamlet far away from the town. He was about thirty-five years old. Till summer came, he would cultivate the piece of land he owned. As soon as summer started, he would leave his wife and children with his father and go up to the town to sell cool drink.

When Janu came in the afternoon as usual, Ahmed told her he was returning to his village the next day. Janu said nothing. She sat silently on the crate, longer than usual. She felt a strange uneasiness. She didn't know why, but she felt a stranger had intruded into her mind and was speaking to her in a language she didn't understand. Ahmed asked her several questions. But she didn't reply. She just sat in silence with her face downcast. Intermittently she glanced up at Ahmed.

Finally Janu got up to go. She couldn't bear to look at Ahmed's face. Looking down at the ground, she asked, "What time are you leaving tomorrow?"

Janu's change of expression surprised Ahmed. "I will be going early in the morning—before you come," he replied in a matter-of-fact way.

Janu walked away quietly. Early next morning, Ahmed was busy with his preparations to go home. He gave the table to a friend for safekeeping. He stacked his bottles and glasses in his wooden crate. When he finished counting the money he had with him—his season's earnings—and turned, he saw Janu staring at him. A strange agitation had taken possession of her mind. Ahmed thought she was saddened by the fact that she wouldn't get her cool drink any more. He took a two-*anna* coin and extended it to her. "Goodbye, Janu. Here, you can keep this."

Janu struck at Ahmed's hand angrily and the coin flew out of his grasp. Ahmed bent down to peer at her face. There were tears in her eyes. He picked up the coin, took out another two-*anna* bit and extended both to Janu. Janu struck at his hand again. The coins did not fly away this time as Ahmed had tightened his grip. "Why do you cry?" he asked her. She did not reply.

It was time for Ahmed to go. He had to start at once if he was to reach home by noon. He lifted the wooden crate, placed it on his head, said goodbye to Janu again and started walking.

Janu wiped her tears and watched Ahmed walking away from her. Ahmed turned to look back after a few paces. Janu was still there, rooted to the spot. When he looked back from the turning at the end of the street, Janu was still there, staring at him. He turned the bend and disappeared from her sight. Janu let out a long sigh.

Janu still comes to town every day to sell milk. When she reached the corner of the street where Ahmed used to sell his cool drink, she would stop and gaze wistfully at the spot for a long time.

(Translated by K. M. Sherrif)

POOVANPAZHAM

Karoor Nilakanta Pillai

To the east of our house lies the *mana*[1] of a powerful landlord family. We were their vassals and dependents. It would be correct to say that we needed each other—as masters and servants. When there was some special occasion at the *mana*—a birthday, an *unniyoonu*[2], a wedding or a *pindam*[3]—we never cooked anything at home. On *thiruvathira*[4], there was *kaikottikkali*[5] everywhere. But our women went only to the *mana* to dance. At the beginning of summer, when the mangoes ripened, we children always hung around the large, tall mango tree at the *mana*, picking our windfall of mangoes and building our little castles in the sand under it. When Onam came, we rushed to tie our swings to the large shady tree which stood in the yard of the *mana*. The *mana* was more than a home to us.

There was a boy of my age at the *mana*—Vasukkuttan. We became inseparable friends in spite of the difference in our social standing. Poor Vasukkuttan! He died three years ago.

His mother almost died of grief. He was her only source of hope after her husband's death. The dreams which sustained her for ten years in her bereavement were shattered. That was three years ago.

The *antharjanam*[6] certainly did not deserve her fate. Every-

---
[1] Mana - The home or homstead of a Namboodiri family.
[2] Unniyoonu - The ceremonial feeding of child with boiled rice when it is six months or one year old.
[3] Pindam - The ceremonial feeding of the spirits of the dead with balls of rice.
[4] Thiruvathira - A festival celebrated mainly by women, which falls in the Indian month of Dhanu (December-January)
[5] Kaikottikkali - A kind of dance, is mainly performed during thiruvathira.
[6] Antharjanam - Literally the one who stays inside the house. A Namboodiri woman.

body who knew her, even those who talked to her just once, were her well-wishers. Nobody could pass her by without shedding a tear at her fate. She had forgotten what happiness meant. What was left for her in life now?

Her real name is 'Unnima' or 'Nangayya' or some such thing. But the women in the neighbourhood had given her another name—'poovanpazham'[7]. It was not really a nickname. She belonged to a place called Poovanpuzha. 'Poovanpazham' sounded very much like it and soon became the popular name for her. The name suited her well, too, for she was fair and plump.

After her son died, I remember seeing her only once. I was at the age when I could consider myself grown up. She was a young widow.

One day Mother called me, "Appu, Poovanpazham is calling you. There, near the wall."

I was doing my homework, trying to solve a problem in maths. Most probably, she wanted me to do some errand for her. I had begun to find this humiliating. At home, all of us, men, women and children were the servants of the *mana*. But I was a High School student now and thought this beneath my dignity. It was our poverty which drove us to work at the *mana*. But working there did not redeem us from our poverty. Everybody seemed to be content with getting their daily bread from the *mana*. Nobody seemed to have any desire to move up in life. I longed for a way out of this eternal slavery in which our whole family was enmeshed. I would be the one to take the lead in this. It would be far more dignified for the women to pluck weeds or cut crops in the fields instead of sweeping floors and washing clothes at the *mana*. As for the men, why shouldn't they go somewhere else for ploughing the soil and mending fences? Nobody at the *mana* would have taken kindly to my studying in an English school, for it meant that they would be left with one servant less to be at their beck and call.

"Blast Poovanpazham!" I muttered as I walked towards the mud-wall which separated our compound from the *mana*.

---

[7] Poovanpazham - Also a kind of thick, fleshy plantains, with a cloyingly sweet taste.

"What is it?" I shouted at the top of my voice much before I reached the wall.

The wall was only as high as her waist. But the ground rose steeply there to be almost level with my head. She had wrapped a shawl around her shoulders. The strands of her long, beautiful hair kept falling onto her face. They knew they could afford to be unruly with a woman who had nobody in the world to call her own. I stopped at a distance of about fifteen feet from her.

"Appu, what a long time it has been since I saw you last! What were you doing at home?"

"I was doing a problem in maths."

"Why are you so busy on a holiday?"

"I am not busy. Is there anything I can do for you?"

"You always remind me of my Vasu. He was only a month and a half younger than you."

She would often burst into tears at the mention of her son's name. I did not know how I could console her. So I just nodded my head.

"God called him back." Her voice did not falter, but I saw grief reflected in her blue eyes.

"Don't know when my turn will come," she sighed.

After a short pause, she started asking me a variety of questions: what did I have for breakfast? In which class was I studying? What were the fees? Which language was more difficult to learn, Sanskrit or English? So on and so forth.

"I nearly forgot what I called you for," she said at last. "Get me a ball of thread and a needle, a thin one. I have some sewing to do."

"Sure, I will get them for you."

She called me near, extended her bare arm towards me and dropped a coin into my hand.

"Will that be enough? Don't be in a hurry. It will do if you get them for me tomorrow. Get back to your homework now. Ah, what was that problem you were doing?"

This is what they call small talk. Why should she be so inquisitive? There was nothing of interest for her in the problem I was doing. "It's a problem about work and time," I replied all the same.

"I have only work, no time. Never mind, tell me about it."

I was getting irritated, but she was my friend's mother. I

described the problem to her: Raman worked twice as fast as Krishnan. They do a piece of work together in ten days. How long will it take for each of them to do the same work separately?

I saw her getting interested. She wanted to know how it could be solved. I told her.

"The things you know!" She gave me an admiring smile—a smile fresh and charming like a rose in bloom.

I sent her the thread and needle through my young brother.

She called me again the next week. She wanted me to buy her a metre of cloth to stitch a pillow-cover with.

"May I go?" I asked her politely when she finished telling me what she wanted.

"You always seem to be in a hurry, Appu," she said.

"It's not that," I said. I did not like to talk to anybody at the *mana* for long. I would become painfully aware of the fact that they were people who mattered, and I was a nobody.

A squirrel ran up the wall squeaking.

"How cute it looks! They say Lord Ram drew the lines on its back. Do you know the story, Appu?"

"As a token of gratitude for carrying mud to build the bridge to reach Lanka. I know the story." I was in a hurry to end the conversation.

"It seems there is nothing you don't know!" That admiring smile again.

Perhaps she was saddened by the fact that her son too would have known all this if he had been alive.

Two weeks later she called me again. I was annoyed. But I went without a murmur. She had no son to do anything for her. She presented me with a small packet. I think she placed it, instead of dropping it, in my hand. I opened the banana-leaf wrappings to find two *neyyappams*[8].

"Appu, eat them. They are for you." I was debating whether to take them home.

I ate both the *neyyappams*.

"Did you like them?"

"Doesn't everybody like *neyyappam*?"

She let me go only after chatting with me a long time about nothing in particular.

---

[8] Neyyappams - A sweet delicacy made of rice flour.

A few days later she called me to pluck some betel leaves from the betel-vine for her.

It seemed she was making a proper servant out of me. I was now in my final year at school. I would get a job if I passed the exam—a job which would fetch me at least twenty rupees a month. I wouldn't work like a serf at the *mana* then. She was trying to make me do as much work as she could before that happened. She might be good at heart, but could she be free of the jealousy of her caste towards 'upstarts' like me?

"But you don't chew betel, *kunnatheramma*[9], do you?"

"I don't. Does that mean everybody at the *illam*[10] is like me? As for me, I haven't chewed betel for about a dozen years now. Even when I did, I never took tobacco with it. Don't bother if you can't climb the tree."

Can't climb! I was far too young to say I couldn't climb the tree on which the vine lay entwined.

"I can climb it all right. Wait, let me come over there."

"Just hop over the wall."

"It's not nice to hop over walls, when there are proper ways to enter."

"You don't have to be fussy about proper ways, Appu. You can always do what you like here. Come on."

I hopped over the mud-wall effortlessly.

"How smart you are!" She was praising me again. It was distressing for her to be reminded of her son who would have been as smart as me if he had been alive.

She stood behind a row of plantains and watched me climb the tree.

"Look, Appu, don't trouble yourself if you can't."

I tied up the ends of my *mundu* at my waist. Plucking the leaves one by one, I deposited them in the fold of my *mundu*. She was standing in the veranda when I came down."Bring them here," she beckoned me.

I went around to the veranda at the back. I shook the betel leaves down to the floor and started stacking them neatly.

---

[9] Kunnatheramma - Atheramma; the word used by members of some lower castes to address Namboodiri women. The younger ones among them are called kunnatheramma.

[10] Illam - The home or homestead of a Namboodiri family.

"How tender they look! I feel like having a chew myself," she said, watching me.

"Take some," she said, when I had finished.

"What do I need betels for!" I said and stepped out into the yard to go.

"Did you attend Kesavan's wedding yesterday?"

"Yes."

"Was it a grand wedding? Were there plenty of guests?"

"There were quite a few."

"What did you have for lunch?"

I described everything in detail.

"Did they bring home the bride yesterday?"

It seemed that I was in for another spell of small talk. There were more questions to come: Did they bring the bride in a carriage? How many of us at home attended the wedding? Did the bride wear plenty of jewelry? etc., etc. It would take a whole day to answer all her questions. I had to cut the conversation short somehow. The best way to do it was to answer her in monosyllables.

"Um."

"Is she smart?"

"Um."

"How do you know that?"

"Well, she looked smart."

"Is she good-looking?"

"Um."

"How is her complexion?"

"Middling. Not very fair."

"Like me?"

"Um."

"Or fairer than me?"

"Um."

"Do you call that middling? How old is she?"

"Oh, sort of."

"Sort of!" she laughed

"Sorry, I was thinking of something else. She is about twenty."

"What were you thinking of?"

"Oh, nothing."

"Come on, tell me."

"I was thinking of her family. They are quite well-off."

"So she is twenty. How old is Kesavan?"

"He is older than her."

She smiled. "Quite natural for us, isn't it? They say it's different for the white men."

Here was an *antharjanam* who scarcely saw the world outside her *illam* talking about the customs of Europeans. The way she said it, one would think she had travelled all over the world. But I shouldn't be rude to her. Poor woman! She had neither husband nor children.

"You are eighteen now, aren't you?"

"Um."

"I was thirteen when I was married. That was twenty years ago."

"Um."

"He was eighteen then."

"Um."

She stood with her bosom pressed against the door. She had wrapped a shawl around her shoulders. But it was more like a belt around her neck with both the ends going over her shoulders and hanging behind her. It only covered enough of her chest to conceal the fact that she wore no *thali*.

Meanwhile my pussy-cat joined us. She seated herself comfortably on the steps and gazed at me. She seemed to find our conversation very interesting.

"Cute, isn't she?" *Atheramma* said. "But she's very naughty too. Sleeps with me at night. She comes in quietly without waking me and cuddles up to me."

"She knows *Kunhatheramma* is fond of her. And she likes the warmth of bodies."

She gave me a look, a sharp piercing look. In an instant her face disappeared behind the door.

"I'll be going along." I crossed the yard and went out through the gates.

I didn't see Poovanpazham for some time after that. Whenever she sent for me, I would say, "Tell her I am not here. She has plenty of time for her silly prattle. I don't have any."

One day, I heard somebody at home saying Poovanpazham was ill.

Around that time, the old Namboodiri at the *mana* married

for the third time. Though the bride's *Kudiveypu*[10] was not so grand, there was a feast for the guests. After I had finished eating, Poovanpazham called me. She was still ill. Perhaps she wanted me to buy some medicines for her. She had no child of her own to do it for her. I went round to the backyard and stood near the steps. She was sitting at the door of her room. Her long hair had been cut short. Her cheekbones were protruding and her eyes were lustreless. Only her eyelashes retained some of the old charm.

"Did you enjoy the lunch?"

"Um."

"I am forbidden to eat anything. I have no appetite either."

"Um."

"The next feast here will be a *pindam*."

"Yes, Appu, it will be a *pindam*."

"Why do you say that, *Kunhatheramma*?"

"Kunnatheramma!..."

She tried to force a smile.

Here was what they called God's plenty: riches, beauty, youth . . .

I stared at her dumbfounded. Had I too, like the others, hurt her with my insolence?

"You may go, Appu." She closed the door before I could say anything.

(Translated by K. M. Sherrif)

---

[10] Kudiveypu - The ceremony of bringing the bride to the bridegroom's house among Namboodiris.

NIGHT QUEEN
S. K. Pottekkatt

There is nothing that attracts me more than the fragrance which emanates from the petals of the night queen in bloom. It is wafted to me by the wind through the darkness from hedges and bushes, filling me with a frenzy of excitement. The night queen is a harlot among flowers. She sleeps the whole day, and after the daylight fades at dusk, moves stealthily through the darkness and accosts men! Yes, the fragrance befits a harlot.

But in my own garden, I would never plant a night queen. You could not see a single night queen among the neat rows of flowering plants in my garden. You will know the reason if you listen to this old tale which I shall unfold before you now.

I was a college student of seventeen then. Seventeen is a dangerous age in the life of a boy. Though they call it sweet seventeen in English, I have given it a more suitable name : susceptible seventeen. It is the age at which any new fancy catches the boy's eye. A boy at seventeen is a harmless, starry-eyed dreamer who tumbles headlong into love, hatches conspiracies around good-looking girls and runs feverishly after new-fangled ideas, only to stumble and bite the dust. He is a perpetual nuisance to editors of literary periodicals, for he is at that age when poetry comes naturally to the worst among the nitwits. In most cases, he shuns materialism and embraces instead, a spiritualism of the Vedantic type. His conception of love follows the same path, making him prefer the love of *'Nalini'* or *'Leela'*[1] to that of *'Vilasathilaka'*[2]. Dante, the Italian poet, would be his ideal lover.

After conducting a thorough investigation into the beauty and character of several girls (without their knowledge or permission), Malathi became lucky to don the mantle of my ideal

---
[1] Nalini and Leela - Two long poems by Kumaran Asan, celebrating platonic love.
[2] Vilasathilaka.

girl. Malathi was a High School student. She was fair, a bit short-statured and plump, the little curves on her chest beginning to show, her face bright and round like the full moon. It was her dancing eyes that attracted me first.

Though she radiated beauty all around, my 'Malu' was a grim-faced girl who never smiled. But I liked her grave expression. I liked girls that way. I detested girls who giggled and frolicked around. Every evening, I presented myself promptly at the balcony of my house to drink in with my eyes the spectacle of her returning from school, wearing a green *pavada*[3], khadi of course, and a white khadi blouse with red spots, her books clasped to her chest. She walked with a swan-like gait, her eyes downcast. She did not know that my days and nights were spent in worshipping her. Throwing away my homework, in which I had to battle with a lot of 'logarithm', 'co-tangents' and various other thingamajigs which my maths teacher Mr Ramanathan Iyer was ruthless enough to burden me with, I set about writing poems about Malathi—about her swan-like gait, about the books which were blessed to be clasped to her bosom.

My heart withers as my eyes behold the
Two little buds that swell at her bosom.

Wonderful! I liked the lines I composed. But, though I wrote them in a fit of love, I was very particular about not looking at her with lustful eyes. Ours should be a love founded on uncompromising idealism. There should be some despair and dejection in it too. I wished to be crossed in love like Madanan. I imagined the scene in which my 'Malu' would fall into my arms like a 'pennant drooping down on the pole'.

Malathi lived in a double-storeyed house, which stood in the middle of a large plot of land, about two furlongs from my house. Her father and I had no more than a casual acquaintance with each other. Just enough to say 'hello' when we met. I doubt whether Malathi, who always walked with her eyes downcast, had ever seen my face.

At night, after supper, I went for a walk. There was a small track that branched away from the road and ended at a huge arched doorway on the western side of the compound in which

---

[3] Pavada - A long skirt

Malathi's house stood. Inside the compound, a few yards from the doorway was a bush of night queens, six feet in height. One day, I made a discovery: standing in the bush I could get a good look at Malathi as she sat reading in her bedroom. The light of the table-lamp gave a clear view of the expressions on her face. She wore a low-cut blouse. As her hair cascaded from either side on to her chest, only a small portion of her white bosom was visible—like a fountain sprouting among rocks. Keeping the English Reader open before her, supporting her forehead with the palm of her left hand, bending slightly towards the table, she would read, or rather, mutter—she never really read loudly—"And Sita wanted to go with Rama . . . " Her voice was so toneless that it seemed she was reluctantly doing somebody a favour by her reading. Sometimes she would start nodding as she read, her head drooping down and down, till it finally struck the table. When this happened, she would put an end to her journey to the window for some time. Watching all this from the bush, I often thought of calling out to her, "Darling, that will do. Go to sleep." But after rubbing her eyes for a few moments, she would resume reading. I would gaze intently at my heartthrob with bated breath as sleep drew her into its fold. The strong refreshing fragrance of the night queen gushed into my nostrils and overflowed into my heart. Every moment in the bush gave me a taste of eternal bliss. Like the idyllic vision of an incense-bearing dream, she glittered before me like a' gem of the purest ray serene. The incense of the night queen clung to every thought and dream of mine.

Sometimes she recited Malayalam poetry:

Ammaikkyu Mathramalla—ellarkkume chenneduth— Umma vecheeduvan Thonnumallo

(And none—not just her mother—liked to miss planting on her forehead a fond kiss.)

The lines seemed to be written solely for her lips to give them sound. When I heard her recite them, I longed to give *her* a kiss on her lips.

Thus, for three months, I silently admired her beauty for an hour every night. The fragrance of the night queen and the vision of Malati's face blended into one and became etched in my heart. My eyes savoured her heavenly beauty every day.

The rains started. *Edavappathy*[3] came and went. *Thiruvathira Nhattuvela*[4] arrived.

But the rains were no obstacle for my visits at night. Sometimes, when the drizzle thickened into a downpour, she would get up and close the window. It was like locking up my heart! Crestfallen, I would walk back with heavy steps, drenched to the skin by the cruel rain.

One night, standing in the bush, I overheard her father speaking to her brother: "I think we should trim and replant the whole lot in the garden. And the whole place is overgrown with weeds and bushes. Let's clear them too..."

My heart was on fire. If they started trimming, slashing and clearing everything, the night queens were sure to be wiped out. The bush was too tall and thick. What would become of me if my haunt of love was destroyed? I had invested all my hopes in those night queens. I would drown in grief like a bird robbed of its nest. How would I ever get a chance to gaze at the angelic face in solitude again?

There was no way out, except to write a letter to her, seeking her intervention to save the night queens.

I sat awake till three in the night and drafted a letter.

Dear Princess of my heart,

I have been worshipping you silently for the last three months, standing in the bush of night queens near the doorway on the western side of your house. I would have liked to go on worshipping you for years and ages without telling a soul—not even you—about it. But 'Man proposes, God disposes'. Oh! It breaks my heart to think about it. Tomorrow your father will wipe out my haunt of love. No more shall I be able to worship at the altar of your love. I, therefore, appeal to you in the name of love to save the bush of night queens, and this humble devotee of yours, from the impending disaster. Grace me with your act of compassion so that my selfless and sacred worship may continue unhindered.

sd/-
A mendicant at the temple of love

---

[3] Edavappathy - The middle of the Indian month of Edavam (the last week of May) when the monson arrives in Kerala.
[4] Thiruvathira Nhattuvela - The spell of heavy rains in July, when Nharu (paddy saplings) are transplanted.

To deliver the letter to Malathi at the earliest, I set out towards her house early the next morning on the pretext of asking her father for a sapling of 'Prince of Wales' to plant in my garden. There was a commotion in the yard. About a dozen of her neighbours were gathered in a circle, talking in excited voices. I wriggled my way into the circle and peered at the cause of the excitement.

It was a snake they had beaten to death—full three feet in length.

A cobra of the first order!

"The fellow was living primly in that bush of those what-do-you-call-them that smell at night. We saw the hole when we cleared the bush. Had to poke about a bit before our reptilian friend came out. What beats me is why we didn't even get a clue about him while he lived so close to us!" Velu, the carpenter who had killed it, laid his forefinger across his nose in amazement. "A proper dandy, with dots and stripes . . ."

The cobra's body was still twitching like the electric needle I had seen at the telegraph office. Velu saw it and became immediately alert. Seizing a thin log of firewood he started clobbering it again. The snake's head was crushed and its blood coloured the soil.

I turned and walked away. I don't remember how and when I reached home. I felt my whole body burning. I almost went out of my head when I thought of the cobra, its mouth open, its head lifted, taking in the fragrance of the night queens as I gazed at the embodiment of celestial beauty. However hard I tried, I could not get the picture of the cobra out of my mind.

I ran a fever the same night. Soon I became delirious. I had nightmares. I groaned, muttered and screamed. I saw snakes everywhere, on the bed-post, under the cot, on the window. . . snakes hissing, writhing and lifting their hoods. "Snakes, snakes!," I screamed. Everybody at home came running and turned the room upside down in search of snakes. As a snake rubbed its hood on my back, I woke up with another scream.

In my dreams, I saw Malathi as a snake-maiden, with the body of a snake and the face of a girl. Her face allured me, but I shrank back in horror at the sight of her body.

I was ill for a month. When I went for a walk the first time after my recovery, I saw a board with the legend, 'to let', hanging on the gate of Malathi's house. I learned from a neighbour that Malathi's father had been transferred to Kannoor and they had all left for Kannoor a week before.

I have never seen Malathi after that. Recently, I learned that she was married and was the mother of two children. The undelivered letter I had written to her was lying in a pile of my old letters. I burned it a week ago.

Whenever the fragrance of the night queen is wafted to me by the wind, the memory of my amorous adventure at the age of seventeen drifts into my mind. It brings alive the images of a sleepy schoolgirl reading her lessons and a cobra raising its hood to strike ... Yes, it is a strange fear that has made me deny access to night queens in my garden.

(Translated by K. M. Sherrif)

A GOOD OMEN

Kovilan

It was a five-hundred-rupee problem. I had five hundred rupees in my pocket. But the number of things I had to do with it... The list was ready a day early. Everything must be settled. I lay awake the whole night reciting the rupee-anna-paisa formula in my mind. When I woke up, Suja asked me:

"When are you going, *Acha*[1]?"

That was before giving me my black tea, which I always had first thing in the morning.

"When it is time to."

My voice did not properly convey the irritation of not getting my black tea. I hurled a question at her:

"What do you want?"

"Buy me a ribbon."

When Rome burns, she will fiddle on the loss of her charred ribbon. Typical of her sex. So I said:

"Not today. After Suran's operation."

She whimpered:

"It's him you think about all the time. A ribbon costs only forty paise."

Expenses were getting out of hand.

As I walked to the bus stand with five hundred rupees in my pocket, there was no ribbon in my mind. I should get into a bus that started from the bus stand, not any that stopped in front of it on its way, crammed with passengers. I had my five hundred rupees to protect.

I thought there was an unusually large crowd on the footpath. Who was that shadowy figure following me? Who was it that watched me while I counted out the money from the locker at the bank? My left hand was on my pocket. Curse the tribe of

---

[1] Achan - Father

tailors who stitch pockets on the left sides of shirts! And the blasted umbrella! The right hand was not used to holding anything except umbrellas. As for pretending to be a heart-patient, the hand did not cover the pocket well enough. Getting a window-seat on the left side of the bus was a bit of pure luck. I heaved a sigh of relief.

The Mother Superior had said:

"Keep the money ready. The rest is in the hands of the Lord."

The doctor pointed to the white spot on the dark film: "Here is the stone."

"What was that?" Suran asked me as we came out.

He had started asking questions as soon as we crossed the gates. Was that a trident St Joseph was holding as he hung in the air above the earth with a halo around his head? How does the water in the pond full of lotuses rise up in the fountain?

The hospital seemed to fill the valley. Suran panted as we descended the road that went down the valley, glinting in the sun.

"*Acha*, don't walk so quickly."

We walked slowly, trying to recollect old stories. This road was just a mud-track.

The road was a mud-track. Men were apes!

What I mean is . . .

It happens to me every time. I intend to say something. But when I say it, it is not what I had intended.

There were narrow mud-tracks from the market to Kanippalam. Even at noon, the wayfarers had their hearts in their mouths as they walked through them. At dusk, when day blended into night, few dared to take the risk. There was a *chira*[2] there in those days. The lonely wayfarer trembled as he approached the *chira*. He stopped and called loudly through his cupped hands:

Kaleeeeeee. . .

He waited for the answering call. Not a step before that. Didn't Kali hear his fervent call which darted across the valley?

Kaleeeee. . . he called again.

The wayfarer was perplexed. What had happened to Kali,

---

[2] Chira - A big pond, generally a public bathing place.

who had made the *chira* her abode? And then the answering call came. Relieved, he offered a third call to Kali to complete the ritual, and walked on.

As the echoes of his calls ran up and down the valley and bumped against one another, the wayfarer felt a cold sweat wetting his temples. Was Kali following him?

Suran asked:

"Is this the spot they call Kali from?"

"I don't remember."

The old pathways were all, perhaps, enclosed by the walls of the hospital and the convent. Anyway, this was not the old valley any more.

Suran said:

"I am going to call Kali."

"A missionary came here."

"Let me call Kali."

"No, you'll be out of breath."

He looked reprovingly at me.

"How scared you are!"

I was scared of what was wrong with him.

The doctor said:

"This is the stone. It can be removed. There is a ninety per cent chance of success. Let us hope your son is not among the other ten per cent."

Why did I tell him about that persevering priest? The man who built a church, a convent and a hospital in the domain of Kali, was also a child once.

So was I.

Suran stopped before the small pond with a ringed wall around it in front of the porch of the hospital.

"Is this the *chira*?"

"This is no *chira*, just another concrete pond."

Having grown up wallowing in mud and water, I could not communicate with a child born and brought up in a jungle of concrete.

There was once a log-bridge across the stream. The bridge that spanned the stream now was of concrete. Motor vehicles brought patients to the hospital along the roads which had devoured the old mud-tracks.

"What's that?"

Suran pointed to the corner of the doctor's cabin as we came out.

The doctor took the film, hot from the machine, and put it into a slot in a square box. A yellow light glowed in the box. The doctor's forefinger zeroed in on the white lines on the dark surface, but did not touch them.

"There is a deposit."

But Ramu Vaidyar said:

"It is just too much bile in his blood. Take four small onions. Soak them in sour buttermilk kept in an iron vessel at night. In the morning, cut the onions into four pieces. Mix it well with the buttermilk and stir. Drinking the mixture for seven days continuously will purify his blood. It ought to work—it is a time-tested formula.

His mother said:

"God gave us a son. Now what can men do?"

"Is it a microscope?" Suran asked.

We were standing at the door of the lab. The nurse who wrote the test report came out.

"Your son? Well, there are some RBC—red blood corpuscles."

"I want to see it," Suran said.

The Sister smiled.

"You can't see what is inside your body."

Suran looked cross—like a calf wrenched from the cow's udder.

"That!" he pointed.

The nurse, who knew the minerals and salts of the body, went down into his soul laughing. Her laughter resounded in her chest.

"You want to see the microscope? Let him have a look. Perhaps . . ."

The golden rays reflected on her upper lip, trembled in the unexpected silence.

"Sister, what made you take orders?"

Why should a bride of the Lord be so concerned about Suran?

The Sister at the X-ray department wore a bored look.

"You are a dumb boy. The sun, the moon and the stars are not the only things which give out rays," she said. "There are fireflies. There are rays in your eyes. At all sources of light . . . don't jump to conclusions. Here the light is produced by electricity. Take off your knickers. Here, wear this *mundu*. Don't know how to wear a *mundu*—stupid. The invisible rays from the source of light enter your body and . . . don't move."

"He didn't take off his waist-chain," the Sister said as she came out with the developed film.

"How would I know? You didn't tell me!"

"Do you know, Sister, where I come from, we tie waist-chains to our young coconut trees when their spikes burst or when they bear fruit for the first time. We are true sons of the soil. A day will come when you too will need at least a black thread at your waist."

While the doctor was searching for the stone in the light of the illuminator, I gazed at what went around the universe . . . no, not the universe! A white line went around the image of my son's naked body on the film.

The doctor said:

"You can admit him on Monday or Thursday. We have operations on Tuesday and Friday."

I was thirsty.

"Ten paise for ice-cooled water. Quench your thirst for ten paise!"

My five hundred rupees!

The notes were safe in my pocket. But this dozing off . . . No, it won't do. I pressed the palm of my hand on the pocket.

"Tomorrow—tomorrow is the day—the draw of the Kerala State Government Lotteries—spend a measly one rupee—reap a bonanza of one lakh rupees—the ticket from rags to riches costs you only one rupee—I repeat, a single rupee . . . "

Suja said:

"Buy me a ribbon."

No, I am not thirsty.

"Ice-cooled water—ten paise."

"Where to?"

"Me?"

"Sleeping ? You can go back to sleep after taking the ticket. We don't charge extra for sleeping. Come on, where to? Gimme change . . . "

I had brought change. The five hundred rupees shall remain

intact.

I didn't know when the bus filled up. I sleep again . . . All right, it needs an extraordinarily large hand to reach my pocket from the seat behind.

As the bus started, I saw the hawkers waving ribbons of various colours with a flourish. Don't try to tempt me. You will get a share of my five hundred rupees only over my dead body.

The departure of the bus was heralded by the roar of the engine raised to full throttle. Soon it stopped, took in goods and passengers, and continued its journey to the next stop. But a yellow light filled my eyes and white lines on the dark patch appeared again.

This is the stone.

Tomorrow—Friday.

After Thursday, it will be Friday. But I was not sure. I folded my fingers to count. Thursday should not slip out of them. I pressed the folded finger-joints on the palm of the other hand.

Friday.

The surgeon's knife met the stone. The sparks flew from my eyes.

"Are you in the operation theatre, Sister? Can I go in and watch it?"

"Yes, you can go in. But you won't be seeing anything then."

To forget everything, I watched the flow of the crowd on the footpath. The crowd fought with the hawkers for six feet of air, for a slice of life. Nobody could fix his feet firmly on the ground. I tried to calculate the number of people who passed a point in a fixed period of time. One coolumb . . . one ampere. But this species, the multitude was not electricity! I think of them as atoms in a colossal flow of current through the circuit called the universe. Caught in the restless flow of masses of atoms, the species of life find their trajectories. I find my orbit: the hospital—the bank— Kanippalam—the operation theatre in the hospital.

The bus stopped again. They were standing on the footpath. I was curious. They seemed to have all the time in the world, the young couple. The man was speaking to her. He was tall. The woman's neck was white and round, but too low for his lips to reach. She couldn't hear what he was saying. The bus could have stopped a few steps ahead as well. Then I too could have heard what he was saying. But the words that fell from his lips filled up her ears, bulged in the blue veins on her neck. Below her neck, inside her red *choli*[3], her chest and ribs, propelled by a laugh, jerked like a piston in a cylinder bore. In the plait of her hair which rested on her *choli* was a red ribbon.

"After Suran's operation."

Today I have to forget all my obligations. Today is Wednesday. Thursday comes next. As my finger-joints folded again, I took up the rupee-anna-paisa formula again. I woke up with a start as the bus moved. They were still there on the footpath. The crowd flowed past them. But they—only they—were unperturbed. The customers of the hawkers, who had taken over most of the footpath, jostled for standing space. But the couple were oblivious to them. In front of them was a bus full of passengers. Curse the conductor. But their world was tranquil, serene. On the road the din of speeding vehicles. Over the maidan across the road, voices mangified by loudspeakers flooded the air. But nothing affected their small talk. The words flew up from her lips. The man bent down to receive them before they faded into the air. Inside the red *choli*, her chest and ribs worked themselves up to a continuous motion. I saw the energy radiated by the motion lighting up a sun in the man's eyes. But the bus left them behind.

Energy became flesh and blood, vitamins in the blood. As an atom of life set out on its journey, a stone blocked its way . . .

Let us hope your son won't be among the other ten per cent. No, not really about my son. About the vistas that will open up to him in the valley of the Kali, across Kanippalam, in the city—the vistas which are not destined for me . . .

The bus stopped again.

It was a ship that sailed on land, taking in merchandise from the ports of crossroads and marketplaces.

Buy me a ribbon.

I craned my neck out of the window to look back up the road. But no, I could not spot the red ribbon in the plaited hair.

The bus moved again. But it stopped at the next turning. I heard a loud gasp and scream. When I woke up the passengers were all getting down. On the footpath, the crowd, its motion

---

[3] Choli - A blouse

arrested, joined the hawkers in silent mourning. On a sudden impulse, I leaned forward on my toes to get a look. But my five hundred rupees! I sat tight on my five hundred rupees. I was the only one in the bus now. I should get down too.

When I did, I saw . . .

The young man kneeling on the footpath. On his lap . . . I recognised the red ribbon in the blood-splattered hair. But there was no movement inside the *choli*.

The young man tapped her, shook her, caressed her. But the sun was setting in his eyes.

The immobilised crown had a tear to shed for this version of the old disaster too.

Excited, propelled by their exuberance, they were crossing the road, when . . .

In the fading light of his eyes, the young man searched for her life all over her body.

I felt the pocket of my shirt.

Safe and sound!

Did anybody see my relieved smile? Nobody would be as clever as to read my thoughts!

My thoughts—

A dead body. A good omen!

Kaleeeeeeeeee . . . !

(Translated by K. M. Sherrif)

THE MODERNISERS

THE DEATH OF MAKHAN SINGH

T. Padmanabhan

Night had fallen when the bus reached Banihal. Makhan Singh stopped the bus in front of Panditji's restaurant as usual. As the passengers hastily got out, he leaned his face on the steering wheel and shut his eyes. He was overcome by an indescribable fatigue and discomfort.

In fact there was no special reason for him to be late with the bus. Usually, there would be several military trucks on the way and he would slow down, letting them pass. But that day, there were no trucks; yet he was late with the bus.

He had been late before, too. But nothing of this sort had ever happened.

When he remembered the reason, he felt his head would split. He had resolved not to think about anything, ever. But could he keep that resolution even once? Makhan Singh said to himself: death is better than this. Why didn't I die that day?

So much had happened. Weren't they uprooted from the land of their birth? Still he lived. Not because he wished to. But it was destined that way. He had calmed down by telling himself: Never mind; the roots may sprout again in fresh soil.

He had been searching. Where was that fresh soil?

He wasn't certain where it was. Sometimes he had the feeling that it was Delhi. In any case, he was sure it would be in India. All that he feels now is that it is enough if he can somehow go on living somewhere.

He must forget the past if he has to live. But, however much he tries, he cannot help brooding over the past again and again.

When he met Bachan Singh recently, he had said: "I am going to the Andamans; there's fifteen acres of land for me."

Fifteen acres! Can't believe it! Why have so much land? Bachan Singh cannot cultivate it by himself. He needs someone to help him. So. . .

Will wheat grow there? Maybe. The soil is very fertile, it is heard.

If only he could get one acre!

Yet, he would never go to the Andamans. Even if he died here! Even death holds forth a solace! Man prizes his pride the greatest. To go away from this soil where his father and grandfather are laid to rest . . .

In Makhan Singh's choking heart, the smoke of memories billowed.

He heard as if from a great distance the noise of the tarpaulin being removed and the luggage unloaded from the top of the bus. He thought: It is very late. Everyone must have had their supper. Only I am late. The very thought of eating nauseated Makhan Singh. He decided against eating.

Getting off the bus, he walked up to the restaurant's veranda. It was as if there was a heavy chain on his legs. It grew heavier as he put each step forward.

When he reached the front of the veranda, he stopped in his tracks. The two of them were standing there. The old woman and the young lady. Their hollow eyes seemed to be searching for them. Like a blade of grass in the hands of one drowning.

Those fragile forms of misery moved over to the lighted patch from darkness.

Makhan Singh was unable to confront them. He turned around. He was aching all over.

His lips trembled; eyes shut by themselves.

If only the earth would open and swallow me!

I am a disgrace even to my father!

Coward!

"Sardarji!" Someone thumped his shoulders.

It was Panditji.

"Panditji."

"What happened?"

He couldn't say anything.

Panditji put his palm on Makhan Singh's brow.

"You have fever."

"Let it be."

"Come. Let us go inside."

He didn't budge.

Why go inside? To avoid seeing them?

"It is snowing."

"Let it snow."

Makhan Singh wanted to lie face-down on that bare earth and weep. He wished to stand before them, his head erect. Wishing thus, he recollected several painful things. He saw his mother, father and wife in his mind's eye. He pressed his chest hard. Memories were breaking out of his heart in the form of blood. He said to himself: I will help them; certainly I will.

He went in with Panditji.

Moonshine spread in the Banihal pass.

A cold wind began to blow from the pass.

He was still sitting in front of the fireplace. There was no fire in the fireplace. But there was fire in his mind. It was not blazing. And so, no one saw it. Yet, he was aware of that all-consuming heat.

All this while, he was brooding. Panditji gave food to everyone.

(They did not have any money on them. I had guessed it all along. If only I had some money with me! They didn't ask for anything. Only stood in the far corner. Like me, they also must have a lot to ponder over.

Can't human beings keep away from thinking about anything?

Then I said to Panditji: Give them something.

He asked for money. I am not angry; I am only amazed. Does one keep an account of feeding one's own mother and sisters, and demand money from them? To think that he is a brahmin. He is a dog!)

Everyone retired for the night; and they too lay down. He alone sat up, thinking.

When the midnight-cock crowed, he got up and walked out. Ramlal was snoring away inside the bus. He said to himself: "He must be sleeping all wrapped up in blankets. It is really cold. Let him sleep! Isn't he young! But I cannot sleep tonight!"

In that cold, he recalled his childhood when he would keep vigil in the fields.

Wheat lay ripe in the fields!

It was before the harvest. Who would be there now?

Makhan Singh sighed. He strolled along Banihal's streets. There was total silence everywhere. The road that crept into the pass shone like a black snake in the moonlight. He took that road everyday. And would take it tomorrow too. But . . .

This moonlight seems to have a peculiar sheen. The colour of blood!

The smell of burning human flesh.

He thrust his hands into the pockets of the old corduroy trousers and walked on.

He was recalling something.

The moonshine, road and hillsides faded from Makhan Singh's vision. He was aware only of the comforting touch of the old corduroy.

Makhan Singh felt the cloth again.

He couldn't bear the thought.

He had bought it in Lahore.

She was also with him that day.

My first . . .

Lahore!

Lahore is now in Delhi!

How contented life was then!

He sighed. If only the past was a mere dream!

But how could it be? Lahore is gone. Rawalpindi is gone. Punjab's . . .

Where were they coming from? He should have asked. The next morning he would ask them everything. He went back to the restaurant. He was dead tired. But couldn't sleep. The forms of that mother and daughter would not fade from his mind. They seemed to be asking for something from far away, weeping. It was for help. He felt infinitely sad.

He should help them. It was his duty.

If he doesn't help them out in this condition, what is the use of his staying alive?

To think that he didn't have any money at all with him.

He would ask Panditji. If he got it, well and good.

God would find a way.

He comforted himself.

Towards morning he dozed off a little. Even in that reverie, a vague memory of them filled his mind like a mist.

Where did he spot them first? Must be at Pathankot. But his attention turned towards them only at Madhopur. There was a special reason for that. It took almost an hour for the search in the bus to finish. Even beddings and boxes were not spared. Standing under the tree in front of the tea-bunk, Makhan Singh enjoyed watching the fun.

The proceedings that day were very strict. It was not just a cursory affair, as usual: each person was individually subjected to the search. People were impatient to have it over and done with. Makhan Singh thought: maybe some high-ranking official is visiting the area.

Munshiji took the register from Ramlal's hands and went through it.

"There are two persons in excess," Munshiji said, raising his still-damp pen towards the sky.

Munshiji is always impatient.

"Where are they?"

They were there.

Munshiji lost his temper. He doesn't talk, once he is angry. He roars.

Munshiji asked, "Don't you have ears? Where are your things?"

It was Ramlal who said: "Munshiji, they do not have any baggage."

"Is that so?"

Advancing two steps, he asked them: "Where are you going?"

"Srinagar."

It was the old woman who spoke up. Makhan Singh thought that her voice faltered.

He got up from under the tree. Something was wrong somewhere. Why does that woman weep? Why does she weep standing at that roadside in Madhopur, in front of soldiers, passengers and shopkeepers?

He saw the old woman producing the tickets from the bundle in her hands.

"Isn't this to Jammu?"

No one spoke.

Munshiji drew something in the air with his pen.

At last a soldier said, "Never mind, Munshiji, this is not your headache! Let them go anywhere. Why do you bother?"

Munshiji flared up. "Oh, is that so?" As he was leaving, he said: "It is also you who did away with Punjab."

Hearing that, Makhan Singh turned pale. He had not forgotten the fate of Punjab. He hailed from Punjab. He had never wished to go anywhere else. His father was a farmer. His grandfather was a farmer too. They had at home swords that were old, but not rusting. But he had never seen anyone striking someone else with them.

It was when things were thus . . . Makhan Singh could not contain himself. Whom did that scarecrow-thin Munshiji have in mind when he said that? Was it aimed at him? If it was so . . . True, he was never vengeful. But whether he could have retaliated then, was another question. He could have, if he wished. But he didn't. That is why Munshiji spoke thus.

Why didn't he retaliate?

Makhan Singh gnashed his teeth. He should have struck back. But he had been away. Later Bachan Singh had said: They hacked your father to pieces. He himself had not witnessed the scene. Then, who did?

It is a son's sacred duty to avenge his father's death. But upon whom should he take revenge?

Thank God Mother was long dead by then. Otherwise, what they would have done to Mother . . .

When I went away that day, my Preetham was with Father.

Nothing was heard of her.

Where all I searched!

Who knows what has become of her.

She might not be dead.

Makhan Singh felt his heart break.

Her name must have been changed. She must be thinking about me and sighing at this very minute as I sit wondering what might have happened to her. We will never meet again.

Oh my Preetham!

Where are you?

In Karachi?

The bus was waiting for him.

Ramlal said, "Let us go, Sardarji."

With a sigh, Makhan Singh started the bus.

As the bus hurtled towards Jammu, leaving behind the landscape of a wild expanse of bare land strewn with gigantic rocks, and corn-fields irrigated by camel-drawn Persian wheels, he thought: Whatever the provocation, I am incapable of harming anyone. Why should I then rack my brains thinking about revenge? What is past is past.

Makhan Singh thought about many other things. It was a few days since he had got the letter from his aunt in Delhi. Her son was going to school. He should send them something. The next week is Roop Chand's daughter's wedding. Shouldn't he give some gift? The old man is too hard up . . . He smiled automatically, thinking about all that. He felt a sense of great contentment. What a paltry sum he spends for himself! All the rest somehow erodes this way and that . . .

He called out good-naturedly to the old cabwallah who took the wrong side, as he passed the military camp:

"Mind your precious life, Uncle."

Stopping the bus near the Rest House, Makhan Singh went to the restaurant he usually ate at. He had forgotten the mother and daughter by then. When he returned, the passengers were discussing them. He heard a young man say: "They were in our compartment till Pathankot."

There was still time for the bus to start.

Someone asked, "Are they going to Srinagar?"

"That's what they said."

"Looks like they are in dire straits."

"Aren't they refugees?"

"Why are they going there then?"

"Her son in the army is sick."

"He must be dead by now."

"Don't say that, brother."

"Oh."

"Isn't she his mother?"

"The other must be his wife."

"God help them."

Makhan Singh was hurt. They were not to be found anywhere, even if he wished to do them a good turn.

He said to no one in particular, "It seems they are gone."

"Where can they go?"

"They are gone for sure."

"What, walk up two hundred miles?"

"They might."

"They had to have at least two new pairs of footwear to do that."

"What about clothes?"
"Still, they left."
"No wonder."
"They were weeping."
"They will freeze to death tonight. That's why."
"Or . . . "
"The young one is pretty. If someone takes a fancy to her . . . "
"Things are like that in Calcutta and Delhi."

As he was heading for Banihal, what they said resounded in his ears. The form of his aunt swam into his mind.

His aunt in Delhi.

The refugee women of Delhi . . . The thought was revolting.

He was leaving behind the crowded, colourful streets of Jammu. The bus is merely crawling, he felt. When he rounded the bend in front of the 'Palace', he stopped the bus suddenly.

The woman and daughter were walking along the road which seemed created only for them.

They halted in confusion.

He didn't look at their faces. But asked, "Coming along?"

The daughter looked away.

The mother's eyes filled with tears. "We do not have money, son!"

Makhan Singh recalled his dead mother. Only she had called him 'son' with such feeling and love.

He said: "You come along."

They still hesitated.

"Get in."

Ramlal opened the rear door.

"God will reward you."

The old woman's voice faltered. The bus moved. Makhan Singh thought wonderingly about them. He was melancholy too. He sighed. Alas! Panjab's offspring are orphaned thus.

Families are broken, relationships wrecked.

But here, a mother has set off, without a second thought, to meet her sick son hundreds of miles away.

She has only love in her heart.

That young woman must be craving to meet her husband. He also must be longing to see her. When their eyes meet . . .

That relationship will never be severed.

Like the mother and wife of that sick young man in Srinagar, had his father and wife survived . . .

He was sad and angry at the same time.

He loved to see life putting forth fresh buds in that fertile soil. The beauty and freshness of, those hillsides sporting lofty pines, and the hillocks dotted by fruit-bearing pomegranates had never been lost on him. He used to glance around occasionally as he passed them. But not that day.

The storm of memories kept up a swell in his heart.

He had met refugees from Punjab on earlier occasions too. But he had never felt anything like this before. What is past is past. One can never return to old times. So, survive somehow in the new circumstances . . . this was what he felt on those occasions. He had decided not to ulcerate his mind thinking about the past. But now, witnessing such love and self-sacrifice, he was led back to the past of his own relationships. He knew very well that he couldn't, but still he yearned: if only he could return to the past!

Familiar faces paraded before the windscreen.

He heard voices of old time through the wind.

His father is calling him. He braked the bus suddenly. It was heading for a chasm! The bus shook violently.

Makhan Singh perspired. How many lives were in his hands!

He remembered his old resolution. He wouldn't think about anything.

Meeting that mother and daughter did it. He shouldn't have seen them.

The bus was moving very slowly.

They failed to reach Banihal before nightfall . . .

Makhan Singh rose as the first rays of dawn fell on the hills. People were preparing to leave.

Panditji was making tea.

Makhan Singh said, "Panditji, I am in trouble."

Putting down the teapot, Panditji looked at the face of that tall Punjabi driver. He had never heard him say anything in that tone.

What had happened? Is it the beginning of some illness? Then he should not stay in the restaurant.

"Panditji, I need some money. As soon as I get my wages,

I shall pay it back."

He was asking for a loan, for the first time in his life.

Opening his empty palms, Panditji said, "Money, Sardarji? I don't have! And look at the time you thought fit to ask for money. Hardly dawn yet."

Makhan Singh's face fell. He thought: I shouldn't have asked. Humiliation for nothing. He stood in front of the restaurant, immersed in thought.

After the lethargy of the night, the noisy life of Banihal was pulsating once again. Shops opened. The shepherds with reddened faces were coming out of liquor shops, although it was early morning. The shepherds, their flock, their dogs, their women and children. What a commotion!

The trucks began to leave one by one.

The racket of the porter-urchins. People went down to the stream with neem-twigs in their mouths, and sleepy eyes.

Gurgling springs.

Makhan Singh was in low spirits. It was time to start.

With a heavy heart, he got into his seat and started the engine. Heaving and swaying, the bus somehow reached the road. As he proceeded a few yards beyond the toll-gate, his legs suddenly seemed paralysed!

The inspector!

Makhan Singh sweated.

He did not have a blot on his career, as yet.

But now . . .

What accursed moment let this devil in!

Was he lying in wait?

Damn him!

The inspector took the register from Ramlal's hands and counted the passengers.

"There are two persons in excess."

Ramlal looked in the direction of Makhan Singh. And Makhan Singh studied the inspector's face.

"Who are they?"

The mother and daughter were in the back seat. The eyes of the passengers turned towards them. They hung their heads.

The inspector asked: "Where are your tickets?"

There were no tickets.

"Get down."

The inspector noted down the driver's number.
Makhan Singh thought: I will lose my job.
What if . . .
Let it go!
He remembered that young man in a sick-bed in Srinagar. He must be waiting expectantly for them.
The bus is to reach there by midday.
But that Panditji . . . Makhan Singh was enraged. Now there is this inspector halting them!
None of these people can understand human misery.
He went near the inspector and said: "They have to reach Srinagar by noon today. That old woman's son is ill."
The inspector said contemptuously, "So what?"
Sparks flew from Makhan Singh's eyes: "So what? So, you should permit them to travel in this bus. They are poor. Let alone how they became poor! If I had some money I would have helped them. But I don't."
Makhan Singh stopped. The passengers were taken aback. His voice was still booming . . .
Again he said: "I shall cut the tickets right in front of you. I will arrange for the money when we reach Srinagar."
The inspector turned around and walked off without a word.
He then said to a policemen who arrived from the toll-gate hearing the commotion:
"These Punjabis can't be trusted."
The blood boiled in Makhan Singh's veins.
"Can't be trusted, eh? I will show you." His pent-up emotions broke loose like the deluge in a dam-burst. Pain, sorrow, anger and hatred blinded him.
Makhan Singh lunged forward with raised fists.
The inspector side-stepped. Some people stopped Makhan Singh. Ramlal caught him around his waist and begged: "Sardarji, Sardarji . . . " Ramlal was seeing that good man in such a condition for the first time.
Makhan Singh blurted out as if in delirium: "Leave me! Let me slash open his entrails! I will die after that."
The policeman intervened: "Leave it, Sardarji. What he said is absolute rot. I apologize on his behalf. Enough . . .
Makhan Singh did not hear him. He said, "I don't want this

job. Let another person take the bus away."

"Sardarji, don't say so. You . . . "

Makhan Singh didn't let him complete his sentence. Raising his palms, he asked him:

"Do you see these calluses? It is not by hitting people that I got them. Not by holding the steering wheel either. It's by tilling the soil that I got them. My father and grandfather were farmers. We have not cheated anyone. Now this fellow says, we Punjabis can't be trusted."

He was terribly angry. The policeman appealed: "Leave it, Sardarji. It is all over; forget it . . . "

"Forget?"

He thought for a moment. "I used to forget. But now? No!"

The policeman was worried.

"How many persons must be waiting for these people? Just imagine."

How many? There is a sick young man. But he will not be able to meet his mother and wife. Why should I then . . .

Perhaps there might be other similar cases . . .

Many such persons would be waiting for their beloved.

"Go, Sardarji."

Makhan Singh thought it over for a moment. Then he started the bus without uttering a word. With a drone, the new bus started to climb the pass. Its wail, as it climbed along the belly of the mountains where the mellow morning sun played hide-and-seek, was painful. Hills towered, one behind the other. No end to them.

The wind whistled and howled.

Hot springs of memories boiled over in Makhan Singh's heart.

A small hill was darkened with a shadow. Another hill in the distance seemed to move in the sun.

Are the hills alive?

Do the hills die?

People were killed in Punjab. Bachan Singh said they had hacked Father into slices. Shall I too kill everyone in this bus? Oh, my chest pains. I feel suffocated. Is the bus going to overturn?

If it overturns . . . jackals will carry off everyone at night . . . from Madhopur. The bus won't fall off. It will hang suspended in the sky. I will then ask, aren't the Punjabis trustworthy?

Oh, such pain. I think I will die . . .

I will go to Lahore. I had gone to Lahore taking Preetham along. But . . .

Oh, what pain . . .

The bus reaches at noon. But I won't reach. I won't find any of those early migrants in Delhi. If I die declaring I have calluses on my palms, wheat would be ripening in Lahore. If anyone in childhood . . . for me . . .

I feel cold; terribly cold. This corduroy from Lahore . . .

The bus was approaching the tunnel . . .

Makhan Singh's memories stopped. He felt a great fatigue. He was being carried off in a current. The bus passed into the tunnel without waiting for the sentry's signal.

Makhan Singh was choking. The dim lights in the tunnel were like the stars of some other world.

As soon as the bus passed through the tunnel and reached the other end, it slowly came to a halt. Opening its door, Makhan Singh fell out.

In the beautiful Kashmir valley, waves of sunlight were spreading.

When Ramlal and the sentries came running, he was lying on the raw earth. Tears rolled down and soaked the cloth that held his beard tight.

Someone among the passengers said: "God saved us. Otherwise, we would now be there, fifteen thousand feet below!"

Ramlal went on crying, like a child: "Sardarji, Sardarji . . . "

Ramlal's Sardarji did not hear that call. He was dreaming of the ripe wheat fields of Punjab.

(Translated by A. J. Thomas)

LITTLE EARTHQUAKES

M. T. Vasudevan Nair

Look, what I don't understand is . . . it is so funny. Everybody used to talk about them with terrified faces. I too used to believe some of it. The *damshtra*[1] will sink deep into the flesh, and . . . grrr . . . it will suck out all the blood. It will chew the bones and spit them out next. All this about poor *Kunhatho*[2].

The *yakshi*[3] appeared twice every day at the upper end of our *parambu*[4], they said, at *ucchakkanam*[5], and at midnight. What we call *ucchakkanam* is the time of the day which begins when Amma lies down in the kitchen for a nap after giving *kanji*[6] to the servants and ends when *Valiamma*[7] gets up to make the afternoon tea. I wonder what language it is!

It was also the time for *Akkara*[8] *Muthashi*[9] to wander all over

---

[1] Damshtra - The long, canine teeth yakshis are said to possess.
[2] Kunhathol, karineeli, etc. - 'Kunhathol' is a young Namboodiri woman. Here she is the spirit of a young Namboodiri woman who used to live in the neighbourhood. In the hierarchy of spirits, Kunhathol and Brahmarakshas are Brahmins, while Karineeli, Parappoodam, Kalladimuthan, Parakkutty and Karinkutty are either untouchables or of other backward castes. They have a reputation for being impish too. Some of them like parappoodam are represented by mixed dancers in temple festivals.
[3] Yakshi - A demi-god
[4] Parambu - The area surrounding a house, sometimes very large with ponds and groves, especially in the case of taravaadus, the traditional joint families of Kerala.
[5] Ucchakkanam - Noon
[6] Kanji - A thin food made by boiling rice in water
[7] Valiamma- Mother's elder sister. Valiachan is her husband.
[8] Akkara - Other side of the river
[9] Muthashi - 'Grandmother', also used loosely to mean 'great aunt' or 'elderly female relative. Here *Akkara Muthashi* is the muthashi who came from across the river.

the *parambu*, picking leaves and roots. They are for making medicines. Only *Muthashi* knows what they are for. *Muthashi* will pass on their secret to the child she likes most in the family. Who else but me!

When *Muthashi* became bedridden, I started wandering alone in the *parambu* without anybody catching sight of me. Amma and *Valiamma* say that spirits might have entered my body then. Ravunni Nair, who waters the fields, says all the troubles started, "after this cursed old hag came here."

But there is another *yakshi* who goes sneaking along the mud-wall of the *parambu*. It is none other than Sarojini *edathi*[10], *Valiamma's* beloved daughter. Nobody sees her, or the *gandharvan*[11], who sits on the steps of the outer pond of the *illam*[12], angling for fish.

Then there is the one who stands at the wooden grill in the western wing of the house, gesticulating at Nanikkutty, who wanders into the *parambu* pretending to graze her goats—my *ettan*.[13] If you ask me, he is the one who is possessed, not me. But who would believe me.

And if I go into the inner courtyard with the idea of having a chat, 'her majesty' lying on the *charupadi*[14], her hair untied and spread out, flipping the pages of a book which has pictures of film stars in it, would shoo me away! The way she walks with her nose in the air! She is my own *edathi*, only three years older than me. But what is the use? Not a bit of kindness in her.

One day at *Ucchakkanam*, I was wandering in the *parambu* when I saw her standing under the mango trees. I was sure it was the *yakshi* they had been talking about. I tried to run, but my feet wouldn't move. I tried to scream, but no sound came out. I closed

---

[10] Edathi - 'Elder sister', also used honorifically. Refers to cousins too in joint families. Janakikkutty, for instance, distinguishes her own edathi from Sarojini edathi.
[11] Gandharvan - In Hindu mythology heavenly musician, husband of the Apsara.
[12] Illam - The home/homestead of a Namboodiri family.
[13] Ettan - Elder brother, also used honorifically.
[14] Charupadi - The stone-couches built in the verandas and inner courtyards of the traditional houses of the nobility in Kerala.

my eyes tight and mumbled, "Arjunan, Phalgunan[15] . . . "

"Janakikkutty." I heard my name called. Not Jatti, as everybody called me. I don't really like anybody calling me that. But here was somebody calling me by my full name. And she had such a nice, soft voice too. I opened my eyes to find *Kunhathol* standing before me. You remember the *Kunhathol* who was married to the boy from Kunnamkulam. The *yakshi* looked just like her. She wore a white *mundu* with *kara*[16], and a *kuri*.[17] Her blouse was white too. She had wrapped a shawl around her shoulders. A spot of red *chandu*[18] on her forehead, rings on her ears and a *kasimala* around her neck.

"Why are you all alone, Janakikkutty?"

I didn't say anything.

I was looking at her mouth when she spoke. She shouldn't feel I was afraid of her. I asked her:

"Where is your *damshtra*?"

Kunhathol laughed. What pretty teeth she had! The *damshtra* would grow only when she wanted to kill somebody, she said. Everybody was sacred to play with her because of her *damshtra*, she told me sadly. Further down the slope of the *parambu* from where we stood, were the ruins of an old outhouse. A maidservant at the *illam* used to live there long ago. Around it was a thicket of palm trees. The *yakshi* went and sat there. She took out betel leaves and arecanut from the folds of her *mundu* and put them in her mouth. I looked longingly at her as she chewed. The *yakshi* glanced at me as she said, "Little children shouldn't chew betel."

I picked up some smooth little pebbles and we played *kothengallu*. Oh, you should have seen her grab as many as five pebbles in one go! Naturally, it was Kunhathol who won. The *yakshi* liked me to call her Kunhathol.

"Tomorrow, you can win, Janakikkutty."

The *yakshi* smiled.

---

[15] Arjunan, phalgunan, etc. - Children were taught by their parents to recite the various names and titles (numbering ten in all) of Arjuna, the epic hero, to regain courage when they were frightened.

[16] Kara - Coloured border of a cloth.

[17] Kuri - A decorative mark worn on the forehead by women.

[18] Chandu - A compound paste of sandal, camphor and turmeric

I didn't mind losing as long as there was somebody to play with!

But *yakshis* keep their promises. Not like my *edathi*. When she says, "I'll give it to you tomorrow," it is only to put me off. The next day I really won!

It is *Muthashi* who now leads me in chanting my prayers at dusk. This started from the day Amma said to herself—in a voice loud enough for *Muthashi* to hear—"The old woman can at least make herself useful by teaching the girl to say her prayers right!"

She is not my real *Muthashi*, but the younger sister of my *Muthashi*, the mother of Amma and *Valiamma*. I have never seen my *Muthashi*. She died before I was born. Amma and *Valiamma* sometimes say nasty things about *Muthashi*. "It is the old hag's sickening ways that made her own children desert her."

When Muthashi was laid up in bed, Amma grumbled: "Drat her! Now I'll have to wait on her all the time. What a nuisance!"

At dusk, when we sat down for prayers, I told *Muthashi* about meeting the *yakshi* and playing *kothengallu* with her.

"Not a word to anybody," *Muthashi* said in a whisper. "I know them well. None of them will do you any harm, child."

When we got bored with playing *Kothengallu*, the *yakshi* and I roamed about the *parambu*. It was then that we saw Karineeli. If you want to know what she looked like, think of *Parappoodam*[19] or our Kali, who comes to sweep the yard and remove dung from the cow-shed. But Karineeli looked a bit younger than Kali. She wore no blouse, but she had a number of bead-necklaces around her neck. I think she chews tobacco with her betel—her teeth have gone all black.

I didn't know who she was when I saw her standing under the tree. But Kunhathol was annoyed.

"Hm, Karineeli!" she uttered.

Kunhathol and Karineeli glared at each other for some time. I have seen Amma and *Valiamma* glaring at each other like that. But this was more frightening. I was scared of them starting a fight. But nothing happened.

"*Thampuratti*[20], why don't you let me play with you?" Neeli

---

[19] Parappoodam - See *Kunhathol*
[20] Thampuratti - Literally, 'lady' or 'queen'. The term used by members of the lower castes to address a woman of an upper caste.

asked Kunhathol.

My friend, Kunhathol, smiled at last. "OK, come."

Karineeli drew a gameboard on the ground. She brought the pieces too — broken tiles. The three of us played *vattu*.

When I told all this to *Muthashi* in the evening, she patted me on my head and said: "There is nothing wrong with you, child. No harm shall come to you."

Once, while we were playing, Kunhathol showed me *Brahmarakshasu*[21]. He was standing on the ruins of the old outhouse, where we played *kothengallu*. He looked exactly like old Kunju Namboodiri who was dead—but three times as tall.

"If we don't go near him or try to talk to him, he won't do us any harm." There were some others who hid behind the bush of honeysuckle and watched us playing. They were Karineeli's chums, *Parakkutty, Karinkutty* and *Kalladimuthan*[22]. They never dared to come out of the bush. Kunhathol would glare at them if she saw them peeping at us and they would scamper back frightened.

One day, a poisonous thorn pierced my foot. Karineeli flew into a rage and ticked off Kalladimuthan properly. "If the wound gets sore and the poor child is bedridden, I'll skin you!"

The next day, there was not even the pain of an ant-bite where the thorn had gone in. They are people who keep their word.

I used to sleep with *Muthashi*, but now I slept at the foot of Amma's cot, next to *Edathi*. 'Her majesty' doesn't like this. She goes to sleep early, except when Sarojini *edathi* comes in for a chat. They jabber away till Amma comes.

I don't get much sleep now. Not because there is anything wrong with me, as they say. It is a secret. The thing is, I am jealous of Kunhathol and Karineeli, who can walk about freely while I lie in bed. It is this jealousy that keeps me awake. Once I saw them walking through the plantain grove, munching something. I ran to the window and called them: "Kunhathol! Neeli!"

They did not even turn their heads. They behave so oddly sometimes.

But Amma woke up and there was an earthquake in

---

[21] Brahmanakshas - See Kunhathol
[22] Parakkutty, Karinkutty and Kalladimuthan - See Kunhathol

the house.

Amma lighted a lamp and everybody came running. I don't know what all that fuss was about. When *Muthashi* too came fumbling and shuffling, Amma roared:

"Lie down somewhere instead of groping about if you don't want to break your neck! Curse you!"

The *panikkar*[23] is very clever. They say he spread his cowries and found out all about my playing with Kunhathol and Karineeli. But he said some foolish things too. Everybody believed him when he said that *Thekkan Chovva*[24] was also among my playmates. They sent Ravunni Nair with an offering of a hundred and one rupees to the temple at Anakkara. Good. It goes to *Bhagawati*, doesn't it? But neither *Thekkan Chovva* nor *Vadakkan Chovva* came anywhere near us while we played. Even if she does, we won't let her play with us. Not till we know what kind of woman she is!

Amma looks so sad sometimes. But sometimes she loses her temper too.

"Let them fall ill or die — what does that man who calls himself their father care!"

But how can Achan, who works in the tea plantations at Valppara, come down here whenever he feels like it? *Ettan* had visited the plantations once. He says Achan won't take in leaves that are too tender. Achan has to watch it even when they grind it into grains and powder. When they sell the tea he hasn't looked over, in the shops, people start grumbling: "Have they started mixing mud with it?" or "If you make tea with this, it will taste like tamarind-water!"

Amma says Achan lost his head when he took that coquette with him to the plantations saying he wanted someone to do his cooking and washing for him. Let that coquette watch it. If she makes too much trouble, I will tell Kunhathol about it. I haven't said anything to Kunhathol so far only because if Kunhathol gets

---

[23] Panikkar - A caste; here an astrologer.
[24] Thekkan Chovva - Astrologically the influence of chovva (the planet, Mars) is considered harmful for human beings. The adjective, thekkan (southern) tagged to it makes it more so, the direction, south having associations with evil and death. Only an ignorant girl like Janakikkutty would dare to be funny about it with her flippant talk about vadakkan (northern) chovva.

really angry, she will grow her *damshtra* and Achan too might get hurt.

I don't like the way *Edathi* and Sarojini *edathi* stare at me even when I sit quietly in a corner, doing nothing. When I stare back, they scamper away, frightened. Ha, they are a bit scared of me too!

I still go to *Muthashi* when I take a head-bath. It is she who rubs rasnadi powder on my head. She is very weak now, but her rubbing is so brisk that it hurts me a little. Then she presses her finger, still smelling of powder, to my nostrils. I have to draw in the smell with my breath . . . I'll never catch a cold if I do it every time.

They stopped me going to school. I heard it was because Achan wrote it was not worth going to school walking two miles. As for my *edathi*, I think she was delighted. It didn't suit her high-and-mighty ways to take me to school with her. They are talking of two miles as if it is a thousand leagues! Kunhathol, Karineeli and I have walked and run back and forth a hundred times between the Illathodi's fence and the bridge over the brook at the far end of Asaripparambu! They must be out of their heads to say I am ill. Now they are looking for a teacher to give me private tuition at home.

Now there is another rule for me to fall in with. No wandering about in the *parambu* at any time of the day. I told this to Kunhathol as we stood by the remains of the old snake mound.

Now Kunhathol and Neeli started coming into the house at *ucchakkanam* when everybody was asleep. We walked through all the rooms. We laughed at the funny postures of the sleepers. *Ettan*, who was gesticulating to Nanikkutty as usual, got wild and came at me with his hand raised. I saw Kunhathol's *damshtra* growing. *Ettan* got away only because I begged Kunhathol not to do anything. Neeli has a way of spitting at people she is cross with. Large red boils will come up wherever the spittle falls. Neeli would have done it too, but for me.

We would sit in *Muthashi's* room for some time playing *thayam*. *Muthashi* liked it too.

One day somebody—I think it was either Amma or *Valiamma*—saw us walking about the house. There was an earthquake again.

Soon the *panikkar* was called. I should have said *panikkars*—

there were two of them. There were some horoscopes to be looked up. And Amma wanted to know more about the coquette who had seduced Achan. I was not the only cause of all the spreading of cowries, drawing of strange columns on the floor, and the chanting of *slokas*. I knew there was somebody waiting out of sight in the southern wing of the house, her ears straining to take in anything that was said about arranging the marriage—Sarojini *edathi*. She is the real *yakshi*, not the ones the *panikkar* are chasing.

They decided to call some great sorcerer from Kalladikkodu. Ravunni Nair went to Kalladikkodu to fix the day and came back with a list of the things for the pooja. I heard them praising the sorcerer's skills. I ran to Kunhathol at once, I thought I should tell her what was in store for her. Nails would be driven into the log of a kanjira tree. A spade would be roasted in a roaring fire. Poor Kunhathol! The sorcerer would make her run for her life. But Kunhathol and Neeli only laughed.

When I told all this to *Muthashi*, she too laughed.

The old sorcerer from Kalladikkodu seated me before him and started the pooja. There were a lot of lamps burning. A large figure like a wheel was drawn on the floor. I was really scared. I felt better only when Kunhathol and Neeli came in and stood behind me. Soon *Muthashi* too came in, shuffling and panting. Now all my fears vanished.

As the nails were being driven into the log, I turned and gave Kunhathol a sly look. Kunhathol seemed to be annoyed. Neeli winked at me, made some gesture about Kunhathol and smiled.

Then the log was set on fire, Oh, the heat and smoke were unbearable! I felt dizzy and fell back. But Kunhathol held me. I was drifting off to sleep.

"It is over, all over. She will be all right now."

I was lying in Kunhathol's lap when the sorcerer said this. I smiled. "Go to sleep, Janakikkutty," Kunhathol whispered in my ear.

Kunhathol had the smell of fresh linen and kalabham.

The next day, *Valiachan*, Sarojini *edathi's* father, came. When will my father come, I wondered.

Muthashi told me later: He has got just two months' leave. Sarojinikkutty's wedding should be done with before he goes back. They have found a boy for her already."

It was someone called Sankara Narayanan, who worked with *Valiachan*.

In the evening, Kunhathol and Neeli crept in quietly. To think everybody had been fooled into believing they had run away!

"Will I live to see Janakikkutty's marriage too?" Muthashi asked Kunhathol. Kunhathol did not reply. She became thoughtful.

When *Edathi* and I went to have our bath in the pond, there was a bit of fun. Bhaskaran, who fished in the pond every day at *ucchakkanam*, was giving Sarojini *edathi* a proper dressing-down. And poor Sarojini *edathi* listened to everything without a word, tears in her eyes! When they saw us, they suddenly walked away, heads bowed, in opposite directions.

The wedding was to be at the *Bhagawati* temple and the lunch, at home. How nice it would be if Kunhathol, Neeli and I could wear *pavadas* and blouses of the same colour.

There was a great to-do in the house after *Valiachan* came. There was always a bunch of guests around. On the day of the *nischayam*[25], there were about fifty people for lunch. I took some *payasam*[26] along with *kanji* to *Muthashi*, lying in bed in her room.

Muthashi wanted a new set of clothes for the wedding, complete with a spotless *mundu* and *Erappu*[27]. She was bent on attending the wedding, well or ill.

Amma didn't think much of it. "Don't make trouble for yourself. You'll have to be carried all the way to the temple. She will come to take your blessings when we start for the temple. You can throw flowers and rice on her then."

The same day *Muthashi* fell down while groping her way to the bathroom. Amma was really annoyed.

"Huh, what did I tell you? Don't tell me you want to go to the temple in this condition?"

"What a nuisance!" I heard *Valiamma* telling *Valiachan* as they carried *Muthashi* to the room.

---

[25] Nischayam - The fixing of the date for marriage.
[26] Payasam - A sweet pudding.
[27] Erappu - A piece of cloth worn over the upper part of the body by women.

"At this age, a fall is enough to make you bedridden for good." That was from Ravunni Nair, the know-all!

Muthashi had high fever at night. They brought a doctor from Padinhare-Angadi. The doctor had a spot of sandal-paste on his forehead.

I went into *Muthashi's* room as she lay groaning.

"I am all right, child," Muthashi mumbled. My friends also came in to look at *Muthashi*.

"Squandered all her property and drove out her children, the cursed hag! Now, when she is good for nothing, she is so kind as to land up here!" *Valiachan* said to those who had come to see *Muthashi*.

"It is hernia," Ravunni Nair said. "The doctor says it is better to take her to the hospital."

"He will send you to the hospital even if you have a cold. He gets a commission for it."

But *Valiamma* had something else on her mind.

"Suppose she croaks before the wedding . . . ?"

"Let her croak."

"She is not the real *Muthashi*, anyway."

But she is the oldest living member of the tharavaadu, and there would be a *pula*[28] if she died. There was not much difference between a *Muthashi* and her sister. Ravunni Nair explained all this to *Valiachan*, who had been living in Bombay for some time.

Valiamma and *Valiachan* went to Thrisoor to buy ornaments for Sarojini *edathi*. Only the jewellers of Thrisoor knew everything about the latest fashion. I had a look at the whole lot. *Edathi* too had a chance to put them on and show herself off for some time.

I prayed for Kunhathol and Neeli to come when the ornaments were kept in the open for everybody to see. But it was late at night when they came. Kunhathol didn't show much interest when I described the designs of the ornaments to her. Of course, she wouldn't. She is a *yakshi* who can conjure up any number of jewels out of thin air. But Kunhathol always covered her neck with a shawl and there was no way of knowing what she wore under it. Neeli did not like anything in gold. She had her necklaces of beads. She liked them to jingle when she walked.

---

[28] Pula – Pollution or defilement caused by the death of a near relative, which necessitates the postponement of functions like weddings.

"That is what is laid down for us," Neeli said.
"Who laid it down?"
"That is the custom."

Muthashi did not take the medicines the doctor with the sandal-paste mark on his forehead wrote down on the piece of paper. It was *Ettan* who noticed it. They called Kunjan Vaidyar then. Some of the guests who came for the wedding peeped into the room where *Muthashi* was lying.

An old woman and her daughter, who had come from Pattambi, said to *Muthashi:* "Pray to God to call you up to him without more suffering. The children are doing all they can for you."

I was standing at the door. The old woman stared at me as she came out of the room.

"She is Kunjikukutty's second daughter, isn't she?"

The woman in the red sari, the old woman's daughter, nodded.

"How is she now?"

"I heard them say she is better now!"

I sat near *Muthashi's* cot with a grain-sieve in my hand. I was given little jobs to do now—there was such a lot of work to be done in the house. I cleaned the oil lamps in the attic and sifted little stones from the packets of green gram.

As Sarojini *edathi* was to go to live in Bombay, *Edathi* was trying to teach her a bit of broken Hindi. They tried it out on me too.

"Jatti, *baahar jaa.*"
"Jatti, *idhar aa.*"

There was such a din and bustle at home all the time.

I tried out the Hindi on Kunhathol and Neeli in the evening, near the beanstalks.

"Kunhathol, *idhar aa!*"
"Neeli, *idhar aa.*"
"You little devil!"

I turned to find *Ettan* staring at me.

"If you start anything like this again, I will give you a hiding you will never forget!"

"What is going on here?" Amma came running.

"If you have any money left with you after everything is over, don't rejoice. This little imp has found a way to spend it all."

"Go inside!" Amma commanded. "Don't stand here in the open at the evil hour."

I signalled secretly to Kunhathol—it's all right!—and went inside. Achan was to come at night, but he didn't. There was an uproar of sorts over that.

But a letter came soon enough. Achan would come only on the day of the wedding. And he would return immediately after the wedding. There was an uproar again and the coquette at the plantation got her share of curses.

There was a great hustle and bustle. Welcoming the guests, showing off the ornaments and saris, telling tall tales. Nobody bothered to inquire whether I was getting anything to eat or whether *Muthashi* was being looked after. How busy everybody was! I was angry with everybody. When Kunhathol, going on her wanderings at midnight, peeped in through the wooden grills on the western wing, I asked her: "What happened to your *damshtra?* Come on, bite them all! Suck their blood."

"Should I?"

"Don't kill them. Just scare them a bit."

Kunhathol looked as if she was thinking over what I had said, as she shook her hair to look every bit like a *yakshi* and peered at the figures who were sleeping in the room, all strangers to her. As guests for the wedding, they had arrived full three days ahead. Sarojini *edathi* had shifted to Amma's room after Valiachan came, while I shifted into this room. Let her learn as much Hindi as she wants. If I have my way . . . oh, let her be.

I was woken up by the sound of people talking and running helter-skelter.

"Bring that pill, someone, quick! She's gasping for breath."

Valiamma was praying that nothing may happen to *Muthashi* till the wedding was over.

I got up and went to *Muthashi's* room. But Amma shooed me away. "Who asked you to come here? Get back to bed!"

They put up the *pandal*[29] the next day. There was a little shed for the cooks in the kitchen yard too. The huge vessels for cooking rice arrived. So did my *pavada* and blouse which *Valiamma* had given for stitching. I didn't like the colour. But the cloth is nice. It is silk!

---

[29] Pandal - A special tent put up to conduct special functions like marriages.

"Do you know why I have bought all these for you? So that you will be a good girl and won't let people say things about you." *Valiamma* stroked my hair.

From now on, I won't say a word to anyone—that is for sure.

I wonder what new games Kunhathol and Neeli are playing without me. They don't come this way at all. But then, who will come here in the middle of all the hustle and bustle?

Muthashi's room stinks of urine. There is a grating sound when *Muthashi* breathes. Suddenly she gestured with her head asking me to go to her. I went into the room. *Valiachan* and Ravunni Nair came to the door and peeped in.

After the *pandal* was erected, they played songs over loudspeakers with their huge mouths turned towards the fields. One of them faced the hill at the back. Let my friends enjoy the music too.

The bridegroom's party was to come in two buses and three cars. *Ettan* would be waiting at the bend in the road to welcome them. They would go straight to the temple from there. The *nadaswaram*[30] troupe would be waiting in the shade of the banyan tree in front of the temple.

Ravunni Nair said to the cooks: "They will be here by nine-thirty. The first batch should be served at ten. Will everything be ready, Embrandiri?"

"Oh, certainly."

The cooks kept everybody sleepless the whole night with the din they made. The house was so full that I could not find place to sleep. The way *Muthashi* lay groaning and grasping for breath, I didn't think she would be able to attend the wedding.

"Touch her feet before you start for the temple. She is *Muthashi's* sister and the same ceremonies are due to her too. Place a *mundu* at her feet too. Not that it will be of any use. Still . . . "

Hardly had *Valiamma* finished her advice to Sarojini *edathi* than Ravunni Nari burst out laughing.

"She will need some cloth soon enough! Don't buy anything costly."

---

[30] Nadasuaram - A small musical troupe comprsing mainly of wind and percussion instruments and usually accompanying traditional marriage ceremonies.

I had thought of having a bath early in the morning and running off to Kunhathol to show her my new *pavada*. But the first thing I saw on opening my eyes was Ravunni Nair, wringing his hands, a scared look on his face.

"Oh, God, everything is lost!"

They were racing towards *Muthashi's* room.

"Uh?" *Valiachan* raised his eyebrows.

"It's all over."

"Don't say a word to anybody. Nobody should get the least wind of it till lunch is over and they get into their buses and cars. Not a word to . . . "

Valiachan stopped as he caught sight of me.

"Jatti, come here," *Valiamma* called me near.

"*Muthashi* is very ill. Don't go into the room. Come on, have your bath and dress. Achan will come now. Come on."

"Poor girl, she doesn't know anything."

"Ravunni, you stay right here. There are enough busybodies around to say the wedding should be put off. And there is no lack of scriptures for them to quote from."

"I'll be here."

I was soon dressed and ready to go. *Edathi* tied a blue ribbon in my hair. They were still dressing up Sarojini *edathi*. They started last night. It took four of them to set a thick braid of flowers in Sarojini *edathi's* hair.

Honestly, when she was all decked up in flowers and jewels, I thought she looked less beautiful than she really was.

"What are you women waiting for? Come on, let us start."

When the women started for the temple, I reminded Sarojini *edathi*, "Don't you have to touch *Muthashi's* feet?"

"There she goes again! Stop fussing around and come with us, will you?" Amma was in a terrible mood. What made her really annoyed was that Achan had still not turned up. Nobody bothered to take as much as a look at *Muthashi* as they trooped out one after the other. I stood in the corridor hesitating.

"What are you hovering around there for? Come out, quick!" That was from *Valiamma*.

I told her I wanted to drink some water and ran to the kitchen. From the kitchen, I slipped out through the back and ran towards the ruins of the old outhouse.

Kunhathol was combing her hair. She was alone.

"Did you see Sarojini *edathi* start for the temple without touching *Muthashi's* feet?"

Kunhathol said nothing.

I was annoyed at her.

"Why do you call yourself a *yakshi* if you can't cure *Muthashi*? How pleased she would be to attend the wedding!"

Kunhathol smiled.

"And I think they were just cooking it up when they said you can fly to the tree-tops whenever you feel like it." Kunhathol gave me one of those looks of hers.

"All right, I will come for the wedding. Call *Muthashi*. I'll be waiting at the gates."

I hesitated. "Go on. *Muthashi* will come if you call her. I give you my word for it."

As I ran into the house, Ravunni Nair stopped me.

"What are you doing here, child?"

"*Muthashi's* . . ."

He did not let me go into *Muthashi's* room. "Don't go in. What are you doing here instead of going to the temple for the wedding?"

"I have come to take *Muthashi* with me."

"*Muthashi* . . . *Muthashi* is dead. We shouldn't let anybody know till lunch is over. Don't say a word to anybody, will you? If you go in and see her now, you will be . . ."

I brushed past him and pushed open the door. *Muthashi* was lying still on the bed. She was covered with a blanket up to her neck. She must be sulking, pretending to be dead. I too sulk like that sometimes—when I am really cross with somebody. *Muthashi* has her ways of playing tricks on people. But she shouldn't die without attending Sarojini *edathi's* wedding. I won't let her.

"*Muthashi*, get up. It's me."

Ravunni Nair smiled a mocking smile from the door.

What did I tell you? Muthashi opened her eyes!

"It's nearly time for the *muhoortham*[31]. Let us go."

Muthashi sat up in bed.

"Do you want to change your dress?"

Muthashi took off her *mundu*, shook it to take out the wrinkles and put it on again. Folding the cloth she was using as

---

[31] Muhoortham - The auspicious hour for a wedding.

a blanket and putting it over her head, she took my hand and walked briskly out of the room. With a mere glance at Ravunni Nair, who still wore the mocking smile on his face, we walked out of the gates. As I expected, Kunhathol and Neeli were waiting at the gates. The four of us ran, hand in hand, towards the temple. Surprisingly, *Muthashi* was running faster than the rest of us. She ran in front and dragged us after her.

When we walked up the sloping lane and came to the banyan tree, we heard the sound of *nadaswaram* being played. As we pushed our way through the crowd of people at the outer wall of the temple, nobody noticed us. *Muthashi* watched everything with a smile. We had reached in time. Sarojini *edathi* and the man who stood near her were getting ready to garland each other.

After the tying of the *thali*[32] was over, everybody rushed towards the platform to throw rice and flowers on them. *Muthashi* glanced at me. I grabbed a handful of rice and flowers and gave it to *Muthashi*.

"Want some?" I asked Kunhathol.

But Kunhathol was looking at the man who had garlanded Sarojini *edathi*. I thought I saw smoke coming out of her eyes. Her *damshtra* was growing. Suddenly Kunhathol leaped towards him as he held a bouquet in his hands and smiled for the photograph. I screamed.

I don't know what happened to me. When I opened my eyes, I saw Sarojini *edathi* and the *ettan* who married her standing beside my bed. Kunhathol was also there—but she didn't try to do anything. They invited me to visit them when I was well.

"I was not alone. *Muthashi* came with me."

"*Bhagwane!*"

At that Amma began mumbling prayers.

"Ask Ravunni Nair, He was here all the time, wasn't he?"

"She was just imagining it."

It is always my 'imagination' when I tell them something I had really seen. I wasn't going to let them think I was lying. So I told them everything—how *Muthashi* came to the temple, how she threw rice and flowers on Sarojini *edthi* and the *ettan*—everything that happened. When I was through, they

---

[32] Thali - Mangalsootra, the string or necklace tied by the bridegroom around the bride's neck as a token of wedlock.

glanced at each other and started whispering.

They let it out that *Muthashi* was dead only after Sarojini *edathi*, the *ettan* who married her, and the guests had left. Never mind. She lived to see Sarojini *edathi's* wedding, didn't she? She lived till the wedding was over. Poor old woman, she was so fond of them all—the women who came to clean up the house said to each other.

Suddenly Ravunni Nair screamed.

"What is it?"

From my bed, I could hear what was going on outside the room quite well.

"I bathed and dressed her, and I should know. I don't know where the rice and the flowers came from!"

There! What did I tell them? They wouldn't believe me then.

"She has entered the girl's body for sure. Didn't you hear what she said?"

Nobody entered my body. We went hand in hand to the temple.

"Looks like she is hovering around here to haunt us."

Ravunni Nair said something about calling a *mannan*[33] to exorcise the spirit at the pyre.

"Otherwise she will always hover around here."

I closed my eyes and lay still for some time. Kunhathol and Neeli came in. Without opening my eyes I drew in their smell as they came near me. I said nothing. Kunhathol was going too far, scaring people with her *damshtra* at the wrong time!

"Go away. I'll never play with you again. Go away."

I heard them going away.

They cut only a small mango tree for *Muthashi*. There was enough firewood left over from what was brought for the wedding.

I caught a glimpse of them carrying away *Muthashi*.

Why did Ravunni Nair say she would always hover around here? I got up from bed.

I saw everything through the wooden grills. The logs were piled up near the cashew plant. They laid *Muthashi* on the pile, placed some more logs on top of her and set fire to the whole heap.

---

[33] Mannan - A man belonging to one of the lower castes. Sorcery was one of the traditional occupations of this caste.

Oh, how hot it would be!

Oh, no! Don't, please! The smoke fills up everywhere . . . I can't see anything. Then, *Muthashi* is walking out of the fire, all wrapped up in a white cloth. No, *Muthashi* won't die. She won't leave me.

She has lot of secrets to tell me before she dies—medicines for burns, cuts, mumps, pastes of herbs and roots . . .

Muthashi was flying towards me now. The white cloth had turned into two wings. Before I could get a good look at her, she was sitting on my bed. I giggled and hugged *Muthashi*.

"What a dear you are! You fooled them all, pretending to be dead!" *Muthashi* smiled. *Chechi*, do you know where *Muthashi* is now? *Chechi*, why don't you wear a white dress like other nurses? Let them all go. I don't care. The one I want is still here. Do you know who? Look, over there in the corner, wearing my silk *pavada*, her hair close-cropped—*Muthashi*!

Come, let us play. Come, *Chechi*, you too. What are you doing? And *Muthashi* too with you? Why do you shout? Who are all these people who come running? Is there an earthquake here too?

Muthashi . . . where are you, *Muthashi*?

Ha, here she is. What is *Muthashi* doing on the windowsill? Oh, no! It's them! *Muthashi* is pulling them in through the window.

"Come on, you silly little girl! We didn't go anywhere," Kunhathol whispered in my ear.

Now there are four of us to play *Kothengallu* and *Vattu*. You two can make a team. Little *Muthashi* and I will make the other. That is fair. What fun we will have! There is nothing more I could wish for!

(Translated by K. M. Sheriff)

THE COURT OF KING GEORGE THE SIXTH

M. P. Narayana Pillai

A telegram from Penang: "Madathiraman sinking. Start immediately."

Such telegrams are sent usually after death. "Sinking!"

So Madathiraman's dead. Dead like a dog. Dead like a log.

The wicked die; the righteous only return. That's the difference.

Only very few return. Because the righteous are very rare. The returning is also described as *moksha*[1].

White hair will turn black. Hair sprouts on baldness. Wrinkled skin smoothens out. The body waxes round; hair on the hands, armpits and chest falls off. Then that on the face. The voice turns into a piping. Teeth fall off. You study in standard seven. From seven to six and from six to five. And, demoted to standard one. Then to the kindergarten; then the palmyra leaf; the days race backward to the first writing of *hari sree*[2]. The days of oblivion. A ritual degeneration into toddling; then down on hands and knees; then crawling; you turn into an infant, a suckler. Finally, one day, you go back the way you came.

Back to Mother's womb.

Then the counting is downward. Ten months, nine months, eight, seven, six. Then the Craving. Then the Aversion, Vomiting.

The unending journey of blood returning to blood.

But . . . where is Mother for that?

Where is Mother? Father? The generations?

The generations are doors opening for the return journey. Doors with brass bolts shining like gold.

One has to return through the aeons. It is *Chingam*[3] the first,

---

[1] Moksha - Salvation

[2] Hari sree - the first letters taught by ancient teachers.

[3] Chingam—Sravan, the first month in the Malayalam calendar.

when one reaches Kollam. It is Christ crucified when one reaches Rome.

Then, the journey without touching any years.

All the incarnations of the past resurrect. The Boar retreats to the Tortoise, the Tortoise to the Fish and the Fish to *moksha*.

From Destruction to Creation, through Preservation. A state in which Creation and Destruction become one and the same.

The wicked die. Jackals tear at their carcasses, as if it was placenta.

Placenta is the only true relative of a human being. The brother whom dogs snatched away before one could even kiss him. He is dragged away through the garden.

The cow eats its placenta. It is nature's fenugreek tonic for her recovery after delivery.

The mother cat, unable to contain her hunger, eats her own litter. Spider babies devour their mother.

Man eats on the sly, for he is intelligent.

Wicked ones who eat on the sly. Wicked ones like Madathiraman.

Stopped me at the *Sivarathri sands*[4]. Snatched away the two rupees tucked away in the folds of my *mundu*. When I begged him to give me back at least two *annas* for a glass of tea, he twisted my arm. He was about to break my fingers.

He should be killed. All the wicked ones should be killed.

The good people live. When they are finished with living, they return.

Gods come down from heaven to the earth. And mate with beasts. Good people are born out of such unions.

Those who do not steal. Those who do not extort.

The sage Mrugaspathy was born thus. He curses Madathiraman, the asura, who polluted his sacred groves, and turns him into a handful of ashes. From the spots where those ashes fell on the earth, cactus, thistle, bramble, oleander and *nux vomica* trees sprout. Bitter leaves. Guava fruit on which the snake has spat its venom. Cactus-milk that turns into a flame.

For cactus-milk to turn into fire, the most potent black magic is needed; one that will send a roast chicken flying. The

---

[4] Sivarathri sands - the banks of Aluva river where Sivarathri is celebrated every year.

blackest sorcery. The fiercest ritual.

A black cat's skull is buried beneath his *tulasi*[5]-bed. Then he is nailed down on a nux vomica plank.

Let us see whether he moves, then. He is pinned down.

Then he won't strip me of my *mundu* in mid-road.

Let us see how he can thrown stones at me. His hands are nailed down on the *nux vomica* plank.

It'll cause him great pain when he moves. Blue blood oozes down.

The blood of the wicked is blue in colour. The blood that courses through their hearts and veins is polluted.

Heads of two dogs on the end of the staff.

The staff turns into a snake. And the dogs become rabid. A snake with the head of a mad dog. Mad snake. Bit him on his face.

That was a punishment for throwing on my face the water with which the remains of the chilly on the grinding stone had been washed.

The emperor Jehangir punishes him.

Whoever it may be, those who commit crimes deserve punishment. Be it Mehrunnisa Begum, be it Madathiraman.

Deserves to be punished . . .

The case moves up from the Magistrate's Court to the Sessions Court. The verdict in the Sessions Court is death by hanging. The High Court rejected the appeal. The last meal. The executioner. The gallows. The noose.

Again, a telegram from Penang. The cremation is over. Do not start.

Didn't I say, no need?

He should die abroad. A death which warrants no release for the soul.

The ancestors refuse to peck at the cooked rice offered at the *shradham*[6]. Only the kakkampeechi pecks at the sacrificial rice, at last. Kakkampeechis are the ancestors of the asuras. The souls of the ancestors of humans are crows. Koels are the ancestors of gods.

The ancestors of Madathiraman are kakkampeechis. He is an asura.

---

[5] Tulasi - basil plant, sacred to Hindus.
[6] Shradham - offerings to the dead.

The war between the devas and the asuras. A telegram from the abode of the gods. Madathiraman should start immediately. To fight in the war on the side of the asuras. Agreed. In the fierce battle that ensued, the asuras are all killed. The sacred *Sudarsana*[7] of Mahavishnu saves the gods. Parts of human bodies rain down from the sky. Headless carcasses. Whose head is this? The black mole and the thin moustache. Madathiraman. This hand. This chest with the welt of a stab-wound. Whose is this syphilitic groin? Whose is this hairy ear?

O Mother! Why do you weep? Your womb that bore the asura is accursed. Your teats sucked by the asura, your lips kissed by the asura and the body that trembled in joy seeing the asura are accursed. Pray that you may be spared the curse. Pray for a boon to enable you to return.

Raman, you put me in the stocks. You whipped me with a ray-tail. You put the dust of the cowhage on my face. You rubbed devil-nettle on my thighs and back.

You starved me. When I was thirsty, you put salt in my mouth—rock-salt.

The cure for insanity is eating rock-salt when thirsty.

Rock-salt is a medicine. What you put in my mouth was not rock-salt. It was salt-petre.

Then you put sulphur in my mouth.

Salt-petre and sulphur. To explode in my mouth in the morning when I brushed my teeth with burned husk.

You of course knew that gun-powder was a mix of salt-petre, sulphur and charcoal. You cheat.

That day I stopped brushing my teeth.

The taste of salt-petre and sulphur still lingers in the mouth.

You came searching for me disguised as an innoculator, didn't you? It was not the dead germs of cowpox that you carried in your bottle or needle. It was the live germs of small-pox that you carried.

The sage Narada appeared to me in the guise of a *lada* physician and told me this. That day I shifted my residence to the sanctum of the temple. But the wicked brahmins threw me out. And chained me at the base of the banyan tree. The very same spot where the elephant Padmanabhan of Ahor Mana was chained

---

[7] Sudarsana - Vishnu's weapon, the killing wheel.

when he was in musth.

As rain and sunshine fell on me, moss slowly covered me. The soles of my feet were eaten by termites. The tips of my toes put forth buds. My hair turned into upward-growing roots. My hands became branches. New fingers. New branches put forth buds. Green leaves. When the leaves ripened, they turned yellow. I flowered in spring. When the butterflies approached me with pollen, I was tickled. When the birds that flew all around perched on my branches, I was contented.

The brahmins cut down the tree, to build a banquet-shed on that spot.

You were the first one who wielded the axe.

The axe used to hack up and burn a leper does not catch leprosy.

Who is it that drowned the eight children of the queen Umayamma?

Madathiraman.

Who killed Maharaja Ayliyam Thirunal, mixing poison in the *neypayasam* of Sree Padmanabhan?

Madathiraman.

Who got from Vazhappilly Kunjikkavu, as bequest, fields worth six hundred bushels of paddy as rent, and mortgaged it? I ask, who did it?

It was Kunjikkavu who bequeathed the property. But it did not belong to her. It belonged to other worthies.

It was the brahmin-property of Ahor mana.

It was the divine-property of Alangad temple.

It was in the will and testament of Kalliksharath.

And the courting of Kunjikkavu.

Who is it that tempted Kunjikkavu with marriage, got her six-hundred-bushel-rent-fields as bequest and cleared out?

Madathiraman.

It is 'brahminicide' to cheat brahmins, and 'deicide' to cheat gods. You won't attain any merit in this world or in the next.

There are seventeen *kuttichathans*[8] under the control of *Palachottil Kaniyan*[9]. Seventeen of them. If he is nettled, the *Kaniyan* won't let anyone off. Didn't you pit him against me and

---

[8] Kuttichathan - An evil spirit.
[9] Kaniyan - An astrologer, here also a magician.

make me mad? You sent me a magic potion, as *prasadam*[10] from Sabarimala. When I was about to eat it, a lizard cackled thrice from the *agnikon*[11].

No! Poison! Don't eat!

I didn't eat.

Then came the *kuttichathans*. Immediately, Perackappally Kunjan went to Chottanikkara and ritually sat in the Devi's presence. And came back with the hibiscus flowers and crataeva leaves taken out of the *nirmalyam*[12] offering to the Devi. The *chathans* went back. And told the *kaniyan* that they were unable to do anything against Kunjan. Then the *Kaniyan* sent the *yakshis*.

The chathans attack during daytime. It is at night that the *yakshis* strike. *Palachottil Kaniyan* keeps the yakshis as his concubines. Under his strict regimen. *Yakshis* with hair as long as palm strands. They arrive at night, jingling their anklets. Not one or two. Several of them. They hold water-frolicks in the temple pond. Their inviting looks lead men astray. The man follows the *yakshi* with a ceremonial piece of *pudava*. Where do they go? To a palace; to a harem. Whose harem? Is it the harem of Emperor Akbar? No. It is the harem of *Palachottil Kaniyan*.

There, Bhajagovindam is sung. The *yakshi* plucks off your gold-girdle, as you embrace her. As she kisses, she licks away your gold-filled teeth.

Then she sucks the blood. When only the husk of the man remains, she will let him loose in the harvested fields, under a spell. There, he will wander about like chicken let loose in a moonlit night, and collapse, dead.

The day you won over *Palachottil Kaniyan*, I stopped sleeping. I haven't slept ever since. Shouldn't sleep at night. If I so much as down my eyelid, my head will be mowed down. The night is a great cheat. Everything is deceitful. A total swindle.

Yakshis move about disguised. Bloodthirsty ghouls. Elephant-shaped demons. Demons looking like children.

Policeman in the thief's guise and the thief dressed as policeman!

Who robs whom?

---

[10] Prasadam - Food, after it has been offered to the gods.
[11] Agnikon - Literally, the fire-corner, a cosmological concept.
[12] Nirmalyam - Offering to the God.

Pandavas head for the wilderness. Bhima in Keechaka's palace.

When is the House of Lac going to catch fire? The temple is also a House of Lac.

Even if the temple burns, nothing will happen to the deity of the temple : Perackappally Kunjan.

The priest comes. The priest goes. The priests are dead and gone. The Varrier women who make garlands for the deity turn old overnight. The Marars die. The temple treasurer is changed. The temple scribe is changed. A squabble over the property of the Bhattathiri. Who is the owner of Kuttikkattu temple properties?

Is it in the son's name or in the son-in-law's name? The case is in the High Court. The verdict, on the *Sivarathri* day, in the month of *Kumbham*.

The temple properties are in no one's name—they are in the name of the deity.

The deity doesn't change.

Neither does Perakkappally Kunjan. The Kuttikkattu temple properties are Kunjan's own by virtue of his being a Shudra.

But one thing. He should not sleep a wink. He should not close an eyelid.

Devils prowl among the tea bushes, to drink the blood of cocks.

Devils and serpents need cock's blood.

The serpents should be worshipped without break. On holidays, officials should venerate scorpions and centipedes, besides serpents. Serpent-worship is to seek protection from *yakshis* and ghouls. Serpents should be fed with chicken blood. The blood of seven fowls such as the rooster, water-fowl, jungle fowl, death's-harbinger fowl, sea-gull, hen quail. All the serpents should be offered worship. Ananthan, Thakshakan, Vasuki, the cobra, the king-cobra, the rat snake, the watersnake, the ear-snake, the betel-snake, the arecanut snake, the tobacco snake . . .

The God of the serpents is the senior Namboodiri of Pampummekkattu Mana. Two serpents are brought in a bottle from Pampummekkattu Mana, and installed in a burrow in the serpent-groves of Varikkattu. People worship them with offerings of milk. Milk such as cow-milk, buffalo-milk, goat-milk, hen-milk, panther-milk, cactus-milk, rubber-milk, breast-milk, milk-powder are given until they are satiated. The saying in

Panchathanthram[13]: "If you feed the snake with milk, it will turn on you and bite you."

Bite whom?

Bite Madathiraman!

The betel-snakes who went crazy drinking cock-blood bite the *yakshis*.

O Krishna on the banyan leaf, deliver me from the betel-snakes!

All because Madathiraman, the asura, has won over *Palachottil Kaniyan*.

Eating flesh is nature's law. Cock eats termite. Jackal eats the cock. Man eats jackal. Man eats man. Lion eats man. The vulture eats the lion. Ants eat the vulture. An Australian creature eats ants. Termites eat that creature. Cock eats termites.

Man eats fish. Fish eats man.

This is not good. One should be self-sufficient. One should not eat the flesh of another creature. One should eat only one's own flesh.

Snakes should eat their own tails when hungry. The elephant, its trunk. The manure for paddy is its own ear of corn.

Madathiraman who is not self-sufficient deserves punishment.

A telegram from England. A Western telegram. Perakkappally Kunjan should start immediately. For England. He should reach the palace of King George the Sixth. Perakkappally Kunjan gets the job of door-keeper at the harem. From today he is in England.

But Kunjan will not eat from the palace. Because George the Sixth is a Christian. So, anything but eating from the palace.

One day Kunjan says to George the Sixth:

"My Emperor, my Lord who feeds me, I am fed up with the onslaughts of Velupillai Raman Nair of Madathi house, of Kunnathunadu Taluk, Rayamangalam village, Pulluvazhy locality. The above-said Raman kills and eats human beings and animals. And collects taxes."

George the Sixth is beside himself with rage: "Hey! I say! Is there another emperor in my own empire?"

Soon the command issues forth:

---

[13] Panchatantra - An ancient Indian classic text.

"Perakkappally Kunjan must go immediately, bring in Madathiraman bound hand and foot, and present him before me."

Kunjan comes with two constables and a bailiff and leads Raman away in fetters. And presents him in the court of King George the Sixth.

The court of King George the Sixth.

Present: King George the Sixth, Queen Victoria, Sree Chithira Thirunal Balaramavarma, Maharaja of Travancore, Vishnu Namboodiri, the young Master of Ahor Mana, Dhanwanthari Moosathu, the Court Physician, and Raman in the dock.

Kunjan starts reading the charge-sheet.

The hearing has begun.

King George the Sixth asks:

"Madathil Raman or Raman Nair of Madathil House?"

"Present."

" . . . Stand . . . Sit . . . Stand . . . Sit . . . "

"What does 'undulation' mean, Madathiraman?"

No answer.

"What does geography mean?"

Silence, still.

"You don't know? Idiot. You haven't learned your lesson."

"How do fleas come into being?"

"Big fleas give birth to small fleas."

"Wrong. Kunjan, you tell him."

"When the larva in cowdung develops wings, it turns into a flea."

"Correct. How do flying termites come into being?"

"When they see light."

"Wrong. Kunjan, you say."

"When termites develop wings, flying termites are born."

"How is a glow-worm formed? Ram must answer this time."

"When the ear-snakes develop wings."

"What are the creatures who thrive on parasitical plants?"

"Parasitical pigs."

"How many British rupees would twenty-seven native rupees make?"

"Twenty-eight."

"Wrong. Twenty-eight native rupees make twenty-seven

British rupees."

"All right. Adjourned."

The verdict next day was to hang Madathiraman. To hang him publicly in the marketplace, like they did to Veluthampi. That noon, Madathiraman had his last meal, with the accompaniment of *adapradhaman*.

The executioner comes bathed, wearing the holy marks. *Palachottil Kaniyan* was sent for and the cowry was cast to fix the time of execution. An auspicious time has to be fixed because the subject is a sorcerer. There is a chance of him turning into a ghoul. Isn't it going to be an unnatural death?

Who is that? Tell him Kunjan is not here. That he has gone to England.

The ghoul should be nailed down. Two measures of pine-gum powder on the *nux vomica* plank. "Kayyittikkuruthy, three bushels full . . . "

Why do you go on asking? Didn't I say Kunjan is not here? Eh? Who is that?

Ha! Is it you?

Don't play a fool with me, I say!

Oooh! Please don't bend my fingers! They'll snap. I shall give you the *mundu*. Don't bend my fingers, Raman. Here it is. The two rupees and four *annas* are in the folds of my *mundu*. Take the money. Don't take the *mundu*. I don't have another to drape around me. Raman, don't leave me like this . . . Please leave the *mundu* on me and go!

Ayyo! Raman!

Oh my . . .

King George the Sixth, where is he?

(Translated by A. J. Thomas)

THE ROCKS

O. V. Vijayan

Mrganga remembered many things: walking over the rocks warm with sunset, he saw the temple of the goddess on the hill beyond the valley. And tugging at Father's little finger he asked, "Father, may I go to that temple?"

"Why do you want to go?" Father asked.

Mrganga said nothing but trotted along behind Father. The birds shot overhead like the little silver fish of the river. There was the scent of dung in the dust and the scent of *tulsi* leaves.

"Mrganga," said Father," you haven't answered me."

Mrganga said guiltily," I want to see that goddess."

"It's a thing cut out of rock," Father replied. " I see no sense in going all that way to look at it,"

It was difficult to make Father understand. All courage left Mrganga as he thought of Father's face growing sombre, forbidding him to go. He felt repudiated. Presently he snuggled against Father again for reassurance. There was something more he wanted to tell Father, but it so overwhelmed him that he could no longer articulate it. It was that as he walked over the rocks at sundown, the goddess on the hill made him think of his dead mother.

He had to cross the valley to get to the temple, but the girl next-door could have taken him. So he ventured again, "Father, may I go with Sunanda?"

"There's no need to go with anyone," Father answered.

There was nothing more to say, so father and son walked on in silence. The rocks were gentle and warm, and their feel on the boy's feet grew vibrant. On his noontime strolls, stalking the hillsides, Mrgnaga would come upon the statues of the serpent gods beside the footpaths or under the strange trees sacred to serpents. He would kneel before them and caressing their granite hooks, ask, "O serpent gods, will you bite me?"

"In you we are well pleased," they would tell him. And they would call him to play in their caverns where the lilies blossomed over the deep water and the blue fish, and where the crypts were full of jewels from the serpents' diadems. There were beds for the child to sleep on, cut in rock and smoothed with the warmth of setting suns.

It was just then that Mrganga remembered his childhood. For again the rocks were warm under his bare feet. Far away the forest stood charred. Beyond the forest the poison churned in the seas, the clouds changed colour and the wind swept on with the myriad voices of the dead. Mrganga scanned the forests with his spy glass. He saw her crouching in the charred tangle. He laid his spear down and as he did so, the palm of his hand was on the rocks. Their touch grew into him and filled him as it did in his childhood.

"Mrganga," said the rocks, "why did you carry a weapon in your hands? You did not want to partake of our peace."

Mrganga was filled with remorse. He wanted to be again the child in whom they were well pleased. And he remembered the goddess of the hill. He never saw her, never touched her granite breasts or anointed her thighs, and so his was innocence wasted away. He wondered if the temple still stood on the hilltop and if the sun set over the hill. No, the radiation must have worn the temple and the hill to dust. "Goddess, Mother," said Mrganga, "why did not I come to you with Sunanda? While Father slept or was out hunting the little beasts, I could have slipped away."

Mrganga stirred himself out of his remembering. Now the deep experience of the rocks was gone. He broke a charred twig and tied a strip of white cloth to it to make the flag of peace. He walked down towards the forest.

The forest was a giant carcass of gesturing cinders. He stood on its edge and raised his white flag.

"I have come without my spear," he called out. "Can you see my white flag?"

He had to wait a while for the thin voice which replied, "Wait there. I'm coming."

She came out of the forest. Mrganga exclaimed in spite of himself, "How terrible! You're burnt all over."

She smiled.

"Why do your grieve over me?" she asked. "Am I not your enemy?"

He caught himself reasoning. He was reasoning like Father would have. This woman is my enemy, he reasoned.

"These are not burns," she said laughing, "but ash and soot I smeared on myself."

She dusted herself clean. Now her skin showed the pallor of the yellow people. She stood before him in her tiny undergarment sagging below her navel.

"Where are your clothes?" he asked.

" I have lost them all in battle, " she said", No one shall spin and weave any more." He moved closer to her.

"Tan Wan," he said, "Can I call you Sunanda?"

"Why?" she said. "Tan Wan is a beautiful name. Do you know what it means in our language?"

"I do not want to know what anything means in your language," he said. "The fathers of my people would have been disappointed in me if I knew."

"Mrganga," she said, gazing with satisfaction at the colours playing on the clouds, "those fathers of the people are all dead."

She stood there and with a sweep of her hand turned his gaze to the far horizon. All the way to the burning rim lay the pollen of death, soft and golden like the dust of the moths' wings.

"It's just you and me now," she said. "All that's left of the two great armies. We are the last surviving enemies."

Tan Wan pulled off her undergarment. She stood yellow and naked.

"Look at me," she said.

"You are beautiful," he said.

She gazed down her breasts at her own body. She gazed below her navel.

"Can you see me bleed here?" she asked.

"Yes, I see the blood," he said.

The cry of the womb went out over the wilderness of the pollen. Mrganga could not hear it, but stood beside her contemplating the far sweep of the dust.

"It is into this pollen," said Tan Wan, "that my son disintegrated. Your spear killed him, Mrganga. And as the thing flamed up his limbs, my little Chen cried, Mother, I'm in pain!"

She stood a while in that memory.

"Mother, I'm in pain," she said. "Sorrow goes no deeper than these few words. Dying, he stretched his hand towards me. He was afraid and wanted to hold mine. I did not touch him. I was a soldier and my duty forbade me. I could not let my hands catch fire. My Chen, who never went out anywhere without clutching my little finger, went alone."

"If you had caught fire," he said, suddenly triumphant, "and I stayed alive, your country would have lost the war."

"True," she said. "But the nations are dead. And no one walks the earth any more save you and me. So the computers tell us. Just the two of us."

He peeled the rag off from around his waist. Like her, he too stood naked. Naked, they held hands. Then hands around each other's naked waists, they walked over the rocks. All round them lay primordial nothingness. The sunset darkened over the dust of the plants and insects and machines and fortresses.

"Tan Wan," Mrganga said abruptly, "my daugher was three years old. She would lie half-wake in the middle of the night and, if she found me at the other end of the bed, she would roll over to me, and reassuring herself, go off to sleep again. She would smile in her sleep knowing, as one knows in sleep, that I was near. Her name was Sita. Once a girl asked her if her name was Gita. Tears came to Sita's eyes, her lips twitched. She cried the whole day : that girl had called her Gita. I scooped up Sita and smothered her in my bosom and laughed. But as the fire spread over her limbs, again I saw her lips twitch."

A scalding wind blew over the pollen of the dead children. The pollen rose. The pollen fell and was quiet again. Tan Wan caressed him below the navel.

"No!" he said. Yet he let her hand be. "Are you not my enemy?"

"The sun is setting," she said.

Under the darkening sky the pools of lava gleamed. The pollen gleamed.

"I remember how the dark used to scare him," she said. "He would cling to me in the dark. Yet I did not touch him!"

She turned her face away.

"Tan Wan!" Mrganga said. "Are you crying?"

He was holding her in his arms. She laid her wet cheek on his shoulder. She pressed her wet lips to his chest.

"I like your breasts," he said.

Her sobbing ceased.

"They are small," she said apologetically.

He let them spill into his palms and felt their heaviness. He wiped the lingering soot from them.

"I have seen your women and the goddesses in your temples," she said. " I wish I had their large round breasts."

"Oh," he said, "what if you had them?"

She said shyly, "I might have pleased you better."

They walked on over the rocks.

"The cry of my womb envelops me now," she said.

"Mythili," he called her.

"Oh, my lover," she said, "may I kneel before you?"

Tan Wan kneeled; Mrganga towered over her, sorrowing like a king, looking down on the fullness of her behind as she kneeled.

The machines that survived over the earth clattered to one another, commuicating passionlessly. An occasional spacecraft strayed back home, bearing the body of its navigator.

Tan Wan and Mrganga came upon a patch of soft grass.

"It is not radioactive here," she said.

"The grass is growing," he said.

"Look," she said. "Flowers in the grass!"

They lay down on the flowers.

"Look at the stars, Mrganga," she said. "So many of them, like the seeds of men wasted in the dark. And just as futile. They spin out through the emptiness, fleeing from the emptiness within. So does the child, as he seeks love, relentlessly feed on the mouldering ancestor. Bloody murder goes on inside his innocence, molecule chasing molecule, metabolism which knows no mercy. There is injustice and desolation within every created thing."

"Don't remind me," he said.

The grass rose around them like incense and roused them. He caressed her all over. He kissed her thighs and her breasts and the slight slits that were her eyes. He kissed her beneath the navel and on the sacrificial blood.

They woke. Their joy had left their limbs weary. Tan Wan rose and started to walk down towards the forest.

"Tan Wan," he said, "where are you going?"

"I'm going to get my spear," she said.

"Why?" he asked, "It is not day yet."

She did not reply but walked on. He made no attempt to stop her. Presently she was back with her spear. She laid the spear on the grass and sat down beside him. She caressed his limp organ with gratitude.

"Mrganga," she said, "your seeds are within me. If you so desire, I will wait for them to sprout again and people this garden. They will become multitudes, great nations. What is your desire, my lover?"

"Burn down the garden," he said.

Tan Wan's face shone. She lit the grass and flowers with her spear.

"God of the Vanity of Creation," she said, "we will no more be your accomplices!"

She lay on him again for the last act of love. When it was over she wept disconsolately and long.

"My love, my love," she said, "the wars are ending within us."

In infinite compassion she raised her spear and touched him where her tears had fallen. Then she laid it in his hand. Gently he touched her breast with it. The fires began swirling through their flesh.

"Peace, my love."

"Farewell."

When it was over, all that remained was the fine dust of gold.

A wind blew over the rocks and the rocks awoke to an ancient memory. The memory of salt waves lashing on them, the memory of incipient life. They remembered it unfolding through the ages in death and slaughter. Those ages were a mere instant in Time. The instant had passed. The wrong had been undone.

The rocks had waited for this knowledge. Once again they were lost in their slumber.

(Translated by the author)

THE BLUE ECLIPSE

Kakkanadan

Now the sky is a dark, deep blue. If I saw this blue filling up a girl's eyes, I would fall in love with her. I would write poems about her. Singing my poems in fine frenzy, forgetting myself, forgetting everything, I would follow her to the ends of the world. When she turned to look at me, the dark, deep blue of her eyes would bombard me (a mere atom), splitting me and releasing the catastrophic energy which would obliterate the planet.

I shall become the blue fog which envelops the whole world. As my intoxicating blue floods the planet, I shall become the sky itself.

Neeli[1], I shall become the sky.

I shall manifest myself as the invisible walls of the Ananga hill, as the cloistered blue glow that spreads itself over the Ananga hill. O, Mother, I shall thrive as your walls, as your mellowing luminescence.

Now the sky is a dark, deep blue.

It was grey a short while ago. In the lake of grey, the palm-leaves swayed gently like driftwood. The wet trees shivered. Dew-drops hung on the rafters which were protruding from the roof. Everything was grey, the swaying palm-leaves, the wet trees, the dew-drops on the rafters. Is grey the mother of blue, or its foetus?

As I am not a painter, as I have not learned the techniques of colour composition, as I was not born to be Lord Ram, the mystery of the working of light on colours has not been revealed to me. I am distressed that I don't know whether grey is the foetus of blue.

---

[1] Neeli : A name which has a very close affinity with the colour blue (neela), common among Dalits.

Now the sky is a dark, deep blue. This I know for sure. It has an ethereal charm. It is unique. Its intoxicating presence overwhelms me. I swoon, I fall. I pass out into oblivion. *Neeli*, I forget everything.

O, *Neeli*, Mother of Blue, the sky, watered by your blue, has made me forget everything, made me fall into a languorous swoon, like a man dead to the world. And I, *Chathan*[2], whom you have taken possession of, I stretch myself on the Ananga hill, the hallowed spot where I found you—like a canopy.

I became *Chathan*. *Chathan* became the sky. The dark, deep, blue sky.

Now the sky is a dark, deep blue.

It had rained a little while ago.

When the day shuffled into middle age, all the shadows disappeared from the earth. The sunlight faded and the sun, which had been a dazzlilng ball of fire, disappeared into a hole in the sky. The sky, which had been a pale blue, the palm-leaves which gave off a green sheen, as if they had been massaged with peacock-oil, and the trees which had worn a coffee-brown mantle in the sun, turned grey.

Then it rained.

The raindrops turned grey as they slid down the grey palm-leaves. The grey raindrops writhed like grey worms on the grey barks of the trees. Raindrops smiled coyly on the grey rafters of the roof.

The earth was simmering in the sun before the rain came. The summer heat broke out into boils of syphilis. But soon they burst open and faded away. Then the sun was quenched by the rain. When the boils burst and the sores disappeared, the earth and I retrieved our beauty. The trees regained their charms. Now only goosepimples would appear as the earth shivered lightly in the rain.

It was the rain that made me handsome. But the sun did not return even after the rain poured itself out. The sun did not venture out even after the clouds retreated. Like a defeated emperor in exile, it took refuge in some ancient, mossy cave in the

---

[2] Chathan : The impish demon (a predominatly lower caste deity) who has an ambiguous l/m sometimes verging on the incestuous l/m relationship with the Mother Goddess.

interior of the woods where the tribe of hunters lived. When the rain died out, the grey drop of water on the tip of the palm-leaf trembled like a young, ripe fruit, and the dusk was all over me. It brought the dark, deep blue with it.

Now the sky is a dark, deep blue. Inhaling the blue, drinking the blue, splashing in the blue, my body turns a dark, deep blue, the inebriating blue of the sky, and I, now identified with the blue, inebriated sky, spread out over your Anaga hill like a pearl-rimmed umbrella; O, Mother, *Neeli*, I your *Chathan*, your worshipper, your humble servant.

Where am I? Is it the begining or the end?

Where am I? On the edge of birth, at the narrow mouth of the dark, damp cave? Or on the precipice of the abyss of death, the abode of eerie silence, where tall tongues of fire leap up from burning oil, where fire-serpents breathe toxic flames and fumes?

O, Mother, fear shackles me!

The fear of the unknown, the fear of being lost, the fear of being unaware of what makes me afraid.

O, Son of Arjun, did this fear strangle you when you were trapped in the *padmavyuha*[3]?

I don't know, says the son of Arjun.

He is right. He doesn't know. Neither do I. I don't know whether I feel the fear born out of ignorance or whether it is grief.

All around me, naked men sing and cry and wring their hands over the agony of solitude, over the insufferable, abstruse, absolute affliction of existence.

Neeli, my mother, ignoramo us that I am, the worst among the greenhorns, yet embracing you, spreading myself over you like an umbrella, attaining the summit of ignorance, the summit of omniscient ignorance, the summit of fine frenzy, I laugh at their senseless cries and struggles.

They are mortals, dogged by death and oblivion.

Fear and grief are for mortals.

The mortal's life begins when the ovum in the mother's womb is fertilised. As the ovum grows, the mortal curls up, hiding his head between his legs, scraping against the walls of the

---

[3] Padmavyuha - A disposition of the army, *Vyuham*, in the shafe of *Padma*, lotus flower, resorted to by the Kauravas to trap and kill Abhimanyu, Son of Arjuna, in the great battle of Mahabharat.

womb, binding himself to the placenta, embracing its bondage. Then he exerts pressure on the walls of the womb, struggles to make his way along the path to the mouth of the vagina. Manoeuvring with his head, torturing his mother, he widens the vaginal tract and emerges, cruel and red-faced. As the umbilical cord snaps, he is free to stare at the colourful visage of the world and cry.

The severed placenta and the freedom which fell on him like a curse frightens him.

He has learned to cry. He cries over deaths and births. His cries become music. His cries create literature, painting and sculpture. His cries turn into trigonometry, bio-chemistry and astro-physics. Love, desire and lust spring from his cries. His cries ring in hoarse-throated slogans, in the spirited challenges of youth, in the roar of revolutions. His cries reverberate in the abodes of religion, in the fields of battle.

But I, your humble servant, your *Chathan*, utter no cries. You have given me the boon of absolute knowledge, absolute oblivion. I need not cry, for I have no sorrow of existence, I do not exist.

Now the sky is a dark, deep blue. My complexion is a dark, deep blue. Is blue the colour of non-existence? Sorry, I don't know.

But I am not what I am. I am not *Chathan*. I am not the sky. I am only the pearl-rimmed umbrella that spreads over you. Does an umbrella have existence? Does it have sorrow?

When I turned eighteen, when the fire of youth burned through the sorrow of my existence, who was the middle-aged woman who thrust me into the cave of sin—the thick-lipped woman, the dark chasm of sin between her teeth widening, her curly locks of hair fallen low on her cheeks, lust glowing in her eyes, the golden hair on her thighs beckoning me?

Didn't the chasm between your teeth open the doors of sin to me? Didn't the intoxication in your eyes eclipse me like the demon, Rahu? Didn't your wet lips electrify me like a hydro-electric project? Didn't the desire simmering in your blood exhaust me like a drug?

In the suffocating room adjoining the barn, the odour of paddy fresh from the fields thick in the air, in the small hours of my adolescence, as I waited for the footsteps of approaching youth, as I hid my tiny sun, aroused to its full strength by desire, as I lay awake with my evanescent fancies, my evanescent dreams, the door opened a crack, and through the crack came in the faint luminiscence. The breathing of the shadow broke the silence of the night and heated up the room. The door closed shut. The door closed shut. The door closed shut.

When the door closed shut, the blue night filled up the room. Something heavy pressed on my bed. Instead of the closed door, a hundred fresh, blue doors opened. Fresh, blue flowers bloomed. As the blue flowers opened their petals, I went to them like a bee.

Then everything moved with a pulsating motion. The walls pulsated, the air pulsated, the smells of the room pulsated. I pulsated. She pulsated.

She?

Yes, Mother, she, she, O Mother.

Like the darkness which swallows the earth at night, like the demon Rahu who swallows the sun, she swallowed me and my sun. That was the solar eclipse.

Spasm after spasm of pain struck me. As I writhed, she grunted, her desire unsatiated. She swallowed me up. The screams of the bedstead grew louder . As my pain became insufferable, I screamed. She laughed and roared—as if she was throwing me a challenge. Her movements became faster and faster, her war-cries louder and louder.

In a brief interval, I managed to ask her, "Why do you swallow me up?"

"A fire rages in me," she said. "From you I have to draw out the waters to quench my fire. Ooh! Ooh!"

She grunted, she groaned, she roared.

"Come into me!" she roared.

In spite of my pain, I relished her grunts, groans and roars. Overwhelmed by the enchanting blue, I longed for them over and over again. When they came again, I wallowed in my painful pleasure.

The rain came early that day. That was why the sky was a dark, deep blue. The dark, deep blue filled my rooms like toxic fumes. I writhed in the frenzy of the blue poison, the blue sin. She was blue-sin in blue clothes.

Neeli, my mother, *Neeli*, my bewitching beauty, was it you?

Was it you who drained away my sun from me? Was it you who relieved me of my mortality? Was it you who unburdened me of my existence? Was it you who turned me into the intoxicating blue? Was it you who tore away my identity from me? Was it you who unmade me? My dark, blue damsel, maiden Parvati, was it you?

O naughty black beauty, the intoxication of your song, the intoxication of your movements, the intoxication of your eclipse, the blue intoxication of sin liberated me, redeemed me from the bondage to all things mortal.

My love, my woman, my mother, I am now spread out over Ananga hill, your abode, enveloping you as the blue sky, rising up as the walls that surround you.

Now the sky is a dark, deep blue. The blue is me. I am the blue sky. I am the dark, deep blue sky that was born after the rain.

Am I eighteen years old? Was it only yesterday that I was redeemed? Or did it happen years ago? Centuries ago? Millenniums and aeons ago?

Now the sky is a dark, deep blue. Does Now mean Yesterday? That dark night tainted by sin? The dark cavern of naked, blue sin, inhabited by the tribe of hunters, in the valleys of time stretching back to a million aeons?

O, Mother, my love, tell me—so that I, the blue vault of the sky shall not crumble, so that I, the intoxicating presence shall not fade away—tell me, my bewitching beauty, tell me, O *Tripura Sundari* :

What does Now mean?
Who are you?

(Translated by K. M. Sherrif)

DELHI, 1981

M. Mukundan

Rajinder Pandey opened the window and looked out. Rows and rows of shops on the other side of the street. Behind the shops a large stretch of plain. One couldn't see the plain from the street. Rajinder Pandey's second-floor room stood facing the street. So he could quite clearly see the strees below, the rows of shops and the plain beyond.

A narrow path ran across the middle of the plain. That was a short cut to the main road leading to Chirag Delhi. The plain was always deserted. Very few people used the path. But one could always see pigs grazing there. On the west was a Mughal tomb in ruins. It was inhabited by doves. One could always hear the doves flapping their wings and cooing.

Pandey stood at the window, looking out purposelessly. His room-mate Kishor Lal was listening to a song on the radio. Pandey was not interested iin film songs, so he stood there, bored and undecided.

He saw Raghuvir and Nanakchand walking up the steet. They were the principal goondas of the locality. Both were young. Raghuvir had spent a couple of days in prison for molesting the girl students of IP College at the bus stop. And Nanakchand had been to jail five times. The last was when he snatched a gold chain from a woman.

Pandey saw Raghuvir and Nanakchand moving on to the plain, through the rear of Ameer Singh's dry-cleaning unit. They sat on a boulder, smoking.

Pandey noticed a yellow shadow moving in from the far end of the plain. And with it another, longer shadow. Moments later he realised that they were a woman in a yellow saree and a man. And later still, he saw that the man was carrying a child in his arms.

Raghuvir, who was sitting on the boulder, turned his head and looked at the man and the woman. He said something to

Nanakchand who too turned to have a look. Then they spoke to each other, got up and began to walk up the path.

"*Abbe* Kishor, come on if you want to have fun."

Rajinder Pandey invited Kishor Lal to the window. Kishor Lal put his finger on his lips and gestured for silence. He was listening to Amitabh Bachchan's song in *Lawaris*.

Nanakchand and Raghuvir were casually walking toward the middle of the plain, their arms flung across each other's shoulders, and taking turns at a cigarette they were sharing. Now, the yellow shadow could be seen a bit more clearly. The woman and man were now almost in the middle of the plain. Pandey could not see her face clearly through the window. But he guessed that she was beautiful. The young man with her was tall and lean. They were a happy family of husband, wife and child.

The young woman covered her head with the tip of her saree, probably as protection from the scorching sun. Nanakchand and Raghuvir slowed their pace. Nobody was within sight of the plain. Even the doves in the ruined mausoleum were quiet.

"*Abbe* Kishor, *band karo* your radio, come take a look, *yaar*."

Pandey again invited Kishor Lal to the window.

Nanakchand and Raghuvir came closer to the family.

"*Arre jaldi*, get up, *yaar*."

Pandey glued his eyes to the little group in the middle of the plain, Kishor Lal got up and moved to the window without bothering to switch off the radio.

Nanakchand and Raghuvir stood blocking the way. With arms akimbo and a cigarette dangling from his lips, Nanakchand looked at the young woman and smiled. The young man's face turned red.

"Give way, you rascals," he said.

Nanakchand and Raghuvir paid no attention to what he said. The young woman blushed and shrank, and hid her face in the folds of her saree.

"*Arre yaar*, what are they up to?" Kishor Lal asked Pandey.

"Let's wait and see. Give me a cigarette, *yaar*."

Kishor Lal produced a packet of Red and White and held it out to Pandey. Each of them lit a cigrette and stood looking at the plain with added interest. There the sun was burning hot.

"They must have been going for a matinee show, *yaar*," said

Pandey. "Where else could they go in this scorching heat?"

"Hi, yellow bird, let's see your face."

Nanakchand forcibly removed the saree from the young woman's face. Her face was extremely beautiful, with fleshy cheeks and large eyes. She had applied kumkum along the parting of her hair, and *chand* on her forehead.

Nanakchand turned to the young man carrying a child in his arms and said:

"*Arre* brother, you're damn lucky. You've got a wife as beautiful as Hema Malini."

The young man lost his patience. He burned with anger. He had the child in his arms. And his wife was with him. Otherwise . . .

Somehow he suppressed his anger and said:

"Friends, what do you want? Such indecent behaviour is not good. Aren't you educated young men? Please . . . allow us to go."

Pressing the child to his chest and holding his wife's hand, he made to go, side-stepping Raghuvir and Nanakchand.

"You can't go. Wait."

Raghuvir put a hand on the young man's shoulder.

"You can't move without our permission, OK ?"

Suddenly the young man slapped Raghuvir on his face. The child began to cry aloud.

"How dare you?"

Nanakchand whipped out a knife from his pocket. The young woman's heart beat violently like a dove's. With her eyes she begged her husband not to get into a brawl.

The young man handed over the child to his wife and stood prepared for the worst.

"Son of a bitch!"

Patting his cheek on which the blow had fallen, Raghuvir turned to the young man and grabbed his shirt-collar. The young woman, with the wailing child in her arms, looked around helplessly. She was trembling all over with fear.

"One more cigarette, *yaar*."

Without taking his eyes off the plain, Pandey held out his hand to Kishor. He lit another cigarette and said:

"*Yaar*, very interesting."

As Nanakchand and the young man were pulling and tearing at each other, Raghuvir moved away to a distance, picked up a large stone and came back. He stood holding the stone over the young man's head. As she saw this, the yellow bird felt drained and helpless.

On the other side of the plain, there appeared a white shadow. A bulky middle-aged gentleman. He had a briefcase in his hand. For a moment he stood hesitantly, watching the goings-on in the middle of the plain. Then he continued walking.

"Who the hell is that pig?" said Pandey. To him that newcomer was a spoilsport, and he felt that he would destroy the whole show.

Nanakchand and the young man were shouting and thrusting at each other. Rahguvir was still holding the stone in his hand. At times he would lift it over the young man's head and the young woman would feel her breath vanishing.

She felt relieved when she saw the gentleman walking towards them.

"Come, help, they're killing my son's father," she cried.

The gentleman began to walk faster. Shaking his heavy frame he hurriedly moved toward the young woman. When he was just a hundred yards away, Raghuvir turned to him and said:

"*Badmash*, get out of here."

He made as if to throw the stone at him. The gentleman was immobilised. He had also noticed the long knife in Nanakchand's hand.

"*Bhago*, run!"

After a moment's hesitation, the gentlemen turned and walked away, not heeding the young woman's plea for help.

"Run!"

With the briefcase in his hand, the gentleman fled, his heavy frame shaking.

"*Shabash*—!"

At the window Pandey and Kishor burst out laughing.

At that moment Raghuvir gave a blow on the young man's head with the stone. The young man floundered. Now Nanakchand gave a powerful kick below his belly. The young man bent like a bow and collapsed.

"Those guys—Nanakchand and Raghuvir—really great, OK, *yaar*?" said Kishor Lal in his broken English.

And Pandey: "Very, very great, OK, *yaar*."

They continued to stare.

"Get up, sister."

Nanakchand grabbed the young woman's arm. She was sitting beside her husband and cryng bitterly.

"Come with us. To that tomb."

He pointed to the ruined mausoleum.

"Please don't destroy me. Please."

Her eyes filled with tears, she folded her hands and begged them.

Nanakchand lifted her forcibly and pushed her forward. The little child lay on the ground and cried loudly. Raghuvir whipped out a handkerchief from his pocket and stuffed it in the child's mouth. The child's eyes popped out. He stopped wailing.

The young woman shook herself free and began to run.

"Bitch—*abbe*, get her."

Nanakchand grew furious. Raghuvir chased and caught the young woman. Then both the young men began to drag her toward the tomb. The doves on the walls of the ruined mausoleum were watching the scene in a disturbed manner.

"*Arre yaar*, they're going to rape her," said Kishor Lal.

He stood staring as though watching an Eastman cinemascope movie.

Raghuvir and Nanakchand carried the young woman to the interior of the mausoleum. They tore the yellow bird's sweat-drenched yellow blouse. They held her pressed against the ruined stone wall. She had by now lost all her strength to resist. Her head turned sideways.

"Who'd be first?" asked Kishor Lal.

"Nanakchand—who else?" said Pandey.

Raghuvir held her against the wall. And Nanakchand unbuttoned his trousers . . .

At that moment Rajinder Pandey's room transforms into a metropolis. Huge skyscrapers grow up there. Rajinder Pandey and Kishor Lal turn into a population of six million. From raised platforms, amidst much fanfare, political leaders wearing khadi clothes and Gandhi caps speechify in Hindi. And in coffee-houses filled with cigarette smoke, bearded, long-haired intellectuals sit around tables and debate . . .

At that moment a little ringdove flies in from the darkness of the tomb and with its young and tender beak pecks at Nanakchand's forehead.

(Translated by V. C. Harris)

THE INFANTRY ARRIVES
Punathil Kunhabdulla

Komukkutty and Vishnunarayanan were brothers. One of them was born in Guruvayur and the other in Ponnani.

Let us begin with the story of the man born in the presence of God. God is still an object of doubt; it will be improper to conceal the doubt too long.

Vishnu's mother gave birth to him on the threshold of a temple. And since God had given her a mouth, the mother, named Kangaru, who had carried him about with difficulty for ten months and underwent pain to give birth to him, ran away from the place. Nobody knew anything about her whereabouts after she had thus run away in fear of the two demons called disgrace and society. Not even her own son Vishnu ever came to know of it.

Vishnunarayanan, the son of God, cried out from the threshold of the temple where he was lying. At first no sound came out; when he opened his mouth air alone came out. Then little by little the sound developed. A priest who opened the door was the first person to hear that sound. Even today it is he who goes on hearing the sound.

The priest did not have any milk at home. He put some *prasadam* into the wide open, greedy mouth of Vishnu.

Vishnu sucked and swallowed it. Then the eyes opened. Opening his eyes, Vishnu saw the wide world. He laughed. Thereupon he saw many people laughing.

He walked. There were many people to accompany him while he walked about.

And he fell down. But not even a child was seen anywhere in the surroundings when he fell down. The priest alone rushed in from somewhere.

Until then he had been a god. Thenceforth the priest tried to make a man out of him.

Vishnu wakes up earlier than the crow, hearing the sound of the river running through the courtyard of the temple. He washes himself in the cold river water, offers worship to Naga virgins and goddesses, smears his wet forehead with holy ashes, articulates the *Panchakshara*[1], learns verses by heart, and studies devotional poems. He is becoming a man.

Having become a man, he wanted to live.

One day, unnoticed by anybody, he swam across the river and reached the other side. While he was walking around in search of a place where he could dry his wet clothes, he heard a question which startled him. "Who are you?"

With his eyes wide open in astonishment, he passed his hand over his forehead from which the holy ash had disappeared. Just then he heard another question. "Where are you going?"

Unable to find an answer to the question, he stood there with a wide open mouth.

When Komukkutty ran past the Ponnani mosque and peringanmala and reached the shores of the vast Arabian Sea, he too heard the same two questions.

Komu's mother cried aloud when she gave birth to him on a country mat spread inside the enclosed veranda of Maliyakkal house. Just then he heard the call to prayer from the mosque.

He grew up, nourished by his mother's milk.

His head was clean-shaven and a *thanda* bracelet was put on his leg.

He learned by heart the letters of the Koran, which Musa Musaliar wrote on a wooden plank scrubbed to whiteness by leaves from the *chedi* plant.

He used to stand wailing before *Ossan*[2], who held a knife in his hand, while the guests who were seated outside ate delicious rice preparations cooked in ghee, and belched with satisfaction.

As he walked to the religious school along the country path paved with shadows of pipul trees, he conversed with the angels.

When it rained he used to sit watching the lightning and the raindrops.

He placed lighted sandal sticks on the tomb of the high

---

[1] Panchakshara - A five-letter mantra, or prayer, to the god Siva.
[2] Ossan - A term for barbers, among the Muslims in Kerala.

priest and offered prayers when his mother was laid up with illness.

In the mornings of the days of fasting, he ate cold rice along with wet *pappadams*[3], unseen by his mother, and later on felt a sense of guilt.

He got accustomed to the sound of sabots.

He offered worship after washing his body in the pond at the mosque.

He longed to see Mecca and Medina.

About that time a great event took place.

One day he looked at his own image in a mirror. He forgot for a few moments God's commandment that one should not look at one's own shadow. He felt ashamed to see his clean-shaven head. When he remembered the beauty of the neatly combed curly hair of the Nair youth named Krishnankutty, tears rushed down his cheeks.

He put down the mirror and ran away. He ran past the mosque. When he reached the shore of the Arabian Sea, Komu heard the very same sound which Vishnu also heard. "Where are you going?"

Finding himself at a loss about the answer to that question, he started running again; Vishnunarayanan was also running along from the opposite side.

In the course of this race both of them saw the untouchable Cheruni women who had come to Ponnani to become Muslims.

They met each other on the highway. They shook hands.

Vishnu kissed the shaven head of Komu. And Komu ran his fingers through Vishnu's tuft of hair.

This was the beginning of their friendship.

Silent moments passed. Even the horizons silently watched them. It was Komu who broke the silence.

"Hello, Namboodiri chap. What is meant by `Who are you?"

Vishnu then put up his hands. He asked, "What is meant by "where are you going?"

"One has to ask the Almighty," said Komu.

They commenced their journey in search of knowledge. They went round foreign lands like Mamparam, Mahe, Tirurangadi and Onchiyam without a passport. They succeeded

---

[3] Pappadam - A type of round thin, fried snack.

only in writing travelogues which they published in newspapers, but not in finding answers to their questions.

Disheartened by this failure, the two turned their eyes toward the hill-top which was being embraced by the fog descending from above. Suddenly— a light on the hill-top.

There stood on the hill a great man who wore a golden cross suspended from a gold chain round his neck and was dressed in an overcoat. He subsisted on wild honey and wild tubers. There was an aura of wisdom around him.

From the hill-top he shouted loudly, "O misguided children!"

Vishnu and Komu sat down like disciples.

Lengthy speeches. Hearing the whole series of lectures, Vishnu and Komu gained their capacity to read and write English without any mistake. (As there were no vacancies in the posts of LDCs and UDCs in any office, they escaped that danger.)

At this stage they turned into two great revolutionaries. Vishnu hated temples, and smashed idols. Komu grew and cropped his hair. He discovered the answer to the question "Who are you?" Brandishing his closed fist in the air, he shouted, "I am Komu, short-form of Koja Muhayaddin."

Temples and idols began to tremble. Mosques and veils were shaken.

On the highways of Guruvayur and Ponnani, along the mountain slopes and riverbanks, across the courtyards of temples and mosques, Vishnu and Komu danced and walked hand in hand.

Thus the age was moving on without any particular conflict when Komu turned to Vishnu one day and asked, "*Man rabbukka*[4]?"

Vishnu stood there as if thunderstruck. He had not expected such treachery from Komu. This calamity took place at a time when they were living like a single heart in two bodies.

The Namboodiri chap Vishnu was intelligent. He decided to try a hand against his opponent. He confronted Komu with a counter question, "What is the meaning of 'Kurukshetra'?"

Komu found himself in a tight corner. He had heard of many *kshetras*[5] and seen many. But what was this Kurukshetra? Where was it?

---

[4] Man Rabbukka - Literally, "who is your God?" from the Arabic.
[5] Kshetra - Ground, field, temple

Komu consoled himself.

How could he know of Kurukshetra? There was no temple near his house. He had not seen or enjoyed Kathakali. The picture of the priest opening the temple door was familiar to him only in his imagination. He had nothing to do with Unnayivarier, who had written an *attakkatha*[6].

Absorbed in these thoughts, they spent seven days and seven nights.

On the eighth day, when Komu was waiting for the Madras Mail at the Kozhikode railway station, Vishnu arrived there with a traveller's bundle.

They smiled at each other.

"To which place?" Vishnu asked.

"To Banares," replied Komu.

"Anything in particular?"

"To find out an answer to Kurukshetra."

"And what about you?" Komu asked.

"To Aligarh."

"What for?"

"I must find out an answer to *Man rabbukka* too."

With outstretched arms the two friends approached each other. They remained united in an embrace until the Mail arrived.

At the junction where the railway line branched out into two, one leading to Aligarh and the other to Banares, they burst into tears.

Vishnu reached Aligarh.

There he saw ragging. And he ate *dunlop*[7] and meat.

With the onset of winter, he saw people dressed in western style. He sighed at the sight of veiled beauties and bearded young men. He visited the dilapidated old palaces of nawabs, walked through the courtyard of mosques looking at the minarets, and greeted his friends with the words, "*Assalamu alaikum*[8]" uttered in an impure manner of articulation. During Ramadan he tried to observe fast. He put on a cap, dressed himself in a *sherwani*[9],

---

[6] Attakkatha - A type of ballet found in Kerala.
[7] Dunlop - The name given to English-style bread at Aligarh Muslim University.
[8] Assalamu alaikun - Literally, "Peace be unto you", a Muslim greeting in Arabic.
[9] Sherwani - a type of long coat worn by Muslims

enjoyed *qawwali*[10], and participated in *mushairas*[11].

In spite of all this he failed to become himself. He was transformed into another person.

At Banares Komu saw the temples. He watched holy men clad in loincloths, and half-naked young women on the bathing steps of Kasi. When they had finished their bath, he went into the temple along with them. He gave groundnut kernels to the monkeys which were hopping around along the beams of the temple. He was thrilled on hearing the sound of the bells rung by devotees.

He saw yogis; practiced yogic exercises. He carried in his hand chains of *rudraksha*[12], put on holy ochre robes, exhibited pictures of Mahesh Yogi and Satya Saibaba on the walls and visited holy places like Badrinath and Rishikesh.

Still he failed to be his own self. He became a different man.

Thus three or four years passed by. Vishnu and Komu returned home. One day they met each other on the highway.

Neither of them smiled. Nor did they inquire about each other's well-being.

Komu had shaved his head and put on a cap. Vishnu had a tuft of hair tied together on the back of his head.

There was no trace of love on the face of either of them. Their eyes wee burning with hatred. They withdrew from each other, as if they were magnets whose like poles had been brought together.

Komu roared, "I am not the same old Komu, remember that you *Brahmin* chap. I am *Baffakki*."

Then Vishnu shouted, "You *Mappila*[13] chap. I have changed my name too. I am Madhok now."

They took out hand-grenades to liquidate each other.

Just then—

They heard the reverberating sound of an infantry from somewhere far, far away—the sound of marching and trumpeting. When the army came nearer, they saw the commander.

---

[10] Qawwali - A popular form of music in question-answer form.
[11] Mushaira - A literay gathering where poets recite their poems.
[12] Rudraksha - Berries of *elacocarpus lanceotatus*, used as beads for rosaries.
[13] Mapilla - Muslim community of Kerala.

A middle-aged man without a sacred thread on his body. He thundered, "Ai—I shall finish b—both of you."
He produced a weapon resembling a sickle.
"D—do you know me?" he asked.
"I don't." The answers of both were blurted out simultaneously.
"Ai—I'm—Sa—Sankaran."
"Have you changed your name?" somebody asked.
"Not at all." He explained, "Only the short name was l—lengthened."
The hand-grenades fell from the hands of Komu and Vishnu.

(Translated by K. S. Narayana Pillai)

THE MESSENGER

Sethu

"May I call you Uncle Kochunni?"

"Why not? Many do."

"Perhaps you don't know who I am."

"Doesn't matter. I have given up trying to figure out the identity of the chaps whom I meet. There are certain things which should remain unknown."

"But . . ."

"No buts. Just take it that I don't want to know who you are."

"But Uncle Kochunni, don't you want to . . ."

"No, I don't."

"I have come from Achuthan Kutty to . . ."

"Oh, have you? That is fine."

"It is too hot over there. The children have their summer vacations now. And they give us first-class fare."

"Really? That is wonderful. These days you can go anywhere if you get the rail fare for it."

"Achuthan Kutty asked me to meet you before I went back."

"Did he? That is surprising. I wonder what prompted the gentleman to entertain such an idea."

"Not anything in particular. Blood is thicker than water, you know. Wouldn't he be anxious to know how you are carrying on here?"

"Ha, that was very thoughtful of you. I suppose you might have seen Achuthan Kutty's blood. But I don't know whether I should let you have a look at mine. I am diabetic and a cut is difficult to heal."

"That is not what I meant."

"Whatever you might have meant, I think one has to be cautious when dealing with things like blood. Machines have taken over everything. You say blood will tell, but most often the machines tell you your samples belong to two different groups. And all the notions our venerated ancestors have been drilling into us about blood-relationship goes phut . . ."

"That is besides the point. But you would hardly deny that Achuthan Kutty is your own son, would you?"

"I am not too sure of that—nobody can be, though I wouldn't like to cast aspersions on poor Devakikutty up there in her heavenly abode."

"Achuthan Kutty has told me everything. I am the best friend he has. Besides, he is the president of our Malayalee *Samajam*[1]. I am the secretary."

"So Achuthan Kutty has become a president? I never knew he had it in him. When he becomes the President of India someday, I am sure you will be his secretary."

"I have to go by the five-thirty Express."

"That means you have precisely fifty-five minutes left. Forty-five if you deduct the ten minutes it takes you to walk to the station."

"Yes, I am in a hurry. But before I leave, there are certain things which Achuthan Kutty had asked me to . . ."

"Oh, I see. Yet another messenger."

"No, no. Don't take it that way."

"By the way, where do you hail from?"

"It is a place quite far from here—down south."

"The messenger from the south—I wonder what that signifies. Looks like I will have to brush up my augury."

"No, Uncle Kochunni, please don't take me for a messenger. I have no personal interest in this. It is just that Achuthan Kutty is my friend and I couldn't bear to see him so distressed. Besides, I myself have been looking for an opportunity to meet you. I have heard such a lot about you."

"I used to have a lot of visitors. The image they have sketched of me is about one-quarter fact and three-quarters fiction. For sometime now, I have been left in peace. Most probably because I don't get a pension and have not figured in any of the honours lists. Now, don't get alarmed. I am not trying to unravel my glorious past with a sigh."

"I already know quite a bit about that."

---

[1] Samajam- a society or club

"If you have heard it from Achuthan Kutty, don't believe a word of it. No doubt, he is the president of your *Samajam*. But a propensity for the plain truth has not been one of his strong points."

"Don't misunderstand me, but I feel you should show a little more kindness to Achuthan Kutty. After all, he is your only son."

"What a faithful messenger you are! So Achuthan Kutty likes to have a bit of kindness from me as well, does he? How sad that kindness has such a low melting point! It would turn to water much before you reached Achuthan Kutty. Even if it didn't, I wouldn't think of burdening you with unnecessary luggage on such a long journey."

"I know you harbour certain prejudices against him. Achuthan Kutty has told me everything."

"I see. In an organization, it is always better for the secretary to have complete faith in the president. It promotes discipline."

"That is not the kind of relationship we have with each other. We live next-door to each other and our families maintain the most intimate of relationships with each other."

"I would call it nothing less than a miracle—to remain on good terms while living next-door to each other. Believe me, you are a saint."

"I don't have much time. What I have to say is . . ."

"I know precisely what it is."

"Don't put me off, Uncle Kochunni."

"It is an old joke—each messenger thinking he is the first. It is the limitation of the tribe of messengers as a whole. As for the receiver of the message—all right, let it pass. Conceal the true, give fleeting glimpses of the false—isn't that the function of messengers, as even those big-shots called diplomats say these days? I don't know how they put it in English."

"Achuthan Kutty has a second child now, a boy."

"Good. A boy and a girl. Exactly what the government has decreed for all couples."

"Uncle Kochunni, I . . ."

"You shouldn't have taken the trouble to come down here to give me the news. A postcard would have done the job. Achuthan Kutty knows my address. The only thing you should take care of is to write the pincode neatly on the card. They say there are about a hundred villages in this vast country which are called Ramapuram.

"It is a pity you are not allowing me to say what I want to. And I have come such a long way to meet you."

"Oh, I am sorry. I was forgetting the fact that I am obliged to listen to every word the messenger says. All right, let us go about it this way. You can tell me all you want to. I will listen quietly without putting a word in. That is what I like about human ears—so meek. Lend themselves to the most ridiculous nonsense ever uttered, without a murmur. Never go in for judgment or discrimination on their own. Go ahead. Just keep in mind the time of your train."

"I have half an hour."

"Thirty-three minutes to be precise. Sixteen and a half for each of us."

"I need more."

"Let us make it eighteen-fifteen then."

"I want at least twenty minutes."

"As you like. You are certainly the best friend Achuthan Kutty could have had. You are so like him in your habits: give a little and take a lot."

"I will be brief. It is difficult to put it neatly and tersely. I will tell you about it as it comes to me. Achuthan Kutty has changed a lot recently. He is always lost in thought. There is something that disturbs him. He doesn't know what it is. Sometimes he behaves so oddly. Do you know what happened a few days ago? One day, at dusk, A *Kuravan*[2] appeared in the colony with a monkey. The performance began. The usual gags a *Kuravan* monkey duo go in for. But Achuthan Kutty seemed to enjoy it tremendously. Noticing Achuthan Kutty's interest, the *Kuravan* pitched headlong into the act. As a result, they reeled off some of the more spectacular stunts. Soon it became difficult to distinguish the *Kuravan* from the monkey. While we gazed bewildered at the pair, Achuthan Kutty suddenly leaped into their midst. The *Kuravan*'s little child banged hard on the drum. Achuthan Kutty was really excited. For the residents of the colony it was the spectacle of a lifetime. The frolic and caper of the *Kuravan*, the monkey and Achuthan Kutty lasted for a long time. Finally when

---

[2] Kuravan - a member of the gipsy-like caste, *Kuravar*.

the frenzy subsided, the three of them scrambled to their feet. Achuthan Kutty rewarded the *Kuravan* with a handsome amount and asked him, "Chum, would you give this monkey to me?" "For slaughter or for love?" the *Kuravan* asked in the traditional manner. "Neither. I just want to make him perform," Achuthan Kutty replied. "But he doesn't know any tricks for himself. And he doesn't perform without me," the *Kuravan* explained. "Never mind. I consider myself a *Kuravan*. Give me that old drum and your costumes," Achuthan Kutty insisted. But the *Kuravan* burst out laughing. His face became red with laughter. "That is just wishful thinking, brother. You have to be really lucky to be born a *Kuravan*. I was born a *Kuravan* by the virtues accumulated in three incarnations."

"Achuthan Kutty roaming about like a *Kuravan*! How disgraceful! But I am afraid your time is nearly over."

"There was another incident. I will go through it quickly. Not that Achuthan Kutty asked me to tell you all this. But I think it will sort of round off what I want to say. Besides, it will give you a fairly complete picture of the situation."

"Yes, go ahead by all means. The messenger's tale is becoming curiouser and curiouser."

"In our neighbourhood—in the company's grounds—a few new buildings were coming up. The workers digging the soil to lay the foundations unearthed an old brass idol of the Devi. Hearing the news, Achuthan Kutty rushed to the site and took possession of the idol from the overseer. He always had a fascination for old things, you know. I learned about his new acquisition only after he had given it a thorough wash and a coat of polish and placed it for display in his showcase. That was three days after the workers had unearthed it. At the first glance, I knew there was something odd about the idol. The Devi had only one eye. And there was only a bare patch where the other eye had been. But the single eye sometimes glowed with the glow of a thousand eyes. Sometimes the eyelids throbbed. Occasionally, Achuthan Kutty and I used to go for a swig late in the evening. After I had had a couple, I would be too scared to look at the idol. There was a red flame in its eye. Achuthan Kutty saw it too. In fact he was scared stiff by it. He thought it was some fierce spirit which had strayed into the house. It was not proper to keep it anywhere but in a sanctified house. I had noticed the change that had come over him after the idol was placed in the showcase. He looked worried and gloomy. A strange fear lurked in his eyes all the time. Sometimes he behaved like a man possessed. He lost his appetite and his sleep and grew thinner and thinner like an animal chosen for sacrifice. He stopped going to the company. His wife was in tears. Finally I took the decision. We had to get rid of it by any means. This was not the place for the Devi. One night we took the idol and went out. It was a dark night. I knew there was a deep, unused well at the corner of the compound. We walked slowly towards it. I could hear Achuthan Kutty's heart thumping. In the thick darkness, I saw the single eye of the idol giving out a fiery glow. Achuthan Kutty's hands shook. I heard him mutter something incoherent. I peered into the well. It was pitch dark inside. I thought I heard the hiss of snakes somewhere among the weeds and bushes. The well was deep. The level of water could not be seen from above. Suddenly I saw Achuthan Kutty raising his arm. Blum! I heard it dropping in the water deep inside. Achuthan Kutty laughed hysterically. We walked away with a sigh of relief. But we had not gone more than a dozen steps when we saw something glittering among the dead leaves. The single eye. Yes, the Devi. Durga. I felt goosepimples sprouting all over my body. I trembled. "Run!" Achuthan Kutty said in a hoarse whisper. He was on the verge of tears. "No," I held him tightly by his shoulder. "We must put an end to it now. Or it will be the death of us," I said fiercely. Achuthan Kutty was still staring at it bewildered. At last, after a lot of prompting from me, he picked up the idol. It must have burnt his fingers. He dropped it with a howl. Picking it up with his handkerchief, he walked towards the well again. At the well he stood still for a minute, invoking the deities of his clan and the spirits of his ancestors. He then drew a circle thrice around his head, chanted a prayer begging forgiveness for all his sins and flung the idol into the well . . ."

"And that was the last you saw of it?"

"Yes."

"I understand. Well, you seem to have taken quite a lot of time. Never mind. Now listen as I tell you my piece. My guru is a person who can say much in a little time. What I shall tell you is all about him. He fills all my thoughts and remembrances now. Perhaps it is because I am too old. But don't be scared. He is not an evil spirit or a ghost. If you ask me how he became my guru, I don't remember. Perhaps I first saw him in a dream. Or perhaps he came in search of me. Either way, words cannot express the grace that flowed from his face. And what did I find in his lustrous eyes? Compassion, affection, detachment ... the whole universe was compressed into them. The first impulse you get at the sight of him is to prostrate yourself at his feet. There is nothing else you can do. And he would have learned everything about you with his inner vision. Kochunni, he said, close your eyes and sit all alone. Tell yourself that you are still here. You are late, Kochunni, he said sometimes, you have wasted a lot of time. You could have started much earlier. Of course, it was just my reluctance to set out on my journey, you know. And as I kissed his feet, he said: what is so troublesome about making a beginning? Remember, everything lies within you. It is only the time that you take to find it out that matters. A few lucky men find it quickly. For others it takes very long—several cycles of births and deaths."

"Uncle Kochunni, I don't understand ..."

"Let us go, my guru said. There was no point in hesitating any more, I was convinced. But there were still some strings attached. Of course, even a strong puff of breath would have blown them away. Most of it comes from one's ego. But ripeness is all, as they say. Perhaps the time was not ripe. When I said it, my guru laughed. Kochunni, he said, our forefathers have dwelled at length on the stages of our life. But that is not what should concern us. It is a discovery from inside. They say a hundred nerves start from the heart. Only one of them goes toward the head. Immortality is yours if you can send your soul out of your body through it. For those whose soul goes out through the other nerves, there is only the unending cycle of births and deaths to look forward to. It is extremely difficult for mortals to cross this last frontier. You have to draw out the *purusha* in you which is as small as your thumb, with the diligence and concentration with which you pull out a thorn embedded in your flesh. What he meant was ..."

"I ..."

"There is such a lot I would like to say about him if ..."

"But I have ..."

" ... little time, right? You are already late, aren't you? Don't fret. None of these trains ever come on time."

"Never mind that. I will run to the station if necessary. But there is something I want from you—a promise. After all, I have come such a long way to meet you. I should have something with me to take back to Achuthan Kutty."

"Do you think I have been trying to deceive you?"

"No, not at all."

"What would you like to have from me, apart from the courtesy due to a messenger?"

"I am asking you for a boon—a small promise. Achuthan Kutty wants to come here to meet you. Promise me that you will welcome him."

"Should I have the fattened calf killed too? I needn't? Well, that is a relief. Sure, he can come down here. As for meeting me, I don't think it will come off."

"Why?"

"I am going on a journey."

"Journey? Where to?"

"Don't you think it is rather foolish to ask a man as old as me the destination of his journey? Just take it that it is a long journey."

"But what shall I tell Achuthan Kutty?"

"Tell him I will be going on a journey."

"Suppose he wants to come down all the same?"

"Tell him I will be going on a journey."

"But if he wants to meet you . . .?"

"You can tell him the same thing—that I will be going on a long journey."

(Translated by K. M. Sherrif)

MEMORY

P. Padmarajan

It was years ago.

Sankara Narayana Pillai was travelling in a car along the national highway, from Trivandrum to Kattanam. Pillai sat in the front seat with a mournful face. In the back seat sat his wife, Kamalamma, his daughter, Shailaja, her husband, Soman Nair and their daughter Preeti, their faces grave, a trace of tears in their eyes.

There was nothing in the death to plunge them into grief, except for the fact that a death was occuring in the family after a long time. Pillai's *appachi*[1], K. M. Gowri Amma had died at the age of seventy-three, suffering from nothing more than the infirmities of old age. When the news of the death reached them, together with the information that they were waiting for Pillai's arival for the cremation, there was the usual alarm and consternation and they had lost no time in getting into a taxi.

When they reached Parippalli, Pillai's thoughts, flitting aimlessly, alighted on his *appachi*. Till his father died, his relationship with her had been very intimate. Even after that he used to visit her when he occasionally went to stay in his ancestral home. The last time he saw her was during Onam when he went to present her with a *mundu*. Unfolding the gold-laced *mundu*, *appachi* asked him with a smile, "Son, don't you know I have no use for any of these gold-laced things any more?"

"You can wear it when you go out, *appachi*. This is a *karalkkada mundu*[2]."

"Oh, there is only one place left for me to go now," *appachi* said with a sigh. Her eyes overflowed with tears. Pillai too was distressed.

---

[1] Appachi - Father's sister.
[2] Karalkkada mundu - a famous brand of hand - woven dhotis.

When Pillai was a child, *appachi* was more fond of him than her own son, Prabhakaran. She had already started considering young Sankara Narayanan as her future son-in-law. When Prabhakaran's indiscretions and excesses began to earn him notoreity, she had written him off with a sob: "You can murder somebody and go to jail for all I care. I have Sankara Narayanan to look after my daughter." Sankara Narayana Pillai still remembered the rush of blood in his cheeks when he heard this. Those were the days when he was developing a fervent intimacy with *appachi's* daughter. For Nair boys, an *appachi's* daughter is as good a *murappennu*[3] as an *ammavan's*[4] daughter.

She was the first girl he had touched in his life with anything more than casual friendship. Finally, when she was married off to Govinda Kurup, a feudal baron from Kainakari, he had even contemplated suicide.

Pillai thought he still felt the taste of her sweat in his mouth after thirty-five years. Though he had not seen her for years, the image of her face floated vividly into his mind. He would certainly meet her today. It was her mother's funeral.

Suddenly, like a flash of lightning, a question struck him: what was her name?

The car was caught in a traffic jam at Chinnakkadai. As the minutes ticked by without her name occuring to him, his pulses quickened in alarm. What was her name? He repeated the question to himself, but, however hard he tried, he could not recollect it. Though he used to call her *podimol*, it was only a pet name. Her real name was . . .

When they reached Kattanam, Pillai was still ransacking his memory for the name. Something had gone wrong with him suddenly, he concluded. Pillai's memory was somethihg of a legend. His colleagues at the Secretariat invariably approached him when they were unsure of the information they wanted. They didn't even bother to verify what he told them from memory. They had learned from experience to take it for the gospel truth. Pillai himself had come to believe that the credibility of his

---

[3] Murapennu - the daughter of a paternal aunt or a maternal uncle. It was more or less obligatory for a Nair boy to choose his bride from among his several murappenu.
[4] Ammarur - Maternal uncle.

memory was as high as that of a dictonary or an encyclopaedia. But here he was, struggling to recall a mere name. A strange terror was taking hold of him. Everything about *appachi's* death and the last rites went clean out of his mind. He struggled like a drowning man in the open sea to get a hold on a simple word which floated by tantalisingly like a piece of driftwood.

He saw a glimpse of her when he went to put the shroud over the dead body. He replied machanically to the inquiries of his relatives and old friends. He realized with a shock that he could remember the names of most of them, while her name still eluded him.

He returned to Trivandrum the next day. But the uneasiness did not leave him. He could forget everything else. But how could he ever forget her name? He was entitled to forget the names of all the women in the world except the one who had first created a flutter in his heart.

Even when he went back to his routine at the office, his mind refused to budge from the enigma which had balked it. It was not any sense of guilt at having forgotten her name that tormented him. It was the fear that something serious had happened to his memory. Of course, he had only to ask Kamalamma to learn it. But as he was able to foresee the embarrassing situation he would be placed in by asking his wife such a thing—his wife, who knew enough about his first love—and the trouble that was likely to ensue, he refrained from such a hazardous course. Besides, a stubborn resistance to taking anybody's help in remembering her name was growing in him. He set himself single-mindedly in pursuit of it.

But this created more problems. As Pillai, who was reputed for his keen intelligence, made all his energies converge onto a point, there were several uncomfortable moments which created both amazement and dismay in his family and among his colleagues.

Sankara Narayana Pillai stored telephone numbers in his memory like a computer. His colleagues merely had to ask him for the numbers they wanted, instead of consulting the telephone directory. Now, when they asked him for numbers as usual, Pillai woke up with a start and groped for them. He gave the wrong numbers most of the time. The senior officers, who had always admired his meticulousness and alacrity in preparing notes and putting up files were aghast at the childish mistakes he made. They were forced to draw Pillai's attention to them—gently and sympathetically at first, but rather sternly afterwards.

Pillai made several blunders at home too. Once he had to employ all the shrewdness and tact at his command to conceal from his wife the fact that he had forgotten the colour of his toothbrush. On another occasion, he did not remember the right wave-band he wanted on the transistor radio and had to fiddle with the band-selector for a long time. He had agonizing mix-ups with the keys of the rooms in the house. All the time, his mind was in pursuit of that female name that eluded his memory.

After twenty-eight days of embarrassments, torments and humiliating defeats, he got the name like a revelation: Vanaja!

Pillai was certain that it was not senility that had made his memory fail. He still had four years left for retirement. He had started wearing glasses only recently. Though there were streaks of grey here and there, it could not properly be said that his hair had grayed. His teeth were as strong as ever. What then had happened?

Naturally, Pillai did not want anybody to learn about the disaster that had struck him. He bought books on the working of the brain, the nervous system and them memory, and read them surreptitiously. When he chanced upon a reference in one of them to the possibility of memory loss in heavy smokers, he gave up his habit of smoking the occasional cigarette (not more than five a day). But in this too, he slipped up badly. Forgetting the fact that he had given up smoking, he once took a cigarette offered by a friend and smoked it to the butt.

At the office, the image he had built up in his long carrer was taking a severe beating. His colleagues whispered to each other that something really bad had happened to Pillai. The list of blunders caused by his failing memory grew dangerously long. One day he created a sensation in the office by addressing Eliamma Philip as Sarah George.

One morning his wife was shocked to find him returning half an hour after he left for the office, with a bag of vegetables in his hand. On another day he forgot the location of the bus stop at which he had been waiting every morning for decades, went to another bus stop, boarded the wrong bus and was late for office. A few days later, he found a file marked 'urgent' missing and turned the whole office upside down in search of it without success. Back at home in the evening, he found the file safe and sound in his briefcase.

As instances of his slips and blunders piled up, making him a laughing-stock in his office, Piilai took voluntary retirement and bid farewell to his office. Though he forgot this the next morning and started for the office as usual, he remembered it in the bus and was able to avert what would have been the worst embarrassment in his life.

His wife, his daughter and his son-in-law were now convinced that something horrifying—something more alarming than the outward manifestations of forgetfulness—had happened to him. Though it made them bewildered and frightened, they soon learned to live with it. Kamalamma promptly reminded her husband on the first of every month to collect his pension. But when it turned out that Pillai was incapable of remembering the figures correctly, she entrusted the job to a nationalised bank.

Pillai's forgetfulness now took on new dimensions. For instance, if his eyes fell on a pencil, he would sharpen it immediately out of force of habit. But after this, he would not be able to remember the name of the object he was holding in his hand. This would set off a furious hunt for the elusive name which, sometimes, lasted several days. As he was aware of the embarrassment which would result from holding the pencil in his hand and asking somebody what it was called, Pillai took care to hide his consternation from everybody. Finally when he got the word 'pencil', he nearly let out a whoop of joy, as if he had stumbled upon a treasure trove.

Soon there was nothing in the house that did not give him trouble: tables, chairs, eyeglasses, windows, the bathroom, the roses in the garden, his left hand, the scooter, his handkerchiefs . . . Though his wife and his son-in-law took him to a psychiatrist, nothing came of it, except that he had to swallow quite a few 'neurobion' tablets.

Once when his son, who worked in Bombay, came home on leave with his wife and children, Pillai's forgetfulness made Kamalamma burst into tears—Pillai, who was the embodiment of paternal affection could not remember his son's name, though he remembered the names of his daughter-in-law and their children perfectly.

As years passed, the cocoon of his amnesia wound thicker and thicker around him. He could not recognize even those faces which looked familiar. Hours later, when he remembered them, he would start crying. It became a routine for his wife or daughter to present a guest or a relative to him with the query, "Come on, can you say who this is?" and for him to stare blankly at the visitor's face for a long time. One evening he sent everyone at home into peals of laughter by stopping Soman Nair, who was returning from office, at the gates and demanding indignantly to know his identity. But the laughter did not hurt Pillai, for he immediately forgot what had caused it.

Pillai now spent all his time in the world of forgetfulness. He no longer felt it humiliating to tell anybody of his handicap. Lying on a couch in the room adjacent to the veranda, which used to be his study, he made futile attempts to recall a thousand things he had forgotten. As his wife reminded him to take his meals at the proper times, he had no problem with his food. Sometimes it took him weeks to recall his own name. He closed his eyes and felt himself tied up inextricably in a million knots which he could not undo. Gradually a thick curtain of forgetfulness separated him from everything: his parents, his sister, his childhood, his friends at the office, the rooms in the house, colours . . .One day he cut a sorry figure before his granddaughter, Preeti, by failing to distinguish between black and green. Rarely, when an event, a face, or a name came alive in his mind, like a bolt from the blue, he broke into a laugh of ecstasy.

But neither Pillai's laughter nor his tears held any significance in the house now. Like an old tubby cat, he leaned back in the easy-chair in his room. He could not even remember the fact that he was now totally incapable of remembering anything.

Pillai entered his seventy-third year. While he was returning home in a car after attending Preeti's wedding, he could not understand a word when his fellow passengers pointed to the flowering acacias which lined the highway and started a discussion on the pros and cons of the afforestation programme.

And then, one day, Pillai performed a miraculous feat. He instantly recognized a relative from Kottayam, whom he was meeting after a gap of twenty years. In a flash, the man's name and any number of details about him occured to Pillai.

"Do you remember when we met last?" the relative who

was well aware of Pillai's forgetfulness, which had become a byword in his family circles, asked him sympathetically.

Pillai remembered it well. They had met at the funeral of his *appachi*, Mrs K. M. Gowri Amma, mother of Vanaja, who had been his *murappennu*. This man, whose name was Parameshwaran Nair, was then in a state of acute distress at still being childless.

He had also mentioned something about making an offering at the temple at Mannarassala. Everything was as clear as day to Pillai.

"You don't remember it, do you? Parameswaran Nair asked in a loud voice, as if he had assumed Pillai was a little deaf.

"No," Pillai said, waking up from a trance.

There was a reason for his denial. He did not wish to prolong the conversation. He was in a hurry to find out how much he could see through the doors of memory which had just been flung open miraculously.

When he peeped in cautiously, his past rushed at him with the force of a tumultuous torrent.

He could remember everything now—even the trivial things that had happened in his long life. He remembered the hushed silence that fell among his colleagues when he mixed up the names of two of his colleagues in his speech at the farewell party in his office on his retirement. He remembered, word for word, the letter written to him by his son, Satish Babu, when he decided to settle down in Bombay, inviting him to live with him in the metropolis. He felt the taste of Vanaja's tears on his lips as she wept uncontrollably on learning that she was to be married off to Govinda Kurup of Kainakari. Going further back, he saw himself walking to school through the fields, and once, on his way home in the evening, being scared out of his wits by the sight of a water snake devouring a frog, and scampering home crying. Exploring deeper into the recesses of the chamber of memory, which had so unexpectedly opened before him, he saw himself vomiting his mother's milk at the age of two and his mother wiping his lips with the tip of her mundu.

But Pillai did not bother to tell anybody about this development. Instead, with an inexpressible delight, humming a nursery rhyme he had learned in his childhood, he pulled open the chests and drawers of his memory one after the other. When it was time for lunch, Pillai remembered it. But without breaking the routine, he waited for his wife to call him.

After lunch, when he lay down for his siesta, there was another miracle. By then, all the events in his life, starting from early infancy, were neatly arrayed in his memory. He could have picked any of them at will. Suddenly Pillai realized with a start that his mind was changing direction and moving into the future.

In his mind's eye, he saw a man with bandages on his hands and legs coming in late in the evening. He also heard distinctly the screams and persistent inquiries that greeted the visitor on his arrival. As he pricked up his ears, he learned from the snatches of conversation that reached him, that the man was none other than his son-in-law, Soman Nair.

Knowing well that it would sound ridiculous, he refrained from sharing his prognosis with anybody.

But late in the afternoon, Soman Nair, who had met with an accident, was brought home with bandages on his hands and legs. There were the same screams and persistent inquiries that Pillai had heard.

This incident took his mind to a razor-sharp alertness. As he tuned his mind to the future, he foresaw the lights going out at nine in the night and coming on half an hour later; Asha, the girl next-door, delivering a baby boy at ten-thirty and Asha's father, Mr. R. P. P. Menon calling to give him the good news; a fire-engine streaming down the road at midnight, its bells jingling wildly. All the three events happened exactly as Pillai had foreseen them.

It was a night of epiphany. Pillai's ecstasy knew no bounds.

It did not take him long to realize that his unique skill, if he could retain and cultivate it, could efface all the pain and humiliation he had had to suffer, and earn for him, instead, boundless respect and admiration. As he lay awake in bed, he foresaw himself going for a walk early in the morning after a lapse of several years.

He knew that no one in the family would allow him to go out for a walk. So he started early, at dawn, before any of them woke up. He saw the world outside the gates after a long time—after seventeen years and nine months to be precise. The road had changed beyond recognition. As he turned left and walked down the road, he saw a large, tall building. Beyond the building, where a barren hillock had stood once, were small, monotonous houses. After that the road split into two like a fork. Turning right, Pillai was greeted by more interesting sights. The young men jogging in tracksuits and the middle-aged men on their morning walks paid no attention to Pillai. The road was lined with tall trees, robbed of their leaves by autumn. There were crows on the branches. One of them let its droppings fall precisely on Pillai's shirt-collar. Wiping it off, he walked towards the stadium. As he entered the stadium, he saw that the health-buffs had only started arriving. On the far side, there were a few who were doing push-ups and warming-up exercises. As they were engrossed in their exercises, none of them noticed Pillai. Pillai stopped when he realized that he had walked quite far from home. He was panting from the exertion he was not used to. But he ignored it. He tried to pick out form his memory the events he liked best, from his childhood to the present. The sun had risen quite high in the sky. The dew-drops on the blades of grass glittered like a million suns. Pillai felt tears of pure joy well up in his eyes as he watched them.

He went to sleep with tears of joy in his eyes.

Early the next morning, before anybody else woke up, Pillai silently opened the gates and went out into the road. He saw the large, tall building and the small, monotonous houses that he had foreseen the previous night. Gazing at the leafless trees and wiping off the crow-dropping from his shirt-colllar, he walked on. As he entered the stadium, he felt as energetic and enthusiastic as a boy.

The health-buffs had only started arriving. On the far side there were a few who were doing push-ups and warming-up exercises. As they were engrossed in their exercises, none of them noticed Pillai.

Stopping to regain his breath—he was panting from the exertion he was not used to—Pillai pulled open the chests and drawers of his memory. He recalled seeing, at the age of seven, a colourful likeness of Lord Krishna, etched by the clouds, high up in the sky, above the branches of the *gomavu*[5] in the yard, and bursting into tears as the wind blew away the clouds and broke up the image. He remembered running up to catch a butterfly perched on a honeysuckle entwined on an arecanut tree, a gnat

---

[5] Gomavu - A kind of mango tree.

concealed in the vines stinging him, and a *kara* thorn piercing the heel of his foot in the same instant, the butterfly flying away to safety and his nursing the smarting hand and foot, his lip twisted in pain. His recollections brought a smile to Pillai's lips. The sun had risen quite high in the sky. The dew-drops on the blades of grass glittered like million little suns.

The glitter filled up Pillai's eyes. He foresaw the sun rising higher in the sky and the dew-drops fading.

Pillai's mind traversed the path into the future through the labyrinths of the grass which was fast losing its sheen. From bright green to dark green, from dark green to the white green of the sun, from the white green to the withering green of the hotter sun, from the withering green to the pink green of the departing sun, and, as the pink green retreated, into the limitless expanses of black green. Pillai could not go beyond the black green, as much as he tried. He tried unsuccessfully to tear apart the veil of black. But shades of black appeared to him in an endless array.

He saw himself wandering out at night once in his childhood, when the fields were full of gnats, and catching three fireflies in a row, locking them up tightly in his fist, and as he stalked the fourth, the three in his fist dying, and their glow giving way to pitch darkness. He saw himself setting off with a lantern in hand to call the midwife, when his mother was in labour to deliver his sister, stumbling on a stone when he reached the temple hunted by Koorattu *yakshi*, falling down with a crash, the lantern going out and the darkness rushing at him with the fury of a huge wave. The shades of black turned on him with the fury of a huge wave. The shades of black turned darker and darker till all light went out of Pillai's eyes.

When Sankara Narayana Pillai's dead body, wet with dew, was brought home, his family was more perplexed than aggrieved. When did he go out? Why? How could he go out without anybody's help?

(Translated by K. M. Sherrif)

A CHRISTMAS STORY

Zachariah

Sidharthan and Pathrose, two friends, brought to their room in a lodging house a prostitute, Ammini. Sidharthan had found her wandering on the veranda after the people in the next room were finished with her.

"Give me brandy and biriyani," she said. She got into Sidharthan's bed, covered herself from head to foot with a sheet and closed her eyes.

Sidharthan and Pathrose sat looking at her for a while. When Pathrose went out for brandy and food, Sidharthan gently lifted the sheet and took a look at her.

Once Ammini had finished drinking brandy and eating biriyani, she got into bed again and covered herself. Sidharthan and Pathrose sat looking at her, their heads swimming in the vapours of brandy. Pathrose prodded her softly with his index finger and said, "Did you come here just to sleep? Remember the two of us who brought you here."

Ammini merely turned her face towards the wall. Sidharthan said, "She's taken us for a ride."

Ammini spoke to the wall, "I have never taken anyone for a ride. It is two days since I had a good sleep. What do you know of my sorrows and sufferings? Let me get some sleep first."

"All right then, if you are so tired, we will also rest," said Pathrose and Sidharthan. They got into the other bed and went to sleep. When they woke, it was late evening. Ammini was seated on Sidharthan's bed, combing her hair and humming a song.

"You're finished your sleep?" Pathrose asked her. Sidharthan listened to the song she was singing:

Oh glorious moonlight, dancing
With a platter full of sandalwood paste

The heart of the jungle flower
Is waiting for you.

Sidharthan hummed the rest of the song silently in his mind. He loved that song.

Then, while one sat on the chair in the veranda, the other took Ammini. After his turn, Sidharthan was filled with a great sorrow.

When it was time for dinner, Pathrose went out again and brought biriyani. When Ammini had drunk and eaten, she sat on a chair, placed her feet on the edge of the bed and said, I am not able to sleep. Shouldn't you also understand my sorrows? What is the life of a prostitute? Look at me. I have a husband and two children. I have a father and a mother, brothers, sisters, uncles and aunts and all. But I am still a prostitute. What does this mean? When I came to you from nowhere and lay with you on your bed, shouldn't you have asked me what this meant? If I had not become a prostitute, what would I have been? I don't understand this. What am I? Am I a wife, a daughter, a mother, an elder sister, a younger sister, a lover or a prostitute?

Sidharthan gently pressed Ammini's feet with both his hands and said, "You're such a simple one. What is your name?"

"You want to find out my name now? My name is prostitute. My work is prostitution." Ammini burst out sobbing. "Is it only now that you want to know my name? With whom did you both lie, a little while ago?"

Distressed, Sidharthan and Pathrose told her, "All right, excuse us. We like you. If you want you can stay here today and tomorrow and all. We won't bother you."

"Then listen to my story first. My lover might come looking for me. My husband might come too. So might my mother or father. What will you do then? If you do not want them to surprise you, listen to this. My husband wanted to make more money to spend on drinks. I found out later that he also had a mistress to maintain. I lay with the men he brought home. He would sit in the veranda and smoke his beedi. Then he would count the money and put it away. Afterwards, he would touch and smell me all over. Even if it was past midnight, I would have a bath and go to sleep with my children.

I still loved my husband. Why? Who is a husband? Why do

I love a husband? Is it my love for the children he gave me, extending to him? Or is it because I imagine that he used to love me once? When I was tired of his counting and smelling, I found a lover. He was a lorry driver. He brings me brandy and biriyani every evening. He gives my children nice toys and dresses. Sometimes he seats me beside him in the driver's cabin and races along MC Road. He takes me to movies. He is the one who kissed me for the first time."

Ammini jumped up from where she was sitting and said, "I was with you the whole day today. Did either of you kiss me? Did you even remember that I have lips? I like to kiss." Sidharthan and Pathrose sat looking at the wall sheepishly. Then Sidharthan said, "No one has ever kissed us either. We'll get some more brandy and biriyani. Will you kiss us?"

Ammini walked up to them quickly and kissed the tops of their heads. "That's all young ones need," she said.

"We are not young ones," said Pathrose, "don't trick us. You kissed us the way our mothers did."

"Then you told me a lie," said Ammini, going up to them and bringing their faces together to press against her soft belly. "So your mothers have kissed you then. I am your mother too. Can you hear your younger brother's heartbeats?"

With great fear, they extricated their heads from her hands and sat staring at her belly, which showed between her saree and blouse. They thought they had heard a heartbeat and that doubled their anxiety.

"That's the son of my lover," Ammini said. "His name is Sidharthan."

Sidharthan nearly jumped out of his skin.

Pathrose asked, "How do you know it is a son?"

"He kicks me, he does somersaults in my womb. Only boys do that. Don't you want to hear his heartbeat again?"

Sidharthan and Pathrose jumped from the bed and said, "No! You tricked us!"

Ammini asked, "How did I trick you?"

"You never told us you were pregnant."

Ammini laughed, ran to them and kissed each of them on their cheeks. "How does it matter to you whether I'm pregnant or not? Your deal is with me, not with my little son. What has he done to you?" Ammini stood looking into their eyes, her own eyes shining with joy.

Pathrose said, "I feel as if there's someone else in the room." Sidharthan asked her, "Why did you give him my name?" Ammini smiled, got into bed and covered herself from head to foot once again. She said to the wall, "Are you afraid of my son? He is the child of my lover. Let him and me both sleep now."

Sidharthan and Pathrose went out into the night and sat at the edge of the backwaters, watching the lights of the ferry boats shimmering across the lake. They heard ships wailing in the distance. Then there was a loud clang of bells. Pathrose said, "Sidharthan."

"Yes."

"Tonight is Christmas Eve."

"Yes, true," said Sidharthan. Lifting his eyes to the heights of the night, where the Milky Way's subdued glow floated like a peel of mist, Sidharthan sang softly.

Beating the holy earthen pot-drum
Of the great Mahadeva
We sing the praise of the new-born one.

Then they went back to the room, opened the door without waking Ammini, silently got into the other bed and lay like statues, their eyes wide open. Their ears were filled with a strange roar which they sometimes imagined to be their own heartbeats and sometimes those of a son sleeping nearby in a womb. Later they were startled by Ammini's voice as she murmured in her sleep. Then once again, the waves of her peaceful breathing flowed over them. "My God!" Sidharthan whispered. "What did you say?" asked Pathrose. "Nothing," said Sidharthan.

Then, like a cradle, their bed rocked them too into a dreamless sleep and into the earth's diurnal rhythm.

(Translated by the author)

THE PARALLEL STREAM

THE SIXTH FINGER
Anand

When he learned his brother was sparing his life, Kamran ceased offering resistance. He asked for a pillow and, when it was brought, he slid it under his head.

The gatekeepers showed in the five soldiers who were commissioned to do the job. It was a large room. Besides the gate keepers, there were only the five soldiers in the room, a priest who stood huddled in a corner and Kamran himself. No one uttered a word.

Two of the soldiers pinned Kamran's hands to the floor. One tied his legs together and sat on them. The fourth one twisted a piece of cloth into a ball and gagged his mouth with it. The fifth soldier was Ali Dost who had six fingers on both his hands. He came in only after the others had taken their positions. Ali Dost folded his legs, sat down at Kamran's head and took out a lancet from a bag he was carrying with him. He held back Kamran's eyelids with one hand and applied the lancet fifty times to each of his eyes. He then took out a lemon from his bag and squeezed its juice into the eye-sockets from where blood was gushing out. At that moment Kamran left out a muffled cry, as much as his gagged mouth would allow—according to historian Gulbadan who also happened to be both Humayun's and Kamran's sister.

His work done, Ali Dost got up and came out of the room. The four soldiers were still holding tight Kamran's hands, legs and head. The priest continued to stand motionless in the corner. Kamran was groaning. And Humayun was pacing up and down in his chamber, restless and anxious to know whether the task had been completed.

It was an exceptionally warm day in the Hindukush Valley. The year, 1553. Month, August. It was the seventh day of Ramzan (Kamran, it is said, regretted he could not carry on with the rest of his fast).

In the outskirts of Kabul, the battle had raged for days. When Humayun sent his emissaries of peace, Kamran arrested them. Some of them were beheaded, while others were hung down the ramparts of the fort in order to stop the fusillades of Humayun's artillery. It was also during this war that Hindal, who was brother to both Humayun and Kamran, was cut into pieces by Kamran's men. Humayun's mind at last hardened like a stone against his brother. Kamran began losing the battle and had to flee. One by one all his friends left him. No one offered him refuge. The Sultan of Gakkar caught him and handed him over to Humayun.

With the war over, Humayun wanted to embark on a campaign to retrieve Hindustan. Before that, he camped at Pirhala in the Hindukush Valley to celebrate his victory. Discussions on the fate of Mirza went on for days. Amirs, muftis, imams and qazis were all of one view, that Kamran did not deserve any mercy and should be put to death. Humayun's mind wavered. Rejecting everyone's advice, he finally decided it would be sufficient to effectively incapacitate him. Thus, this hot August, on the seventh day of Ramzan, a day before the emperor's campaign to retake Hindustan, Kamran was blinded by Ali Dost who had six fingers on both hands.

Coming out of the cell, Ali Dost paused for a moment to look at himself, his hands and clothes soaked in blood. He had carried out a variety of punishments in his career but this was the first time he had blinded somebody. The blood that had gushed out had fallen on his face and almost blinded him. Wiping his eyes, he had continued his work. When he looked at Kamran's face after completing the job, it dawned on him that his victim would no longer be able to see him. He did not know why, but he was not relieved by that knowledge. When the slaves poured water on his hands, he washed away the blood mechanically. Then he wiped his hands with the towel they held out.

After such deeds people like Ali Dost are entitled to a treat in the pub house. Ali Dost did not go there. He walked towards the barracks. But he didn't go in. Instead he untethered his horse, walked with it for a while, and mounted it.

The horse galloped through new pastures, new lands and the darkness of the woods. At sunset he reached a village on the edge of vast fields. Ali Dost was exhausted. Dismounting from the horse, he sat on the ground against a hayrick. The hay and the earth were comfortably cool, probably from the previous day's rain. Suddenly Ali Dost had a bout of nausea. He retched violently. A great relief swept over him when everything inside was thrown out. He took deep breaths to tide over the exertion.

The commotion brought an old woman out of her hut. When she found it was a soldier, her curiosity changed to anger. Flailing her hands, she yelled: "After plundering the poor of their little paise and getting drunk, you fellows get only this place to come and empty out your bile?"

"No, mother, I am not drunk," Ali Dost muttered, still gasping for breath. "Someone else is. I am vomiting for him."

This was the first time he had opened his mouth after carrying out the deed. But he didn't know what he meant by those words. Like the bile he was spewing, a few words too spilled out of him. That was all.

What might have been in Kamran's mind when he said he had to abandon his Ramzan fast? Couldn't he have continued it even after he was blinded? Or, was it because he did not want someone else's help to know the rising and setting of the sun? Kamran lay prostrate before his tormentors for his eyes to be plucked out. That, however, did not mean he repented his deeds and was accepting the punishment gracefully. In fact, Kamran was never one to willingly lose anything. It's just that in the circumstances, he chose his life rather than his sight. That was all.

The victor in a battle kills the vanquished. Kamran too had done this. It is done to prevent the enemy from gathering strength and rising once again. For the same reason it is necessary for the vanquished to save his life so he can take another chance. Babar built an empire just with his strength and skill. Sher Shah Suri took it away from his son. If fortune had favoured him, Kamran too could have achieved what Sher Shah did. He had staked his claim to the empire not as Babar's son, but as a strong soldier. He could not therefore understand the 'crime' people said he had committed. If an ordinary Afghan—not a Turk or a Mongol or any relation of Babar—could defeat Humayun and occupy the throne, then why not he? If captured, Humayun would have been beheaded by Sher Shah or Sher Shah by Humayun and no one would have seen the necessity of any trial for that. Why, then, had all these amirs and muftis and imams and quazis arrayed against him with all their books and laws?

Kamran sent a message through Munim Beg, to Humayun, that he wanted to meet him. Humayun agreed on the condition that Kamran would not betray the least emotion. When he heard this, though his head was splitting with pain, Kamran laughed loudly.

As expected, it was Humayun who burst into tears when he saw the bandaged face of Kamran, "Oh, the vanities of this perishable world! I stained my hands with my brother's blood. I did not listen to the dying words of my revered father," he cried.

"If this is how you feel, why did you do the deed?" Kamran asked dryly.

"It was not my decision, Kamran. It was the verdict of law. I am an emperor too, the same way I am a brother. I too have to obey the law."

"How beautiful!" Kamran exclaimed. "Protecting the position of the emperor is the necessity of the emperor and not of the law, Humayun. Law serves the one who sits on the throne. It does not ask how he reached there. But it comes down heavily on those who claim it. I too have beheaded people and burnt them at the stakes. I did not quote books for doing that, Humayun, I have not come to you with this splitting headache of mine, to hear your philosophy."

"What have you come for?" Humayun asked submissively.

"I have come to congratulate you. To celebrate the death of brotherhood. I spat on its face long ago. Even if the reasons are different, you too have done just that today."

"Don't say such things, Kamran. Your greed for power made you forget you are a brother. Yet, I saved your life, on that count."

"You will not understand, Humayun," Kumran waved his hands to show it was useless to talk to him. "You have always been polluting politics with your foolish sentiments. You spoiled its purity by inducting fathers and sons and brothers into it . . . At least today, I thought, you had finally liberated yourself from it. No brother will any longer be a threat to your throne."

Speech had exerted pressure on the muscles of Kumran's face. He pressed his hands against his head and groaned.

Humayun could not stand the sight. Nor could he understand his brother's arguments. He called the guards and asked them to take him away from there. When they had left, Humayun fell into a deep reverie. In one way, he felt it would have been better to have killed his brother. A dead Kamran might still haunt his thoughts. But where is the time for an emperor for such musings? And if they persisted, there were always the opium pills for him.

Humayun called his chiefs and announced the ceremonial opening of the campaign to take Hindustan.

Hindal is dead. Askari defeated and imprisoned. Kamran blind. Riding on his favourite horse, in the midst of the army moving towards Hindustan, Humayun was suddenly engulfed by solitude. The Mughal army was a moving city which includes not only soldiers and officers and ministers but also the wives, servants and cooks of the king, traders, courtesans, dancing girls and even moneylenders who followed the soldiers. A confusing mass which raised a deafening noise and clouds of dust. Humayun has led this army a number of times—sometimes as a victor and sometimes as a fugitive. These three brothers of his were never with him then. Perhaps the brothers were his worst enemies, not the Sultan of Gujarat, or the Rajputs or Afghans. Separately and jointly, they kept attacking him even when he was wandering in the deserts of Thar and Sindh alone, after being driven out of the country by his enemies. And yet, it was not during those days of running from pillar to post, but now when he was confidently on his way to regain all that he had lost, that he yearned for the love of brothers who already were blinded or imprisoned or dead.

Once, as young boys on a ride, Humayun and Kamran saw a dog lifting its leg against a tombstone. Kamran observed: "The man who lies buried here must be a heretic." "Yes," was Humayun's reply, "and the dog's soul that of an orthodox brute."

There were many complexities and contradictions in the character of Humayun. He was not orthodox, nor was he a heretic. He could melt sometimes with benign brotherly love and, at other times, could commit the most cruel deeds. Again and again he forgave his brothers who had raised their swords against him. When a battle was won or a city captured, clad in red garments, he would sit on his throne. Till his anger subsided and he put on his green garments—and that would often be days after his soldiers had been out in the city plundering, killing, raping and doing whatever they liked with the population. Humayun was a very good soldier but a highly incapable ruler. He always delayed his decisions. Opium had blunted his brains. Mughals who claimed descent from both Timur and Genghis Khan had shown interest in collecting works of art along with their professional skill in cutting heads. Humayun too was interested in arts and pleasure. But he rarely got any time to remain in one place and lead a peaceful life. Whenever he found time he was absorbed in astronomy and literature. He wrote poems.

Even with his willingness to accommodate other points of view, there was one area in which he had no confusion—that empires should be ruled by dynasties and that the right to the throne belonged to the eldest son of the deceased emperor. He would not compromise on this.

After fourteen long years, today Humayun was going to re-establish the correctness of that doctrine. Shaking off the loneliness that had overcome him for a moment, Humayun marched ahead. It was a cloudy day. It would be raining all over Hindustan, he thought. Rivers would be overflowing. Towns and villages would be engulfed by waters. Till the rains subsided, winter began and the festivals of the Hindus concluded, he should spend his time on the banks of the Indus, organising his army, training his soldiers and planning the operation. Humayun tried to compose a poem in his mind.

Way back in Pirhala, guarded by soldiers and attended on by physicians, in his world of darkness and pain, Kamran too was trying to compose a poem. (Kamran was better than Humayun in poetics, says Gulbadan.) These two brothers simply did not understand each other. One believed that the right to rule a people belonged to a dynastic hierarchy. The other believed it went by right to the strongest person. They were blind men who opened their eyes only before mirrors.

There was yet another blind man whose eyes failed him even before a mirror—Ali Dost. He could see everything else, but not himself. Standing behind the cluster of huts, he watched Humayun's army marching in the distance. Villagers shuddered at the thunder and the clouds of dust which enveloped men, horses, elephants, everything. It was like a moving thundercloud.

When convinced that the army was moving away from the village, the villagers sighed in relief and returned to their huts. Ali Dost alone stood and stared.

It was the first time he was dropping out when an army moved. He had no explanation for it. The onward march had been announced days in advance, yet here he was this night, beside the haystacks in the village, eating the bread offered by the villagers and staring at the endless play of clouds in the sky.

No battle was alien to him. He had never looked upon any king with feelings other than of docile submission. There was a category of people those days who had no attachments to family or country and no roots or relations to claim obligations, and whose only consistent activity was to follow this direction or that, with this king or that. Ali Dost was one of them.

He had reached Hindustan as a little boy, in circumstances he himself could not recollect. He grew up serving Turks, Afghans and Mughals. It was the Sultan of Gujarat, Bahadur Shah, who had first exploited the induration process in this soldier. Every soldier kills in the battlefield but that is to save his own life. To kill or maim a man who has done nothing to you, or who cannot do anything to you since he is in chains, is something that everyone cannot do. So kings always retained such people as their palace guards without wasting them in the battlefield. Their duty started after the battle was over. Ali Dost, from his tender years, specialised in jobs such as cutting prisoners' limbs, castrating them with boulders, impaling culprits on stakes, etc.

When the artillery commanded by the Ottoman Turks and Portuguese soldiers smashed the fort of Chittor, Bahadur Shah's victory was assured. Ali Dost and his friends stood by waiting for the Sultan's orders on things to be done after the battle was called off. Rani Karnavati and other women remaining in the fort, jumped into flames. The males, to the last one, rushed out of the gates to end their lives by the swords of their enemies. Left behind were the children. When the soldiers cleared the wells after the battle, Ali Dost stood by and counted their bodies. When the number exceeded three thousand they stopped counting. The Rajputs did not leave much for Ali Dost to do.

When Humayun's forces captured Champanir from Bahadur Shah, Ali Dost and friends were inherited by the Mughal emperor as part of his 'war loot'. Led by Alam Khan, one of the principal officers of Bahadur Shah, they were brought to Humayun's camp for a banquet. Softened with food and drink, Alam Khan revealed the treasures hidden in the fort. So immense were the treasures that the emperor almost danced. The whole camp burst into celebration. In the disorder, a clique of palace underlings did something indiscreet. Extremely incensed with what had happened and intoxicated with drugs, the Emperor, clad in blood red, sat on his throne. He ordered a variety of savage mutilations to be inflicted upon the revolting soldiers. Ali Dost and friends dutifully complied. With the deafening shrieks of soldiers roasting in the flames and the wail rising from the town, the emperor's mood was ecstatic.

It all quietened by evening and an eerie silence fell over the palace. Sitting in a corner of the durbar room which had been cleaned after the day's macabre doings, in the sullen light of a candle, the imam on duty foolishly read that chapter of the Quran which speaks of the ruin that befell the masters of the elephant from their attempt to destroy the sacred building at Mecca. Humayun, who took this as a reflection upon himself, ordered that the imam be trod to death by an elephant. The interceding of the moulanas was in vain. The strong hands of Ali Dost twisted the imam into a ball and carried him to the elephant. Since he stood at a distance, Ali Dost's body was not soiled. The *mahout* was dirtied all over with splattered pieces of brain and intestine.

This was how Ali Dost had grown up.

In the battle for Bengal, Ali Dost came over to Sher Shah, but then, in the battle of Chausa, he found himself among Humayun's men.

From then on it was flight, for five long years. Along with a routed and demoralised army, looking for refuge, they moved across plains, mountains and deserts. Till, at last, on the other side of Hindukush, Humayun bowed his head before the Shah of Iran.

That night at Chausa, had he cared, Ali Dost could have managed to stay behind in Sher Shah's army. He would then have been around to rout the army of Maldeo of Jodhpur and to kill Puran Mal of Malwa by deception. Who can say, Ali Dost might have been assigned the task of capturing the surviving daughter and sons of Puran Mal. He might even have been the man selected by Sher Shah to violate the girl and to sell her to the *bazigaran* and to castrate the boys. But people like Ali Dost never speculate in this manner. They are not particularly concerned about who they serve.

As the emperor's convoy moved on, the dust gradually settled. The rows of trees on the other side of the maidan again became visible. But Ali Dost did not see anything. His eyes, perhaps, were still clouded with dust.

The old woman came out and took his hand in hers. She said: "What is it that is troubling you, you never told me. If it is the thought of sin, my dear boy, you must understand why no retribution can ever fall on you with so many sultans, rajas and subedars to bear that burden on their heads."

"It is not sin, no; it is something else," he said.

"I can give an answer only if you tell me, is it not?"

"It is not the answer that is eluding me, mother, it is the question itself. I cannot see anything, mother, I have gone blind!"

"Do one thing, son," she placed her hand on his shoulder. "Get your horse. Go to the next town. There will be drinking pubs there. And also dancing girls. Cool your head for some time. You will be alright."

He looked at her through his vacant eyes.

Delhi and Agra fell into the hands of Humayun. Thus he proved again that the right to the throne belonged to the Mughal dynasty and, within the dynasty, to the dead ruler's eldest son.

Victorious and satisfied, he withdrew to a quiet and happy life in the palace in Delhi built by Sher Shah. Though he was barely fifty, he had grown old and exhausted. He might have started seeing his end nearing. The sight of the old graves and sepulchers of Delhi often brought to his mind the thought of the Great Beyond and he felt an inclination to depart from this world. He made all arrangements, through Bairam Khan, to install Akbar, who was only thirteen years old at that time, as the emperor after him. He spent most of his time in prayer and reading. He reduced his dose of opium to four pills a day and planned to further reduce it to two. After drinking a portion of his dose for the day mixed in rose water, while coming down the stairs of Sher Mandal, the octagonal red sandstone and granite palace built by Sher Shah which Humayun converted into a library, on that fateful Friday evening of the first winter after his settling in Delhi, Humayun stumbled and missed his footing and fell down and died.

Kamran lived for another year. Discoursing with the ambient darkness, he gradually came to terms with the fact that he had lost the game. He decided, finally, to journey to Mecca along with his faithful and devoted wife Chuchak Begum. The costs were met by the emperor. En route, pirates looted the party. Again the emperor helped him. Favoured thus by the emperor, the blind man performed three pilgrimages to the holy city. The third time he did not return. He died at Mecca.

The dispute between these two men came to pass in this way. But don't believe even for a moment that the notion of the eldest son's right to the throne has triumphed over that of the right of the strongest contestant. Who can say, the story might have swung completely the other way round. Irrespective of the conclusions, at least some of you might argue that the discussion is totally irrelevant for us today as we firmly believe the rightful ruler is someone elected by the country's citizens through a free franchise.

What is left to be told is the story of Ali Dost. What happened to this man jaunting from villages to towns to inns to liquor shops to dancing girls? Could he locate the question which was evading him? Or, did he sink from darkness to even deeper darkness? We do not know. Jauhar, Gulbadan, Bayazid and Abul Fazal do not say anything about it. In fact we hardly know anything about the man. Also, historians abandon this wretched man at the point where they say he applied the lancet fifty times to each of Kumaran's eyes. Whatever was said of him thereafter is our creation. But there is one thing all of them wrote in their histories—that Ali Dost had six fingers on each of his hands. We do not know the significance of this small detail nor what they wanted to convey by it. Yet, taking a cue from this tiny unconformity, we went ahead to create this little story. Since we have now reached a stage from where it is impossible to proceed further, we too will have to drop the story here, as the renowned historians before us had done at, perhaps, a more appropriate stage. Who can say, Ali Dost might actually have gone along his usual path, the narrow, lonely and probably sad path his type of people are condemned to follow.

Coming out of his cell, he might have entered the pub house to celebrate the treat that was due him. He might have been enriched by the customory gifts he received from the emperor. Raising dust and clamour, he too might have moved with the troops of the emperor to Hindustan. He might have taken a valiant part in the battle of Sirhind. He might have toiled hard in the gigantic test of sawing off the heads of man after man to build the acclaimed *sir-i-manzil*. People with freakish physiques need not necessarily veer off the beaten track to become men of moments. Nor is it mandatory for supermen to emerge to alter the form and pattern of practices which are common to specified periods in history.

(Translated by the author)

THE RAZOR'S EDGE
C. V. Sriraman

Brahmachari listened to everything patiently. The eyelids, half-closed in rapt attention, suddenly rose. The flesh beneath the eyelids rippled. Pulling up the shawl which lay dishevelled on his flush, radiant body, Brahmachari spoke.

"You have my sympathy. But the things you just told me... mass orgies with several women in bed, drawing yourself in to the darkness of oblivion with the senselessness induced by several intoxicants at the same time—drink, smoke, tablets, injections... You may get away with it by using the English word—preservation. But I think Kali has entered your soul, a raging Kali." Brahmachari was silent for a moment. Then he said:

"*Kamathuranam na bhayam na lajja.*"

"Brahmachari, tell me, can I redeem myself?"

"Do you yearn for redemption?"

"I feel it is impossible for me."

"I yearn for it. I long for it with all my heart. I would die for it."

"That means you have stepped into the path of redemption, however distant your object may be. Have you read the Gita?"

"No."

"Read it once—at least as a seeker of knowledge. There are many good translations. Do you know who wrote the preface to the first English translation of the Gita? You will be astounded to hear the name—Warren Hastings. You will be more astounded if you read what he wrote: "the writers of the Indian philosophies will survive when the British dominion India shall long have ceased to exist and when the sources which it yielded of wealth and power are lost to remembrance." Hours had passed as he sat spellbound by Brahmachari's eloquence. It was this that had persuaded him to visit the ashram. He had no illusions of transplanting his life instantly in a virtuous soil. But to spend a few hours conversing with a man of exceptional intelligence was certainly a rewarding experience.

He looked out of the window as Brahmachari immersed himself in dedication again. Meadows and clusters of trees stretched as far as the eye could see. The cows of the ashram grazed freely in the meadows. A cow rubbed its back on a tree. There was a hail of flowers. The white flowers fell on the cow's head and neck.

Brahmachari spoke:

"I was trying to recall the lines from the Gita."

"Yathathyapi kauntheya
Purushyasya vipanchithaha
Indriyani pramatheeni
Haranthi prasabham manaha.

Oh, son of Kunti, the fickle senses corrupt the mind of even an industrious and intelligent man."

"Brahmachari, advise me. Tell me, can I redeem my ravaged mind . . ."

"You can. Do you know the story of Vilwamangalam Swamiyar?"

"I am sorry. I know very little about such things."

"Vilwamangalam, a Brahmin by birth, lost his head over Chinthamani, a dancing girl. One dark night, going through the rituals of his father's *shraddham* in indecent haste, he crossed the river on a drifting log and went to Chinthamani. But the log turned out to be a floating corpse and what he had taken for the rope his wife gave him, a snake. Even Chinthamani began to dislike his ways. She tried to reform him."

As he listened, the face of a girl, one of the many he had visited in his forays into the underworld, flashed before his eyes vividly. The words she spoke in her strident voice were kind.

"Yes, I am here to sell my body. But aren't you very late already? Go home, please."

"Was that how Vilwamangalam turned over a new leaf?" he asked impatiently.

"Only momentarily. Not long after that, he became infatuated with a married woman of noble lineage. He became distressed over it and blinded himself. He wandered for years, his restless soul on fire, before he could get salvation. It happens to all who stray into sin. But redemption is within their reach. If they strive for it. And strive for it they must, incessantly . . ." Brahmachari paused to reflect for a moment.

"Do you know what the path of redemption is like? The *Kathopanishad* says:

> *Kshurasya dhara nishatha durathyaya*
> *Durgam pathaha thath kavayo vedanti*

Like a razor's edge. Somerset Maugham quotes the same lines in his novel, *The Razor's Edge*."

Suddenly Brahmachari smiled. A captivating smile.

"Perhaps you wonder what I have to do with literature. I used to read about four hundred pages of fiction every day. My first MA was in English literature. The MA in Sanskrit and Malayalam came later . . ."

He was glancing at his watch. Noticing it, Brahmachari said:

"Don't worry. You can stay here today and leave tomorrow morning."

He was delighted at the invitation. A night in this abode of peace and serenity, lulling his restless soul, forgetting himself in the flow of Brahmachari's words of wisdom which soothed him like balm . . .

"As I said, redemption is never easy, but . . ."

Brahmachari's next question caught him unawares.

"What is it that enslaves you more, addiction to drugs or . . ."

"All I know is that both have enslaved me equally."

"Intoxication is not unknown in the scriptures. Balabhadra's fair complexion often ran out of his body—afraid of being intoxicated!"

"Brahmachari, shall I tell them to get the hot water ready for your bath?" The voice came from outside the window.

"Not necessary. I haven't had a temperature for four days in a row now. I will take a dip in the pond instead."

As she turned to go, Brahmachari said:

"If you could spare a minute, Sister." Brahmachari turned to him. "Sister lives in the shadow of grief. She fell in love with a man from a different faith when she was in college and eloped with him. But she was betrayed in her love. Finally she reached here. How strange are the ways of karma!" Brahmachari paused suddenly, but picked up the thread of his speech even more quickly.

"Look at the flowers that adorn the gardens and meadows of the ashram. Then look at Sister with the same eyes. You can think of her only as a flower. I am reminded of the old poem: *Kusume Kusumolpathy, shrooyathe ne cha drishyathe.* No flower takes its life from another. Such a thing has never been seen or heard. But a woman's face makes a liar of the poet. A woman's face can be a lotus. But on the lotus her eyes bloom like two little blue lotuses!"

He was looking intently at her. She was young. But more than youth, it was her lineage that showed on her face. In her white robes she looked like a bouquet of jasmines. It was the expression of complete detachment that made him gaze at her face without batting his eyelids. Brahmachari's voice woke him up from the trance.

"By the way, I have a problem in law to get cleared up from you. I had gone in for law too. But not finding any use for it, I didn't appear for the examination. Isn't there a clause which binds a wife to live with her husband? Begins with the word, 'restitution' . . ."

"Restitution of conjugal rights," he completed it for Brahmachari.

"But I suppose it is not applicable to registered marriages since a registered marriage is a contract."

"I am also of the opinion that it doesn't apply. Since a registered marriage is a contract, I think the man is only eligible for compensation if the woman refuses to live with him."

"Oh, Sister, you are still there," Brahmachari said ruefully, glancing out of the window. "You may go, Sister."

Her face betrayed no emotion as she walked away through the lush foliage of the ashram grounds.

Brahmachari went out, had a bath, dressed and came back into the room. Sitting cross-legged on the floor, he was soon lost in meditation. There were no rippling muscles on Brahmachari's body. But how wholesome the body looked! A body moulded by yogic postures . . . He gazed longingly at Brahmachari's body.

Oh God!

If only he could sit like that at least for a minute—his thoughts concentrating on a single point, the reins of his mind held tightly in his hands . . . Hours later Brahmachari woke up from his trance, as smoothly as if it had lasted only a few minutes.

"There have been avatars for all purposes—*amsha-avatars* and *Poorna-avatars*. But this is the avatar I worship."

He did not understand. Realizing it, Brahmachari pointed to the idol in front of him.

"Do you know who it is? Maha Varaha Moorthy. It was not the preservation of life on earth that this avatar took up as his mission. It was the deliverance of the Earth Goddess—deliverance from the bondage of Hiranyakasha, the asura."

"Brahmachari is summoned to the *parnasala*[1]," an inmate of the ashram announced. Brahmachari ignored him.

"I made the idol with my own hands—from clay."

What an exquisite piece of work! His respect for Brahmachari rose when he learned that he was also a sculptor.

"Come, Swamiji calls me. Let us pay our respects to him."

They walked across the green carpet of grass, under the canopies of the shady trees.

"We call it Swamiji's little cottage, *parnasala*."

Yes, he thought, the name suits it well.

Swamiji was sitting on a cot. His complexion was resplendently fair. Though he would not have been mistaken for a European, he certainly looked like a north Indian. Swamiji wore a woolen cap. Under the saffron shawl was a black pullover.

Brahmachari introduced him to Swamiji. He bowed to Swamiji.

"I won't be able to take the Gita class in Jnanodayam Hall today," Swamiji said to Brahmachari. "It is my asthma again. You can fill in for me. There are seventeen foreigners. You can speak in English."

He would have liked to accompany Brahmachari. He was looking forward to Brahmachari's Gita class in English. But as he turned to follow Brahmachari, Swamiji said to him:

"Could you please spare me a few minutes? I have certain things to discuss with you."

He sat on an old wooden chair. Swamiji gestured to him to pull his chair closer. He obeyed.

"I hope you have already taken a round of the ashram. I wish I could take you around and show you everything. But I

---

[1] Parnasala - Sacred tent; hermitage

can't move a step. My asthma has been troubling me for a long time. Can you suggest a good cure for asthma?"

He shook his head helplessly.

"I just wondered," Swamiji said in a weary voice.

There was a sudden ringing of bells followed by a chorus of voices chanting prayers. The evening prayers deepened the tranquillity of the ashram.

"I have seen a thousand and ten full moons," Swamiji said, holding his asthma in check.

"But a fear haunts me. Not the fear of death. God has told us what it means.

"*Jathasya hi dhruva mrityuhu*
Dhruvam janma mritasya cha."

Swamiji stopped at the end of the first couplet and scrutinised his face.

"What is born dies. What dies is born again. If you know this fundamental truth, there is no room for regret. But I built this ashram. When I came here, it was a jungle of thorns and weeds. I had everything cleared. I grew all the trees. I built everything—brick by brick—to make it my ashram. Let me be frank with you. I am worried about the future of the ashram. What will happen to it after my death? Who will look after it?"

Either Swamiji's emotions were making his voice thick, or his asthma was overpowering him. The pause lasted longer this time.

"I passed my FA in 1918 and entered government service. But I was not happy with it. As I was going to the city by train to take admission for BA, I met my guru. He was the embodiment of divine grace, the repository of meditative powers. I founded this ashram with his blessings. Like Prahlada, I always prayed for the realization of my only wish—a boon to free me from all desires . . ."

"Swamiji, my mind always flies away from my grasp. What should I do to control it? I have come here to seek your advice," he interrupted Swamiji's recollections.

"How lightly you talk about it! How impatient you are! You should first try to understand that the wise see the human body as two different entities; *prathyaksha sareera* and *dharma sareera*. *Dharma sareera* is what remains after the passions have been subdued. It is a state of complete self-restraint. It takes continuous effort to reach it. The first step is to give up one's desires." Swamiji stopped as a severe attack of asthma struck him.

A servant of the ashram brought a plate of *uppumavu* and a glass of black coffee, spiced with cumin seeds, and placed it before Swamiji. Swamiji tied his muffler around his neck and pulled down the sleeves of the pullover.

"I can eat nothing when I have this attack of *asthma*. In fact I am terribly hungry. I would have liked to eat a good meal. But look at the state I am in."

He gazed sympathetically at Swamiji as he struggled helplessly with his chronic affliction. Swamiji loosened the muffler a little.

"The Upanishad says:
Bhasmantham Sareeram . . ."

"The *pranavayu*, the life-force of the dying man, dissolves into the *prapanchavayu*, the driving force of the universe. The body turns to ashes. So what shall the living do to attain death?
Om kratho smarakritham
Smarakritho smarakritham saara . . ."

Suddenly Swamiji's voice rose. Wrath and disgust—not against anybody in particular—hardened his voice.

"Is there anybody to remember me after my death? Do you know what is happening here? Last year I wanted to name one of the newly constructed halls after me. But nobody liked my suggestion. Finally they took another decision. The ashram will provide the land. I may have a hall built at my own expense. They have already chalked out the plinth area.

"I want your opinion on a legal problem. That is why I asked you to wait. Is there any way to evict a tenant from one's land?"

"Yes, there is. To have a house constructed on the plot for your own use."

"I got some land as my share in the family property. There is a tenant living on it. I have had a good offer for the plot from a man who wants to have a cinema theatre built on it. But the deal is on only if the tenant can be evicted. The solution which you just suggested had occurred to me. I transferred the rights of the plot to a friend of mine and had him file a case to get the tenant evicted for having a house constructed."

Swamiji got up with great difficult, went over to the cupboard and took out a file.

He took the file from Swamiji and ran his eyes quickly over the documents.

"This is quite adequate, Swamiji. The tenant can be evicted once the applicant proves his bonafide intention to have a house constructed."

"So it can be done!" Swamiji smiled, keeping his asthma at bay. "Once I get the tenant evicted, I will sell it. With the amount I get, I will have a prayer hall constructed, to be named after me . . ."

Swamiji looked out of the window, watching the prayer hall coming up in his mind's eye.

The man who sacrificed the whole of his life in pursuit of his ideal, the mortification of desires . . . Here he was, fondling yet another alluring desire . . .

"You can go to sleep now." Swamiji took out a bed sheet from the cupboard and gave it to him. He also gave him a rushmat.

"You may sleep in Brahmachari's room. I won't get any sleep . . . I will spend the whole night panting for breath and sneezing. You will spoil your sleep if you lie here with me."

He went to Brahmachari's room, spread the mat on the floor and lay down. The mat smelled of camphor.

The peace of the night. The fragrance of the flowers in bloom blown into the room by the gentle breeze. No thoughts of street whores entered his mind. The faces of men he had fleeced did not appear in the darkness to haunt him. Neither did the truculent laughs of the men who had swindled him echo in his ear.

Oh God! What a relief!

Why didn't he think of coming here earlier, he wondered. It was not sleep that came to him, but a kind of gentle languor. He closed his eyes and dozed off. He felt a pleasant coolness when he woke up. As he pulled the bedsheet over his head, his body pressed against something soft. He felt the hot puffs of air expelled by the whispered words.

"You should be ashamed of yourself, saying all those things about my face and eyes to a stranger! Wake up, I say . . ."

He was shaken violently.

"Never mind that. But why did you ask him about all those legal things? Are you afraid somebody will come to take me away? Do you think I will go away from you? You have never

ever tried to understand me... As the round, full breasts pressed against him, he felt a wave of nausea rising in his throat. Long, thin fingers fondled his cheeks and crept into his hair. Suddenly they stopped dead. The body recoiled as if bitten by a snake. As it scrambled to its feet and ran, it struck the table with a thud. Something crashed to the floor. Was it the idol of Maha Varaha Moorthy? He wept bitterly at the helplessness of a being called man which tried to get rid of desires.

(Translated by K. M. Sherrif)

AKBAR'S UPANISHAD

Pattathuvila Karunakaran

I sat reading in the armchair; she sat reading on the mattress spread on the floor.

Etta![1] she calls.

I play deaf.

Etta! she calls again.

Yes.

Listen to this. She reads: "Manu, the law-giver of the Hindus has laid down only one vocation for a Sudra; to serve the upper castes."

Yes, I say.

Etta, are you a Sudra?

At your service!

Her interest was the Vedas. She reads Vedas, chants *mantras*. My interest was different.

Listen to this! I read aloud from the book about the revolution of Russian Sudras: "It was just 8.40 when a thundering wave of cheers announced the arrival of a short, stocky figure with a big head, set down in his shoulders, bald and bulging. Little eyes, a snobbish nose, wide, generous mouth and heavy chin, clean shaven now, but already beginning to bristle with the well-known beard of his past and future. Dressed in shabby clothes, his trousers much too long for him. Unimpressive, to be the idol of a mob, loved and revered as perhaps few leaders in history have been."

Who was this smart guy, she inquires.

Lenin!

Etta!

Yes.

Are you really forty-three years old?

Yes, really and truly.

---

[1] Etta - Vocative from Ettan, elder brother. Also used honorifically

Shall I pluck off your grey hairs?
No.
I saw Ajitha yesterday.
Where?
At the bus stand. She was selling the Red Book.
Alone?
No. There were quite a few onlookers. What are you thinking?
Nothing.
Listen! : "Now Lenin, gripping the edge of the reading stand, letting his little eyes travel over the crowd as he stood there waiting, apparently oblivious to the long-rolling ovation, which lasted several minutes. Lenin said: November 6 will be too early... On the other hand November 8 will be too late. We must act on the 7th, the day when the Congress meets, so that we must say to it, here is the power! What are you going to do with it?"
Ajitha looked very weak, she says, which group are you in?
Before my hair turned gray, before you were born, I was a pupil in Sage Namboodirippad's ashram, I reply.
What did you learn?
Servitude. Namboodirippad is a Brahmin, isn't he?
She had long, curly hair. She never kept it combed. She chewed the tips often.
Etta, do you like me?
No.
Shall I read from the Veda?
Yes.
She reads: "The soul has no sex, but the body is male or female. In the Vedas the soul is referred to as 'it', not 'he'. 'He' would signify that Divinity is male. It is unqualified and neutral. This is *advaita*."
Wonderful, I say.
She gets up, gathers her hair in her hands and holds it over her forehead in a bunch.
How do I look?
Not too good. You look like a yogi.
She would have preferred to look like a *yakshi* rather than a yogi.
Shall I make a sandal-mark on my forehead?
Whatever you like. Don't disturb me.

She comes nearer and sits on the arm of the chair.
Edathi[2] won't like me sitting near you.
You shouldn't sit too near.
Suppose I do?
She tosses the bunch of hair and it spills all over her face.
What did Namboodirippad teach his Sudra disciples, she asks.
Armed revolution.
Oh my! What is the revolution for?
To give the land to the tiller.
Father's land?
Yes, that too.
The whole of it? How shall we live then?
One should work for a living.
Should I work too?
Yes, you should too—along with the bloke who marries you.
My God!
I read again: "In a certain upstairs room sat a thin-faced long-haired individual, once an officer in the armies of the Tsar, the revolutionist and exile, a certain Avseenko, called Antonov, mathematician and chess-player; he was drawing careful plans for the seizure of the capital."
Etta, who do you really love?
Your sister, my wife.
Look, didn't you quarrel with her yesterday at 8.30 p.m. sharp?
Yes.
Why?
Just for a lark.
No. Shall I tell you why?
H'm.
Because you put your arm around my shoulder.
I played deaf.
Edathi had seen it.
Will you please shut up.
Etta, do you quarrel with everybody?
Uh huh.
No wonder. It's because you went to learn armed revolution.

---

[2] *Edathi* - *Ettan's* wife; elder sister

How old were you then?
Fourteen.
What happened?
I joined the insurrection. At Vayalar.
Why?
To capture power for the *Sudras*.
And they gave you hell, didn't they?
No, we sowed the seeds of revolution among the people.
Etta, you are old enough to be my father.
I am.
Why do you want a revolution now?
The revolution is not for me alone.
She brushes the hair away from her face and opens the book.
Etta, do you know what the *Kathopanishad* says? She reads: "Awake, arise, stop not till the goal is attained!"
She shuts the book and stares at me.
Now power has come into the hands of Namboodirippad, the sage who initiated you into revolution!
Yes, but Namboodirippad is not a *Sudra*. He is a blue-blood!
Listen : "Lenin was reading the decree on land: All private ownership of land is abolished immediately without compensation. All landowners' estates and all the land belonging to the Crown, the monasteries, and the church lands with all their appurtenances are transferred to the disposition of the township land committees and the District Soviets of Peasants' Deputies until the Constitutent Assembly meets. The lands of peasants and Cossacks serving the army shall not be confiscated."
Etta, all land belongs to God.
Yes, you can say everything belongs to Lord Vishnu Namboodirippad. But *Sudras* should get the right to till it and reap the fruits of their toil.
Ajitha and I are of the same age.
Yes. But her hands have the strength to fire a gun.
They beat her up badly.
Whom?
Ajitha's mother.
She didn't tell them anything. She just smiled.
They kicked him with boots.
Whom?

Gopalan, you know, the one who lost his arm. The cops got him.

I read: "At two o' clock, the land decree was put to vote, with only one against, and the peasant delegates wild with joy . . . so plunged the Bosheveiki ahead, irresistible, overriding hesitation and opposition . . ."

Edathi didn't want to marry you, she says with a secret smile.

How do you know?

I know.

Did she tell you?

She told Mother. Reasons: a) you were too old, b) you were not much to look at.

How old were you then?

Nine. Mother said your family was rich.

She edges nearer.

Edathi had had several good proposals.

What happened to them? Weren't the families rich enough?

Oh, stinking rich! But *Edathi* liked none of them. Father got wild and abused her a lot. Finally she told him to choose anyone he liked.

Please leave me for your Veda.

Edathi nearly cried herself to death the day you first went to see her.

Please go to your bedroom and read.

I love you, Etta.

Thanks.

Shall I go for a bath?

Yes, at once. And don't forget to put a sandal-mark on your forehead.

She left the room, but was back in an instant.

Feel my forehead. I think I have a temperature.

I felt her forehead.

Hell. It was cold.

Etta, your hand is warm.

She left me again.

Phew! I read again: "At 2.30 fell a tense hush. Kameniev was reading the Decree of the Constitution of Power; until the meeting of the Constituent Assembly, a Provisional Workers' and Peasants' Government is formed which shall be named the Council of

People's Commissars."

The historian chronicles excitedly:

"For this did they lie there, the martyrs of March, in their cold Brotherhood Grave on Mars Field, for this thousands and tens of thousands had died in the prisons, in exile, in Siberian mines!"

I heard the gush of the shower in the bathroom, with her singing in accompaniment. She would be back after the bath, pretending to dry her hair under the fan. She wouldn't leave me alone.

I resume reading: "There were bayonets at the edges of the room, bayonets pricking up among the delegates, the Military Revolutionary Committee was arming everybody. Bolshevism was arming itself for the decisive battle with Kerensky, the sound of whose trumpets came up with the south-west wind . . ."

The gush of the shower and her singing stopped. The bathroom suddenly became quite.

Etta!

What is it?

Please get me a towel from the wardrobe.

I heard the loud thump of my heart.

Don't get alarmed. *Edathi* is upstairs.

The door opened a crack and she put her hand through to take the towel.

Let me recite a *mantra* for you, she says through the crack in the door: "*Thamevaikam Janetha Athmanam Anyavachopi Munchana*! This means, know only thy soul. Give your ear to nought else." Edathi is fast asleep!

I opened the book and, with an effort, went back to the Russia of winter 1917: "Kerensky, with the Cossacks, was making hurried preparations to take Petrograd. The Revolution in peril! People's Commissar Trotsky spoke to the workers: March towards Petrograd! The moment is decisive. We've won power; now we must keep it. Our debates are now in the streets. For each revolutionist killed, we shall kill five counter-revolutionists!"

She asks in a choked voice from the bathroom:

Etta, can I borrow a shaving blade of yours?

No.

Oh, you're stingy!

What do you want a blade for?

I want one.
Ask your *Edathi*.
OK. Forget it.
The historian notes: "Three battleships lay anchored in the harbour, their guns trained on the gateway to Petrograd."
She says loudly: *Etta*, the soul need not be a part of life. That is why it is ageless. The soul redeeming itself from life . . .
"Next morning, Sunday, the 11th, the Cossacks entered Tsarkoye Selo, Kerensky himself riding a white horse and all the church-bells clamouring. Petrograd woke to bursts of rifle-fire and the tramping thunder of men marching.
"Over the bleak plain on the cold, air spread the sounds of battle, falling upon the ears of the roving band as they gathered about the little fires, waiting . . . So it was the beginning! They make towards the battle, and the workers' hordes pouring out along the straight roads quickened their pace. This was their battle, for their world. For the moment that incoherent multiple will was one will."
She came out from the bathroom. She had wrapped a bath-towel around her body which barely covered her breasts. Her manner was that of a fully dressed woman.
Can I put on the fan, she asks.
Put on a sari first.
Oh, don't rush me. Let me dry my hair.
Don't let *Edathi* see you near me in this outfit.
You are an old man, aren't you?
She puts the fan on.
If *Edathi* sees us here now she would say, "That's cute! The virgin offers herself to the revolutionary! Beat it!"
"The pickets of Kerensky's Cossacks came in touch. Scattered rifle-fires, summons to surrender. They were met by the Red Guards of the Revolutionary Army and workers armed with strange weapons! In that decisive confrontation, the Revolutionary Army, the army of the poor, surged like a human tide. The sailors fought until they ran out of cartridges, the untrained workmen rushed to the Cossacks and tore them from their horses. The Cossacks broke and fled leaving their artillery behind them . . . The old workman swept the far-gleaming Capital with his hand in an exultant gesture. "Mine," he cried, his face all alight, "all mine now! My Petrograd!"

Etta, didn't Namboodirippad pay homage to the martyrs of Vayalar before he took his oath of office?

Yes, he did. He took his oath, and the next thing he did was to have Mandakini beaten up.

Etta, you're jealous.

Yes, I'm jealous of Mandakini.

Etta, have you heard of *Allahopanishad*?

What Upanishad?

It is an upanishad which extols Allah and calls Mohammed Rajsollah.

No, I haven't.

Allahopanishad was composed at the time of Akbar.

(Translated by K. M. Sherrif)

BROKEN GLASSES

M. Sukumaran

One morning, as I sat reading the paper in the veranda, my spectacles, which I wore for longsight, slipped from my nose and fell to the floor. I gazed wistfully at the fragments of the lenses which had been my windows to the world for a long time. Picking up the frame, I saw it was intact, without as much as a scratch. This was quite reassuring. Frames are always costlier than lenses.

I tried to read the paper, moving it back and forth before my eyes to get a clear vision. It was no good. I could not read a single word. I folded the paper, deposited it on the table and went into the bedroom.

My wife took a long time cleaning up the mess made by the broken glasses. She picked up each tiny speck, making sure that none remained to prick the soles of my daughter's little feet.

The incident created a stir in the household. Of course, my wife did not bother to inquire about how the glasses were broken. She knew my habit of getting wild at her when I was at a loss for answers or explanations. But my mother insisted on learning how it had happened.

She knew I never lost my temper with her. So she pestered me with her questions. Did they slide off your nose when you bent down to pick up something? Did you knock them off the table with your hand accidentally?

Or is it the handiwork of your naughty daughter? And why now, after all these years? I don't remember anything like this happening ever since you started wearing glasses.

They fell down and broke, that is all I know, I muttered wearily.

Not that it was something to lose my sleep over. I knew an optician in the city who could fix me a new pair in an hour's time. I had taken care to preserve the ophthalmologist's prescription.

Financially too, I was far from being in a tight corner. I had just taken an advance from my Provident Fund. Despite these reassuring thoughts, my mind was overcast with dark clouds of depression.

I lay on my face in bed for a long time, shutting my eyes lightly to invoke the elusive sleep. My daughter tickled me on my ribs and the back of my neck with her tiny fingers. But, getting no response from me, she soon left me alone.

My wife came into the bedroom shortly. Aren't you going to the office today?

No, I replied, without turning to look at her.

She did not ask anything more. She knew quite well that without glasses I was as good as blind.

Before long, Mother came in again. Son, what is the matter with you? Why should you feel so helpless just because your glasses are broken? Such a silly thing shouldn't bother you, especially since there is no lack of opticians in the city. Come on, get up.

I said nothing. Turning over in bed, I hid my face from her.

It was the beginning of an unusually hot summer and my wife and mother were in the process of gathering reinforcements to combat it. We had a ceiling fan in the bedroom. But it was too suffocating to sit under it for long. Mother found hand-fans carved out of the fronds of arecanut palms. She filled the new eathern pot we had bought for the summer with water to the brim, dipped pieces of sweet rush in it and placed it on a small heap of wet sand. She sprinkled water on the floor frequently and spread wet pieces of cloth on the wooden frames on the cot on which mosquito nets were hung. Along with my wife and daughter, she too toook cold baths in the morning and in the evening. At night they abandoned their cotton beds for the thin rush mats spread on the floor and lay awake for a long time, cursing the cruel summer before falling asleep.

The earthern water-pot had to be refilled several times during the day. My daughter's head had been close-cropped to prevent her catching cold from sweat. She was given a thorough massage with sandal-paste before her bath. She ate sweet curds twice a day to keep her skin from getting boils.

I stopped going out of the house altogether. Even my appearance in the veranda became a rare event. I spent the whole day in the bedroom, emerging only at meal-times.

As usual a copy of the daily was delivered early in the morning every day. Without my glasses I had no use for them. My wife kept them neatly in chronological order in a pile in the loft, out of reach of my daughter, who would have torn them to bits if she had got her hands on them. My mother, who slept late and woke up late, would be jerked out of her mid-summer dreams by the rolled-up newspaper falling with a thud on the veranda.

I stopped brushing my teeth and having baths. I lost my appetite. It was as if the summer had bored holes in my body, for all the water I drank seemed to run out through them, and I instantly longed for more.

My wife knew I had not applied for leave. She reminded me of it at least once in a day. Looking intently at me hibernating in my cave of silence, she asked: what does all this mean?

No wiser than her, I just shrugged my shoulders.

Had anything happened really, I asked myself. My broken glasses certainly did not present an irretrievable situation. But the weight of an inexplicable sense of loss tormented my family, becoming more and more oppressive as each day passed.

My wife and mother engaged themselves in preparing dried vegetable wafers and cookies. These wafers and cookies, assiduously prepared in March and April, would carry us through to the next summer. The sticky flour-paste, squeezed into quaint shapes on the cloth spread on the floor, took just a few hours to dry up and shrink. The cookies dropped into the simmering coconut oil bloated up like a crop of brave new ideas.

But my throat was parched. I pushed aside the cookies and reached for water. I could have drowned in the water I drank.

Two weeks had passed. The walls of the bedroom appeared to me impenetrable, like the walls of a fortress shutting me out from the world. Spiders had been busy and their webs formed a thick layer on the ceiling. Lizards shed their tail-ends and chased flies on the walls.

At night in bed, drawing me feverishly to her, my wife sobbed. What happened to you? Why should you be so grief-stricken over a pair of broken glasses? How brave and unruffled you were, a pillar of strength, as you led your colleagues in their struggle for their rights! How often have you left home at dawn and returned home late in the night after a hectic day! Aren't you supposed to be in the thick of the strikes and demonstrations which are to be organised soon? When did the Party faction in the office meet last? What about the memorials and gates to be erected in honour of the martyrs? If you idle away your time at home, what will happen to the annual conference and the leadership camp? What will they do at the seminar on the social commitment of poets? Who else can arm the rank and file of the party in the town ideologically? The quota for the strike fund was yet to be filled up, you told me a few days ago. And here is pay-day coming up.

I listened patiently to everything she said. But I had nothing to say in reply. Earth had caved in on the gold-mine of my words. My brain went through the alternating states of the ferocity of the hound and the stunned numbness of the fallen hare.

Mother stopped asking me anything. She just hovered around me with tears in her eyes. A finger moved in her mind's eye, making scrawls on my destiny determined by the distant stars, as her lips mumbled offerings to temples which would ensure peace and prosperity to her family. The god of her clan, sleeping under a neem tree in the yard of a little house in a remote hamlet in Palakkad, appeared to her in a dream. No harm shall come to my subjects, it decreed.

Another week passed. Kerosene became scarce and we were compelled to use firewood for cooking. The smoke from the kitchen spread all over the house, sending us into fits of coughing.

I slept through the day and lay awake the whole night.

Suddenly a strange fact occurred to my wife. Though I had absented myself from the office for more than three weeks without giving even a hint about my whereabouts, nobody had turned up to inquire about me. For a union leader, this was certainly an unusual experience. I nodded in agreement as she volunteered to ring up the office to find out what was happening there. It was just as I had guessed. Most of my colleagues were on long leave. A few others were continuing their unauthorised absence. The office superintendent was perplexed, to say the least. But he was somewhat relieved to find that a few of them had started reporting for duty during the last few days.

The next evening they came—the top leaders of my union. They all had new glasses on, I noticed. They were not in a mood to exchange pleasantries or discuss our singular situation.

They brusquely asked me to accompany them, taking the frame of the broken glasses and the ophthalmologist's prescription. As a disciplined trade union activist, I was bound to obey them.

I was back in the wide open spaces at last. I took in the air, light and fresh, in deep breaths.

The car drew up at a reputed optician's store in the city and we got down and walked up to the counter.

Taking the frame and prescription from me, the optician offered to fix me a new pair of glasses in an hour's time. But what he remarked in passing caught my attention. Several people in the city had had their glasses broken or scratched and, stranger still, some had suddenly found their glasses giving only a blurred vision. The oddest thing about the whole affair was that it happened to them all on the same day. He looked back with satisfaction on the fact that he had been able to cater to all the customers promptly.

Our next destination was the union office. The office was crowded. There were only a few among the members gathered who were without a new pair of glasses. They were young men who had not yet been troubled by longsight.

The Central Committee member arrived late. He was not wearing glasses. Of course, he did not need glasses to make a speech.

The Central Committee member began his speech with a reference to the broken glasses. Comrades, as we all know, a number of people here have had the experience of their glasses breaking, getting scratched or suddenly giving them blurred vision. This may have been due to the sudden, brief tremor that was felt in these parts a few days ago. However, a plot hatched by one of the monopolistic cartels of lens manufacturers cannot be ruled out. Whatever the cause, the need of the hour is to overcome the crisis at any cost. Keep your prescriptions safely with you. Remove your glasses and put them away at the slightest hint of a tremor. Keep the glasses in their cases when you are not wearing them. And don't forget to wipe them clean regularly.

We applauded as he concluded his speech. Soon he left in a car, to speak at another meeting.

We drove to the optician's to collect my glasses. The union

leaders dropped me at home soon after.

At home, everybody was waiting eagerly for my return. The table was laid for a sumptuous supper. We chatted and joked as we ate. My daughter's lisping was music to my ears. I threw down bits of food to our greedy cat under the table. We ate until we could eat no more. It seemed ages since we had enjoyed the happiness and comfort of our home!

As I washed my hands, my wife inquired: shall we go to bed right away? No, I replied, you can turn in. I have a lot to read.

I reached for the pile of back issues of the paper in the loft. Bringing down the pile—a whole month's— I sat down in the armchair in the veranda and started off with the paper that was delivered on the day my glasses broke. My new glasses gave me a clear and sharp vision. I read through the papers without missing a single word. Minutes and hours passed. A cock crowed in the distance. Hymns flowed from the loudspeaker in the temple nearby. I was reading the last line of the previous day's paper when the paper-boy appeared at the gate. The rolled-up paper came sailing through the air and landed at my feet. I picked it up, unrolled it and read the headline in bold letters with joy:

Peace returns to Indo-China. End to China-Vietnam War.

(Translated by K. M. Sherrif)

BEFORE THE COCK CREW

N. P. Mohammad

A moist wind brushed against Seethi Thangal, and the khadi shawl, which had a zig-zig black border, slid down his shoulder. Thangal rolled up the shawl and put it around his neck.
 A palanquin came up the lane. *Kavum-keyin, thayyada-thayyada*, the bearers hummed. Thangal turned to look. It was the *Amsom Adhikari's*[1] palanquin. There were two women escorts, one in front and the other behind. Looked like Moosa Kutty Haji's wife was on an outing.
 It was a cool, pleasant day. He had set out quite early in the morning. Bavaji would be waiting. A couple of games of chess would see them through yet another day. He had to go to the Anjappura market in the evening. Thangal put his hand into the pocket of his *jubba* to make sure he had not forgotten to take the prescription for his daughter's *kashayam*[2].
 The wind was chilly. The banyan tree in Bavaji's yard groaned. Bavaji was sitting cross-legged on the *charana*[3] in the veranda. There was a crowd of *cherumakkal*[4] in the yard.
 Oh, they were to take the *kunhikkuthiras* to the *Kaliyattu kavu* today.
 Thangal recognised Nayadi and Kariyathan among them. They stood in circle. Some of them had *kunhikkuthiras* in their hands—*kunhikkuthiras* made of bamboo splints and decked with

---

[1] Amson Adhikari - The title of the revenue officer who was in charge of an administrative division called *amsom*.

[2] Kashayam - An ayurvedic preparation.

[3] Charana - A kind of couch fixed on the wall, common in large ancestral homes of joint-families in Kerala.

[4] Cherumakkal - The common name for Dalits in the Malabar region of Kerala. At the annual festival at *Kaliyattu kavu*, the *cherumakkal* took out processions carrying *kunhikkuthiras*, small horse-shaped figurines.

tender fronds of coconut palms. As they waved the *kunhikkuthiras*, the others, whose hands were free, clapped. Then they all sang in a chorus:

> Mohammed Ali Mappila
> Shoukath Ali Mappila
> Kayiykkum panathinum
> Danniallatha Gandhi thandaro
> Gandhi tandaro . . . ⁵

They have made Gandhiji a *thandan*⁶, Thangal mused. They used to sing a ballad about the godown and coconuts owned by the Marakkars of Chaliyam collapsing in the monsoon rains.

Times and songs had changed.

The *kunhikkuthiras* swayed to the left and the right in the hands of the dancers. Suddenly Thangal's eyes fell on the 'red-caps' who seemed to have materalised from thin air. Bavaji always treated policemen with respect. He got up hastily from the *charana*⁷ as soon as he saw them.

"Ha, Nair, what's up?"

"*Mooppar*⁸ wants to see Thangal immediately."

"Who, the Head Constable? Or the Sub-Inspector?"

"No, the Circle Inspector."

"*Ya, rabbi*, the Circle! Go with them, Thangal. We can have a go at chess tomorrow."

---

⁵ O, Mohammed Ali Mappila
O, Shoukath Ali Mappila
O, Gandhi Thandar who lusts
Neither for money nor for wealth
O, Gandhi Thandar . . .

⁶ Thandan - The cherumakkal used certain exclusive terms for addressing or referring to members of each of the upper castes. Through the Ali Brothers and Gandhiji did not belong to the case-hierarchy known to them, they have assigned castge-appellations to them. Thus the Ali Brothers become Mappilas(the name for Malayalee Muslims) and Gandhiji a Thandan. The line of reasoning in Gandhiji's case is not very clear (Thandan is the name of a backward caste, whose main occupation is toddy-tapping).

⁷ Charana - A kind of couch fixed on the wall common in large ancestral homes of joint-families in Kerala. Also Charnpadi

⁸ Mooppar - A term of respect for elderly men and for men in authority.

Bavaji went inside.

Thangal hesitated for a moment. The policemen were waiting. He had nothing to say to them. He felt the chilly wind enter his insides too. A flurry of thoughts rushed through his mind at lightning speed.

There was no way they could have found out. Bavaji's caretaker, Johnny, was the only one who was likely to have seen it. But Johnny had decamped the same night.

Nayadi and his troupe were dancing and singing at a furious pace. Let them. It was their day of rejoicing.

Thangal felt his head swelling. The two policemen took up position to his left and right. Thangal lowered his eyes. All he could see now was the tip of his nose. It had reddened considerably. Everything else was hazy. For a split second, Thangal ventured to glance to his right from the corner of his eye. Oh! It was Balan Nair.

"Nair."
"H'm?"
"What is the matter?"
"Uh huh."

What did the humming and hawing mean?

There was no reason for Balan Nair to be so distant. It was only last Saturday that Thangal had treated Balan Nair to tea and vada at Kunhalavi's restaurant. The proverbial memory of policemen. There were occasions when it was better not to remember anything.

There was still a long way to walk.

Suddenly it started drizzling, the raindrops pricking them like pins. Thangal opened his umbrella. The drizzle quickened and threatened to thicken into a downpour.

As they reached the bridge, Thangal glanced up at the thick wall. The legend was clearly visible: repaired 21-7-1942.

A train shook the bridge as it sped away with a roar.

The day would remain etched in Thangal's memory till his last breath.

He got the postcard from Calicut in the evening.

Raman Nair arrives at eleven.

Decoded, it meant a military supplies train would pass by at eleven in the night. Raman Nair should not be allowed to reach its destination.

There was little time left.

There were two of them, Sekharan Nair and Thangal. They had brought two small paper packets with them. The fuses were to be lit from both ends simultaneously. A deafening roar would follow and they would scamper away in opposite directions under cover of darkness.

Another bridge would be destroyed.

The packets were opened and the fuses were pushed into the insides of the railings.

Neither of them spoke a word. But their hands worked deftly. Thangal laid the train for the charge from one end and Sekharan Nair from the other. The train drew a thin black line along the bridge.

Thangal placed a beedi between his lips and lit a match. The sputtering flame struggled with the darkness.

"Darling . . ."

The beedi fell from Thangal's lips. Sekharan Nair switched on the flashlight. As the faint beam drew a triangle of light, two figures that lay locked in embrace on the bridge scrambled up hurriedly.

"*Guruvayoor-appa!*"

"Nair!"

The woman dressed in black got up first. The buttons of her *kuppayam* were opened and the heavy breasts which hung down on her chest heaved. The dishevelled hair stuck to the sweaty face.

Pathumma—daughter of Khauju, who husked paddy at Bavaji's.

The man got up panting.

"Who are you?" Thangal asked sharply.

Sekharan Nair's flashlight came alive again.

Johnny, Bavaji's caretaker.

A tremor went through Thangal. Had he seen anything?

Pathumma took to her heels. Johnny trembled with fear.

Thangal and Sekharan Nair were no less scared. What if Johnny squealed to the police?

"Beat it, you rascal!" Sekharan Nair found his voice.

Oh, what a relief!

The bridge was plunged into darkness again. There was the rustle of Johnny dusting the mud off his *mundu*.

"What are you waiting for? Scram!"

Poor fellow! Thangal said to himself. Sekharan Nair's hands shook as he switched on the flashlight once more.

Johnny was running across the fields.

Would he squeal?

He had to be taken care of before that happened.

The shaft of light came hurtling from the north. The rails became faintly visible. The whistle was deafening.

The train thundered across the bridge wrathfully.

Sweat had made their clothes cling to their bodies. As they walked away, it was Sekharan Nair who found a way out.

"We'll send some toughs from the seaside to chase him out before he squeals."

They headed for the seaside to assemble their followers. But when the seaside toughs came with sticks and blazing torches Johnny had already disappeared. He had packed up and fled by the next train. The search went on till the small hours of the morning.

It was Sekharan Nair who confirmed Johnny's flight the next afternoon.

Like everybody else, they too talked excitedly about the dynamite which was found on the bridge. That was definitely Johnny's handiwork. Rumours roamed about like street urchins. Soon, stories about the dynamite on the bridge died a natural death.

"Hurry up!" one of the 'red-caps' commanded.

They crossed the bridge and reached Anappadikkal.

At the mosque, the novices who learned theology before becoming *moulavis* could be seen taking a stroll in the veranda. A bus had just arrived.

Some of his acquaintances smiled at him. Some said, *assalamu alaikkum*. But were they looking at him rather oddly? Didn't a few avert their eyes when they saw him?

The policemen's gait became stiffer. Thangal felt his mind becoming a churning flux. He was desperately in need of some clear-headed thinking.

He would learn everything before long anyway. Thangal glanced at Kunhalavi sitting in the restaurant. Kunhalavi was deliberately looking away. There was time to sit in the open veranda adjacent to the restaurant and have a cup of tea. The policemen wouldn't mind that.

His eyes scanned the veranda. A crow flew off the bench and disappeared into the distance. Bunches of documents lay scattered on the table. The bench was empty. There was no sign of Sekharan Nair who used to sit on the bench, his head drooping, as he drafted documents.

Thangal started. The pain in his head became agonizing.

Walking up the road to the court were a few lawyers. Their black gowns flapped in the wind.

Thangal's eyes probed the walls enclosing the court grounds. There was a large patch of tar near the gates. Though his eyes had dimmed, his memory was crystal clear. Thangal stiffened.

He knew what had been written on the wall.

It was past midnight. Thangal stood guard as Sekharan Nair dipped the brush made of coconut-husk in a bucket of tar and wrote the message on the wall.

The dark, bold letters came alive:

Do or Die.

The message Gandhiji gave to the nation before he was arrested and imprisoned in Ahmedabad Fort.

8 August! A torrent of events!

The three words which spelt out a political activist's plan of action. The three words which proclaimed the nation's freedom.

The words unleashed a storm.

Do or Die.

Thangal's eyes glistened. Memories flooded his mind. The final hours of darkness before the dawn when the nation waited breathlessly for a ray of light . . . blown-up bridges, derailed trains, towering edifices devoured by raging flames . . . The waves of violence uprooted everything, like a herd of wild elephants gone amok . . .

The wheels of a speeding lorry rolled over a mud-hole, sending muddy water flying into the air. Thangal didn't hear the lorry coming. His mind was roving in the sleepless nights when grenades exploded and telephone poles crashed to the ground. When the roar of the lorry shook him out of his reveries, the muddy water had already made round 'rupee' marks on the shawl. As Thangal turned the clean side of the shawl up, the Registrar's office came into view. The police station was housed in the southern wing of the same building.

The long walk had been exhausting. Something was pricking at his joints.

There was a palanquin in the yard. Who would come to the police station in the *Adhikari's* palanquin? Thangal cursed himself for his absent-mindedness. Moosa Kutty Haji, the *Adhikari*, dealt in real estate, he knew. Perhaps the deeds were made out in his wife's name. But the *Adhikari* had only to summon the Registrar to his residence for such work.

"Oh, Thangal."

The Head Constable gave him a look and went inside. He came out immediately with the Sub-Inspector. The constables who had accompanied him moved aside. The Sub-Inspector took his hand and led him in. As they entered the office, Thangal saw—

In the lock-up, Circle Inspector Appu Menon's right foot rose into the air. The heavy black boot slammed into Sekharan Nair's jaw.

Thangal shut his eyes tightly. When he opened them, blood was trickling down Sekharan Nair's mouth, making a pool on the floor where two of his front teeth lay. Thangal felt a cold sweat drenching him. Something was being wrenched out of him.

"You'll have to take it out of my dead body."

Sekharan Nair, you are a true patriot.

The boot struck again, against a wall of determination.

Sekharan Nair was crumbling, fading away. Only the sheen of oil in his dishevelled hair held out.

"Did you see that, Thangal?"

The Sub-Inspector's question struck him like a blow on the head. The Circle Inspector turned and smiled sweetly at him.

"Water . . ." Sekharan Nair groaned.

"Water!" Appu Menon laughed. His broad chest heaved and the cross-belt of his chest shook.

"Hello, Thangal. Won't you sit down?"

"Water . . ."

Sekharan Nair, I am helpless.

"Sit down. That is what benches are for."

Thangal sat down and rubbed his knees.

"Scoundrel! When did you get the idea that police stations are made for any riff-raff who feels like relaxing?"

The change of expression was swift, deliberate.

Thangal jumped up from the bench. His eyes fell on the lock-up.

Sekharan Nair lay motionless on the floor. The pool of blood had become larger.

Appu Menon pointed towards the lock-up. "Get in there."

Appu Menon's hand rose again. The slaps resounded. Thangal rubbed his smarting cheeks.

As they entered the lock-up, Sekharan Nair's fingers twitched faintly.

"Thangal, I know everything. Now, tell me who else was with you when you made the bombs. Where did you hide them?"

"I don't know anything."

"I know you know."

"But I . . ."

"Oh, I am afraid I am getting quite forgetful," Appu Menon smiled broadly. "You will only be a witness in the case."

"You can't make me an approver."

"I have made approvers of scores of Congressmen more hard-boiled than you."

"So you won't?"

The punch on the underside of the belly caught Thangal unawares. He bent double as the pain shot up to his brain.

"Bloody fools!"

"One Zero Three Four!"

Constable Balan Nair clicked his boots. His right arm rose stiffly in a salute. "Sir!"

"Bring them here."

"Yes, sir!"

Blood was draining out of Thangal's face. His defences were crumbling. Words froze on his lips: Sekharan Nair, I won't betray anybody. I won't be a traitor to my country.

Balan Nair brought in two burqah-clad figures. Thangal looked down. The bottom of the silk burqah was frayed at the edges. The silver *padaswarams* on the smooth, white feet were still. Thangal shifted his gaze. The feet under the hem of the burqah were old and wrinkled.

Thangal felt dizzy. He gripped the iron bars tightly. His knees were buckling.

Appu Menon lifted the veil from the face of one of the figures.

Thangal saw tears running down his wife's face.

"Allah!"

Thangal's khadi shawl slipped from his shoulder. It fell in the pool of blood near Sekharan Nair. Bloodstains obliterated the mud-stains.

Appu Menon lifted the veil from the face of the second figure.

"Son!" Umma's voice dissolved into a sob.

Sekharan Nair's feet moved. "Water . . ." Life was ebbing out of him.

"Don't misunderstand me, Thangal. I will hand them over to the constables tonight—only for the night." The monstrous claws of darkness struck Thangal. Light drained out of his eyes. As he fell into a bottomless pit, he heard a distant voice asking him:

Now, for the last time, will you be our witness?

Thangal's dry lips moved.

UNICHIRAM VEETTIL UNNIATHA HAD FIVE BRAVE SONS

U. A. Khader

Unichiram Veettil Unniatha had five sons. Petting them and playing with them, laughing over their little pranks, Unniatha brought them up in a manner befitting the renowned *taravad* they were born in. As Mathottam Kunithazine Mammath Mappila, who had often watched the capers and caprices of the lads remarked, they grew up into five, fair, full-blooded young men capable of filching the hearts of the fair sex.

As the *Karanavar*[1], Raman Kutty Nair, who had a heart so tender that it melted at the sight of his nephews, always measured out generous quantities of paddy for the consumption of the members of the household, Unniatha's responsibilities were confined to removing the husk of the paddy, sifting the chaff and mud, and cooking the rice into various dishes as and when required. Raman Kutty Nair merely thought that the paddy, on its way from the fields to the hungry mouths of his *taravad*, was just taking a routine passage through his hands. The income from the *taravad's* property was meant for his nephews. So let them live comfortably with it. This was how he explained his generosity to his wife and his in-laws. When his illustrious ancestors of the Vannankandy *taravad* had acquired the vast tracts of land of Unichiram Veedu, they were providing for the generations to come.

---

[1] Karanavar - The head of the *taravad*, the ancestral home of the traditional phase, matrilineal family in Kerala. In the transitional phase, when the old order of matriarchy *(marumakkathayam)* was giving way to patriarchy *(makkathayam)*, the *karanavar* was torn between the love for his sister's children and the responsibility towards his own children, who lived in their mother's taravad. Unniatha and her children are making the best of the old order before it collapsed.

Raman Kutty Nair spent his nights at his wife's *taravad* which lay across the river at Nelliadikkadavu. He would set out for his wife's house well after nightfall with an electric torch in hand. He never had any supper except what was cooked and served by his wife, and Lakshmi Kutty Amma had little to complain about. The boat would be waiting for him at the landing even if it was midnight. The boatman, Mammath Mappila knew precisely the timings of Raman Kutty Nair's arrival and departure. As the swinging beam of the electric torch lit up the dark Palarakkavu lane, Mappila would pull the boat to position and say aloud to himself in his sing-song voice: "Nair has come! Nair has come—after sending his sister and nephews to bed!"

As a rule, Raman Kutty Nair did not speak a word to Mappila at this time of the night. As a northerner he knew his ballads too well to forget that there was no instance of Ponnopurath Ambu Nair ever uttering a single word to anybody on his way to his wife's *taravad*, Thacholi Meppayil. It was not deemed an honourable thing for a Nair gentleman to do. Moreover, the gods who presided over the destiny of Vannankandy *taravad*, whom he had woken up from their peaceful slumber in the attic to take his leave, would not take kindly to his fraternising with a monotheist. As Nair emerged from the lane, he would turn the beam of the torch towards his own face for identification. This would provoke another impish solliloquy from Mammath Mappila: "Here comes the Nair whose only word is mum! Here comes the Nair who left his tongue locked up at his *taravad*. Lakshmi Amma is a happy woman, for Nair won't open his mouth except to eat his supper."

Nair never bothered about Mammath's senseless prattle. You don't pay attention to every tramp on the road who wags his tongue a little too much. A fool's tongue is as slippery as an eel, Nanootty used to say. Nanootty himself was quite liberal with his tongue on occasion—on the day of the festival at the temple and on the ten days preceding it. So much so that one expected him to get a sound thrashing from his more irate listeners. But they forgave him his licentiousness, for, till the festival was over he was a *theyyam*, the oracle of the gods. His rituals began with the partaking of a bottle of toddy. Now toddy, as we know, does not spare even *theyyams*. Naturally it excited the depths in Nanootty. That was Nanooty's business. But what price Mammath Mappila, who drank no toddy, gibbering at him at this time of the night? Nevertheless, it was a relief that he was ever ready to forsake his sleep to ferry his lone passenger across the river. It was prudent to keep him in good humour. Nair started his return journey to his *taravad* early in the morning. Lakshmi Kutty Amma didn't give him any breakfast. At his wife's *taravad*, they didn't have proper breakfast in the morning, only *kanji*. That was the custom for the Nairs of Vadoor Thekkethodi since time immemorial. Tea and snacks for breakfast was yet another of those new fangled ways the Nairs who lived on the other of the river had taken to. It had come to the notice of Kunhiraman Nair, Lakshmi Kutty Amma's brother. "If you want to cultivate a taste for tea and snacks, you too can go west," Kunhiraman Nair had told his sister more than once. "Unichiram Veedu is not a holy of holies where you and your children cannot enter. Times have changed. I know all about the partilineal laws of inheritance. If they don't know it, I will enlighten them."

But Raman Kutty Nair refused to rise to the bait. Quibbles and squabbles did not become gentlemen. Discretion is the better part of valour, as everybody knows, and as Perumalpurath Ambi learned from experience. Though Ambi had forgotten to take his wallet with him when he left Elaneerthodi Madhavi's house after one of his amorous adventures, and though there had been as many as a hundred gold coins in it, he was prudent not to publicise the incident. As a result, the honour of Perumalpuram *taravad* remained intact. Madhavi, of course, bragged about her luck to all and sundry. But who would believe the likes of her? Nobody paid any heed to her tall talk even when she had a palatial mansion built for herself and a fretted copper roof for the Meloor temple. Nor did anybody find it remarkable when she had three ponds dug for bathing the elephants at the Keezhoor temple and offered a whole course of fireworks for the temple festival. Nobody said a word against Ambi. Raman Kutty Nair knew the whole story. That was why he chose to maintain a stoic silence when Lakshmi Kutty Amma harried him with home-truths. Lakshmi Kutty Amma had quite a lot to say: about the gods who slept uneasily in the temple of the Vadoor Thekkethodi *taravad* and about their children who had already gone to sleep in the next room. The children were getting into bad company with nobody to guide them, she lamented. She stressed the word 'nobody'. She detested her brother, Kunhiraman Nair, who was far from being the embodiment of generosity when it came to measuring out the paddy for the expenditure of the household. She resented the way he coolly packed off sacks and sacks of mangoes and jackfruits to his wife's *taravad*, Elanthoor Thodi. Kunhiraman Nair, who chased away the Mappilas who came from the east to sell raw bananas, had an explanation ready when his nephews demanded anything from him: the lone struggle he was waging to make both ends meet in the household. One would have thought that Raman Kutty Nair was deaf, the way he stretched out on the bed, his eyes open and shut for alternate spells, as Lakshmi Kutty Amma poured out her grouses, his expression as dispassionate as a hermit's. Finally as she turned down the wick of the lamp, Lakshmi Kutty Amma would say: "Why do you sneak in every night like an apparition? I suppose you find it a virtue to eat the rice I cook for you. But don't think this will go on forever. I will do something one of these days."

Nair, who was relieved that the light had been put out, would find his curiosity aroused. "What will you do?" he would ask her.

"Kill myself. Do you think I don't have the nerve for that?" Lakshmi Amma's voice would take on a menacing edge.

"The time of your death is predestined." With this parting shot, Raman Kutty started snoring. Nair was fastidious about his food. Even for supper he wanted thick curds, butter and, of course, fried *pappadam*. In spite of everything, nobody had told him till date that all these were new-fangled ways they had taken to, west of the river, and that it was impossible to introduce them here in the East. Lakshmi Amma did drop a hint or two at times, and she did fail to provide him with all the dishes he wanted. But Kunhiraman Nair had always maintained an exemplary decency in his dealings with him. So, amidst grumblings and naggings, amidst the endless incantations of the household expenses as evidence of the hard times they were going through, he got his curds and butter. He got fewer fried *pappadams* than he would have liked to have. But his wife did it on grounds of health.

"You are in your fifties. It is not good for you to take too much of coconut oil—or salt."

When he finished eating his rice, grinding pieces of *pappadam* into it, he had only his mattress and pillow to think of. Lakshmi

Kutty Amma's tales of woe were always unravelled when he was having his supper. But the mattress and the pillow gave Raman Kutty Nair precisely what he longed for—a sound sleep.

Nair woke up unfailingly at dawn. Getting up he would head straight for the temple-pond to brush his teeth and take a dip. There were few who went to the temple-pond that early. As there was nobody to talk to, Nair finished his ablutions in two ticks. Returning to the house, he would get a bowl of *kanji* if Lakshmi Kutty Amma had woken up. Raman Kutty Nair had learned this habit of drinking *kanji* so early in the morning after he started living in his wife's house. Or had he really started living in his wife's house? He only spent the night there. His days were spent in his *taravad*, on the grounds outside the walls of the *taravad*, and in the premises of the temple. It had been the exclusive temple of the Vannnankandy *taravad*. Though the government had taken over its administration, and though the fellows who now performed the poojas were government servants, there was nothing wrong in continuing to call it the family temple. There was a short cut to the temple from the *taravad* across the field, which the women of the *taravad* had been using for a long time. Nair would ruminate over all this as he walked back to the house with a wet bath-towel wrapped round his waist. After changing into his clothes, he didn't stay a minute longer. He was very particular about leaving before the children woke up. Lakshmi Kutty Amma used to say: "Ha, that is rich! Keep the identity of their father a closely guarded secret! But Unniatha is lucky. Her children know everything about both their father, Krishnan Nambiar and their *karanavar*, Raman Kutty Nair. I am not complaining. I suppose they should get the best of everything. It is their *taravad*."

As he sat in the boat, Raman Kutty Nair was still pondering over the invectives Lakshmi Kutty Amma had flung at him the previous night. As he rowed the boat with his long pole, Mammath Mappila kept up his incessant chatter. Now he was on the story of the arrival of Achuthan, younger brother of Krishnan Nambiar, from the 'Gulf'. It appeared that Achuthan's wife and their children talked and behaved in a sort of 'English style'—Mammath Mappila rambled on. Achuthan's arrival was news to Raman Kutty Nair. He wondered why Krishnan Nambiar, Unniatha's husband, had not told him a word about it. Nambiar had recently taken to maintaining long spells of silence, he had noticed. Was Nambiar trying to ape him in maintaining a stoic silence and a nonchalant, unruffled front before his wife and children, Raman Kutty Nair wondered for a moment. That was unlikely, he decided. If Nambiar had a fault, it was his habit of shooting his mouth off at the slightest provocation. In other words, the chief weapons in the armoury of this Nair from Pallikkara were his licentious tongue, the rich crop of words he used on various occasions, and a booming voice that could be heard a mile away. The first thought that then occurred to Raman Kutty Nair when a proposal came from Krishnan Nambiar for Unniatha was that it was unlikely that the *taravad* would have any problems from the harmless young man. Of course, he had learned from Nanu Mooppar, who had brought the proposal, about the idiosyncracies of the members of Krishnan Nambiar's *taravad*, each more amazing than the next, and of the gay, boisterous atmosphere which always prevailed there. But it was, beyond doubt, the best match Unniatha, his only sister, could ever have had, he had thought with contentment as he licked the payasam at the wedding feast. Considering the fact that his five sons had grown up into robust young men and that Unniatha still retained some of her old charms, it was a mystery why Nambiar had recently taken to wearing such a down-in-the-dumps look on his face. Good for him if he doesn't become bedridden, fretting over whatever is in his mind. When old men fret, there are two ways they end up; either they croak, or they run away to Kasi or Rameswaram or wherever world-weary men flock to become ascetics. Either way, it would be a great loss to his sister and her sons. He had to make the necessary arrangements before that happened. The future of Unniatha's sons was inextricably linked with the destiny of the *taravad*.

Tying the boat to the stake in the landing, Mammath Mappila accompanied him as far as the toll-booth. "The boys are still idling at home, aren't they?" Mammath Mappila asked him.

"Which boys?" was the question that sprang instantly to Raman Kutty Nair's lips, more as a reflex than anything else. Not that he liked to set up a conversation with this lowly Mappila. But the question dropped involuntarily.

"I meant your nephews. Proper bums they have become, loafing around the village the whole day. Don't you think it's time they did some work for a change?"

Oh, Mappila was talking about Unniatha's sons. There were five of them. He often remarked that they were like the five Pandavas. "Oh sure, they are," Lakshmi Kutty Amma had retorted. "And the battle of Kurukshetra won't be long in coming!" But Nair knew better than to take women's foolish banter seriously. And spending the night at his in-laws' didn't necessarily mean that he had to be a hen-pecked husband. So he had ignored the retort. But now this Mappila was at it too. "They have gone wild without a leash," he was saying. "They will create havoc sooner or later. Time you did something to bring them to book."

There was something in that, of course. The Mappila wouldn't think of asking why none of them thought much of going to school. Such things didn't come to his notice. But what was he driving at then? Perhaps one of them had had some coconuts plucked from the *parambu* of the *taravad* and sold them for whatever they fetched. And, of course, boys will be boys. They wouldn't be averse to flirting with some of those *cherumis*[2] who came to cut pine-leaves from the corner of the *parambu* for weaving mats. Without waiting to get Mammath Mappila's allegations clarified, he walked briskly toward Unichiram Veedu. It was noon when he reached his *taravad*. Unniatha was waiting in the veranda with a glass of *sambharam*[3]. She had fixed the *sambharam* as soon as she saw him from a distance walking up across the fields.

A sister will always be a sister, Nair mused. Only siblings can know each other so intimately. The *sambharam* was cool and tasty. Unniatha had mixed exactly the required amount of salt and chillies in it. Sometimes Raman Kutty Nair couldn't help recounting his sister's midas-touch with food and drink, to his wife. It was a useful exercise too, for it kept Lakshmi Amma's mouth shut till he went to sleep.

Raman Kutty Nair gulped down a full jug of *sambharam* and stretched himself on the easy-chair in the veranda. He closed his eyes and tried to imagine himself being transformed into one of his illustrious ancestors—Sankaran Nair, for instance. Or Kitten

---

[2] **Cherumi** - A woman belonging to the caste of untouchables called Cherumakkal or Pulayar.
[3] **Sambharam** - Buttermilk garnished with green chillies and ginger

Nair. There was a cool breeze from the west, rustling the leaves of the banyan tree which spread its canopy over the family temple. Unniatha was still there in the veranda, gazing at him. Nair was reminded of the ballad about Kunhunnooli, the sister of Othenan Nambiar of Thacholi Meppayil, leaning against the carved pillar in the veranda of her *taravad* and extolling the virtues of the man she loved. It was easy to remember the stories if you knew the ballads. Raman Kutty Nair knew each one of them by heart. Like Kunhunnooli, Unniatha too had, perhaps, her praises to sing. But Nair knew that it was futile to expect her to come up with anything as fervent or vivid as the word-picture of the valorous deeds of young Kunhambu, Kunhunnooli's sweetheart and son of Aringodar, arch enemy of the chieftain of Nadapuram. But let her say her piece, he said to himself benignly as he glanced expectantly at her.

"The children's father[4] is still here."

"Will he be staying for lunch?"

"No, he has been waiting to meet you. Shall I call him?"

Unniatha's behavior appeared to him bit more polite than necessary. There was something she wanted from him, he reflected calmly. The lull before the storm. Unniatha revelled in going to the extremes—it would either be prolonged indifference or outrageous aggression. As Krishnan Nambiar had waited for him till noon, the latter appeared more likely to be the course of action. He glanced at Unniatha once more and said, "Tell him to come here."

Krishnan Nambiar had already reached the veranda. He began his speech by declaring that his affection for his children was unbounded. That was fine. Going further, he drew Raman Kutty Nair's attention to the fact that he loved his wife more than any man would. Very creditable of him, Nair thought. Nobody could dispute that. But what followed was mere maudlin stuff. He regretted that none of his five sons had paid any attention to their studies. Poor Nambiar! It must have been sheer ignorance which made him have visions of his sons, armed with the riches of English education, proudly ascending the rungs of the civil service. The same reason could be attributed to his grouses

---

[4] 'The children's father' - In a traditional family in Kerala, the wife never referred to her husband by name.

against the Nairs of the Vannankandy *taravad*. Raman Kutty Nair chuckled.

"You find it funny, don't you?" Nambiar's voice was gruff.

"Well, you said the children are going astray. It should have brought tears to my eyes. But you see, Nambiar, there are no tears in my eyes. I don't know why."

"I should not have expected a man like you to be moved by it," pat came Nambiar's retort.

"I see." Nair nodded his head gently. Perhaps it had been decreed in the scrolls of fate that he, the *karanavar* of Vannankandy *taravad* and a man of standing among the landed gentry, should listen patiently while his brother-in-law called him names. The scrawls of fate could not be wished away. Nair leaned back leisurely in the easy-chair to take in the rest of Nambiar's utterances. Nambiar seated himself on the broad parapet which bordered the veranda while Unniatha stood beside him like a dutiful wife. Raman Kutty Nair took a quick look around. How wonderful! The five Pandavas had positioned themselves at strategic points in the yard. One of them leaned against the stone platform around the basil plant, while another stood under the platter of *bhasmam*, the holy ash, hanging from the rafter on the roof. The third and the fourth hovered hear the steps to the veranda. The youngest, Sahadevan Nair, struck a belligerent pose, his right foot lifted on to the rounded brick below the *gulikanthara*[5]. The eldest broke a twig from the basil and fiddled with it.

"Amma," he said, "tell him what we want. I am tired of waiting."

Raman Kutty Nair wondered whether he was in the court of Duryodhana. In that case he should have a reply ready for the Pandavas. As he pondered over this in silence, Krishnan Nambiar suddenly said:"Achuthan, my brother has come from Dubai."

"So Mammath Mappila tells me."

"What did Mappila say?"

"He told me Achuthan had come."

"Did he tell you anything more?"

"Not much."

---

[5] Gulikanthara - a raised plinth built for the demon, Gulikan, an ancient Dravidian deity.

"Well, let me tell you. Achuthan was pained at the sight of my children—the heirs of Vannankany *taravad*, mind you—loafing around like bums. He has offered to take them to Dubai. He says they can earn quite a bit of money there even if they don't do anything in particular."

"You mean to say, begging is such a lucrative profession over there?"

"Why do you have to be so nasty?" Nambiar turned to his wife. "I hope you heard what your dear brother said. If they make a decent living there, I am not the one who should rejoice. If they come up in life, Vannankandy *taravad* will take the credit, not me."

Krishnan Nambiar got up. Bhiman Nair lifted his mace. "*Acha*, you should have been a little more lucid. We need money for our NOCs. The only way to get it is to partition the *taravad*. Land prices have gone up like anything. These Dubai Mappilas will give anything for a piece of land. When we come back we can buy property worth all the assets of the *taravad* put together. The *taravad* must be partitioned in any case. We must get our share. Ammavan can live permanently at his in-laws' for all we care."

The Pandavas were adamant. Unniatha seconded her sons' proposal. Nair glanced at Nambiar again. Nambiar twirled his mustache. "I don't want a paisa of it. Everything is for your sister and her sons. Doesn't everything belong to them? As for me, I have my own share at my own *taravad*, which is more than enough for me. But I won't let you rob my wife and children of what rightfully belongs to them. I love them too dearly for that. You may have different views, of course. That accounts for the way your children are conducting themselves. From what I gather, the *karanavar* of Vadoor Thekkethodi is more interested in his own children than the children of his *taravad*."

Thereby hangs a tale, Nair mused as Nambiar concluded his campaign. He got up and went down into the yard. He had not gone half-a-dozen paces when Unniatha called him. "Etta, where are you going in this scorching heat without an umbrella?"

That was a legitimate question. The sun was scorching hot at noon. He had been careless not to have taken an umbrella. But before Raman Kutty Nair could reply, the Pandavas came running to him with his umbrella. Opening the umbrella, Raman Kutty Nair said: "I must see Kannan, the document writer. He will have to prepare a statement of partition for Vannankandy *taraad* before we go to the Registrar's office at Thacharakkunme. Kannan is the right man for the job. He knows everything about our *taravad*. If they are all heading for Dubai, partition seems to be the only way out."

So Nair was getting down to business. Unniatha and her five sons silently wished him all success as he set out to look up Kannan. It was a sight which brought tears of joy to their eyes—the sight of the *karanavar* of Vannankandy *taravad* setting out resolutely to facilitate his nephews' passage to the Promised Land. Raman Kutty Nair was moving with the times . . .

U.A. Khader too was watching Raman Kutty Nair as he walked away into the distance. All is well that ends well.

(Translated by K. M. Sherrif)

THE COLONEL
V. K. N.

The Colonel who had moved into the ground-floor flat over the weekend seemed an early bird. He left the place before the crow about the place had time to let off its ritual calls thrice-over at crack of dawn, and returned only after it had gone off to sleep. And so the Colonel's lady must be in absolute command of the house, Payyan thought. It was as if the top brass and his lady, between themselves, had demarcated their respective areas of command: his the regiment, hers the house. Even then her ladyship looked inclined to make herself scarce in her theatre of war.

Like a good neighbour, Payyan tried to call on them on Monday morning. The uniformed batman who answered the doorbell said that the Colonel had already left. The Colonel's lady? She too had left. A dog barked inside the house as if in confirmation.

After that, for five days running, Payyan rang the bell but the jawan had the same old story to tell: both his mistress and the master had gone their separate ways and there you are. So, Payyan thought, it would be hard to meet them in the circumstances, he being a bird of the other extreme, early to bed and late to rise.

He decided to track the Colonel down the next Sunday morning. He went down and rang the bell at nine, an hour after breakfast. The door opened and, without giving time to the orderly to sing his refrain in the negative, he walked into the living room. The place looked chic with curtains of the right shade, sofas and cushions of the right foam rubber, the walls replete with old Picasso prints and curios of rare oddity. The objects matched one another and wherever they did not match, matchboxes had been placed as the perfect match work.

Payyan looked about him cautiously for the invisible dog

that had barked on his first ever call, when curtains of the bedroom door parted and the Colonel's lady appeared, tall and smiling and with easy manners. She was dressed in a chocolate-coloured saree with matching sleeves. Buxom in her sleeves, she looked like a person who loved to be coddled by . . .

"Good morning, Payyan here," he said, "a journalist living upstairs."

"Good morning, nice to meet you."

She sat down on a diwan and waved Payyan to a chair opposite.

Payyan thanked her and said he had been calling for almost a week now and . . .

"Funny," she said. Payyan could have left a note with the jawan and she could have fixed an appointment earlier.

Payyan thought he must have looked foolish when he said that what was so obvious had not occurred to him.

"So you live upstairs," she said, "how do you like the place?"

"Not too bad," Payyan said, "it's a bachelor's apartment" . . . and before he could finish, the blow fell.

"Of course, of course, one up on mine for certain," Payyan said.

"When I moved in," she said, "the lawn was a shambles, and one of the first thingg I did was to hire a *mali* and lay a few beds of roses. It'll be lovely in winter when they are in bloom."

"I'm sure it will be," Payyan said, looking across to the lawn through the glass doors and seeing in his mind, roses, roses, all the way. Let a hundred roses bloom, he thought, and let a hundred Colonels lock themselves in combat.

"That's a Tanjore bronze, isn't it?" he said, looking at a Chidambaram Shiva on the mantelpiece.

"Yes, I bought it in Madras," she said. "I was there a couple of years."

Then he spotted a brass icon of the Buddha on the bookshelf and said: "The Bodhisattva too looks serene, as he is duty bound."

"I bought it in Chowringhee."

"While you were in Calcutta?"

"Yes."

Time went by and when the Colonel still did not put in an

appearance, Payyan said:

"Maybe the Colonel is still asleep. Could I see him too in a week's time or so?"

"Just a minute," she said, "will you have some tea?"

This must be a ruse, Payyan thought. She might be buying time to show off some of the crockery she must have picked up in Leopoldville, Nicosia or Sheffield. He was not interested and declined the tea with thanks.

But a veteran, after all, is a veteran.

"That cost me only one hundred ruppees," she said, pointing to a battle-scarred record player sitting on a coffee table in the fifth corner.

"Where did you buy it?"

"Gaza."

Payyan had been told that Gaza was out of bounds for army wives but did not argue the point.

"How does it look?"

"I'm sure it plays tops," Payyan said, and now about the Colonel."

"You want to see me in my uniform too?" she laughed, throwing back her head and extending her right hand to Payyan: "Well then, meet Col Renu of AMC."

When he came to, Payyan made an effort to rise from the chair but the lovely Colonel said: "Stay back for elevenses and . . . later on for lunch . . ." Payyan stayed much more than that.

(Translated by the author)

THE SECOND TRADITION

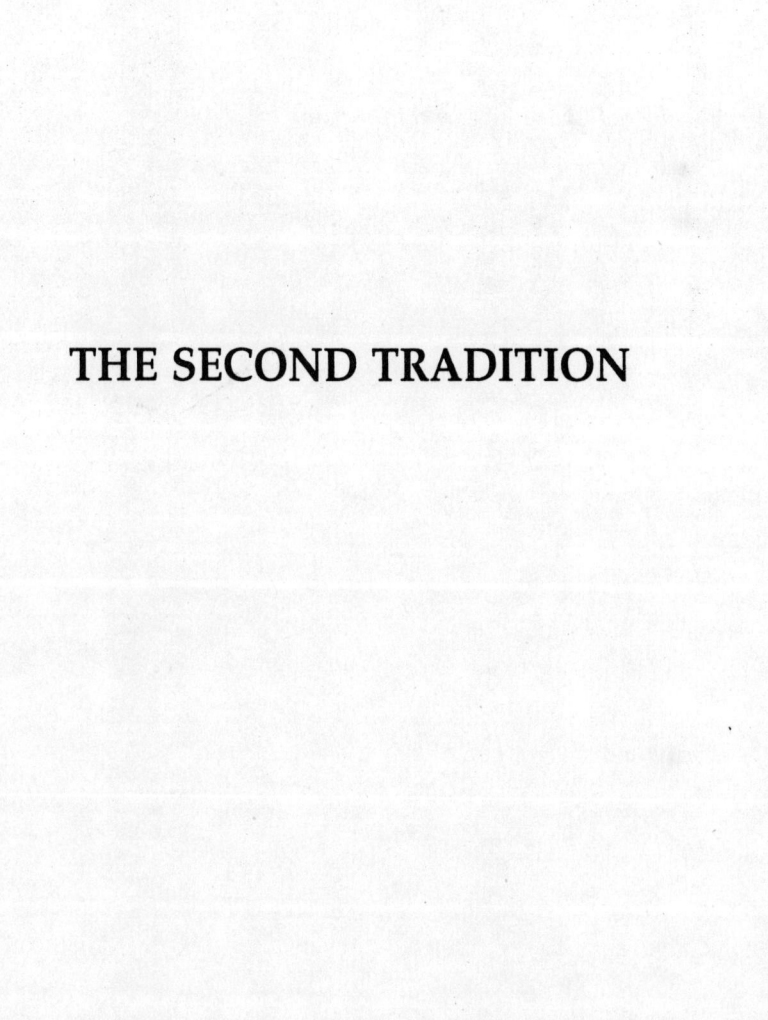

COME BACK

Lalithambika Antharjanam

Whenever I see women agitating for their rights, I am reminded of Bhanumati Amma. For no particular reason. I even catch myself unconsciously addressing young women activists by that name. But, quickly, I correct myself. O, what strange forgetfulness this is! What might be the cause for such absentmindedness in me? Today's girls obviously do not know about Bhanumati Amma. What will they think of me?

Our land has not yet produced women who will be remembered and whose names will mean something to posterity. If we did produce any such, no one is the wiser for it. Once a young poet teased me—"Oh, here's a precious clique, boasting of the traditions of the Rani of Jhansi or Padmini Devi. Tell me, is there a single Malayali woman whom you can name in any field, art, literature, social work or even music?"

I got angry and said, "Maybe not, but there have been mothers to give birth to and rear the great men, such as we have."

It might have been a protest born of an inability to give a fitting repartee. But, either out of a sense of pride or a feeling of insult, I did not even bother to remember any name. Bhanumati Amma used to say: "Our race will improve only if a few women thrust ahead, forgetting traditions and orthodox expectations. Men grip us by the nose and neck, and then tease us if we do not sing or speak. Sisters, we have to bite that hand till it lets go of us. It might hurt . . . let it!"

She was like Tennyson's *Princess*. If women want to improve, they must create a land for themselves and muster courage. It should be a land which has art, literature, sculpture and all. Even politics and martial arts must be taught. The objective: for woman to live in this world without man's aid. Bhanumati used to explain: "In that good country, there will be no place for silks or perfumes! No powder or cosmetics. Not even a mirror. We will cast away all emotions that render us weak and vulnerable. I will consider it a success if I can train some five hundred women between five and twenty-five as volunteers. They will, then, take over."

I could never bring myself to wholeheartedly support Bhanumati Amma's ideals. But her sincerity and sense of pride touched my heart. She dreamt of her future solely in relation to the future of womankind. How to restrain society from mocking and demeaning women? How to mitigate the damage wrought by the constraints within which they lived? She believed in nothing but self-perfection. Bhanumati was not some sophisticated woman trapped in a void. She was a young, beautiful, well-bred, educated girl. She could have aspired to a good job or a comfortable marriage. Or, she could have lazed at home, like her peers, chattering and gossiping. There was no need for her to enter the social field to earn notoriety.

But how long could a passionate girl like Bhanu suppress the flames in her heart! She saw around her so many fellow women wasting their lives trapped in ignorance and slavishness. Painted wooden dolls. Why not try and kindle a spark of life in their breasts? At least she could try, even if it meant dying in the attempt. Her enthusiasm to safeguard the dignity of womankind bordered on the crazy. Slowly, she was able to externalise her ideas and they began to spread around. Soon a women's organisation was born.

To begin with, it was a few women getting together and organising a women's association and a library. To raise money for their activities, they had to organise meetings and cultural festivals. Girls from well-to-do families—are they meant to be out begging in the streets? Or be actresses on stage? Many a guardian frowned. But their daughters and sisters had travelled far and could no more be restrained by angry looks from their elders. All revolutionary movements have something formidable about them. People stared in astonishment as they saw seemingly meek girls transformed into little lionesses.

They needed a roof over their heads. How long could they depend on the kindness of fathers and grandfathers? They had not set out for this work, banking on others' help. Bhanumati Amma took a house on rent. It was a neat and convenient house with a large compound, near the city. It could accommodate some fifty women. During their spare time the women held spinning and tailoring classes. They convened debates and conducted study classes on child care and nursery training. One thing led to the other. People exclaimed in astonishment: "These young girls are really something! They have been able to achieve in one day what we would have taken a hundred years to accomplish."

I remember now how Bhanumati Amma used to manage everything with courage and tact. She had no time even to pause and reflect. It was a question of survival. Even sceptical grandmothers who, at first, dismissed the venture as crazy, realised its seriousness. The women's home was an institution which inspired pride in women, where nobody bothered about caste or religion, where there was no hierarchy of rich and poor. Any woman who observed the simple and austere principles of the sadanam could live there. Women flocked from far and near. They listened to Bhanumati Amma with admiration and implicitly obeyed her. The young girls were willing to even sacrifice their lives for Bhanumati, who was respected as an elder sister.

Those were times when the tides of the independence struggle were surging over every shore of the country. The colonial authorities regarded any well-led organisation with deep suspicion. Bhanumati was no political activist. In fact, she was of the opinion that politics should not be allowed to intrude into social work. Yet she was not prepared to dismiss from the sadanam wives and sisters of national leaders, either imprisoned or in hiding. There was talk that some national leaders even came there in secret. The police intelligence wing kep the sadanam under close surveillance, day and night. Bhanu would say, "Very good. Our government maintains propriety. Wouldn't it have been terrible had there been no guards for a women's hostel?"

Not surprisingly, it was the government's suspiciousness and sanctions that enabled the sadanam to grow apace. The more the authorities obstructed, the more united people became. Donations and contributions multiplied. The movement's enthusiasm redoubled. Inside the hostel, art and aesthetics flourished. The clarion call of free thought resounded . . . Handloom machinery and spinning wheels worked incessantly. Are these really our girls doing all this? Our girls who, till yesterday, could only sing or dance or cry? People used to point to Bhanumati Amma and say, "There goes the secretary of the sadanam. One must learn from her if one wants to do social work."

I firmly believed history would cherish the name of this dedicated social worker.

It was at about this time that a good mariage proposal came Bhanu's way from an unbelievably good family. Bhanumati's people found it a good match. Anyway, she could not go on endlessly with her social work. Moreover, according to them, marriage was the proper foundation even for social work. In our country, there are so many restrictions on an unmarried woman. She is denied admission to most spheres of social life. She has no voice. There will always be an aura of suspicion around her. The respectability of an unmarried social worker is as tenuous as a soap bubble: someone just needs to sneeze to blow off her institution's, and her, reputation. Bhanu's mother knew this. So she tearfully entreated:

"My child! Please consent. This organisation and association will not last for ever. I would like to see you with a wedding locket round your neck before I die."

But Bhanumati shook her head in negation. "No, Mother. You people misguide girls by talking like this. The country won't go to the dogs just because I don't get married. Let me see if I can live respectably without getting married."

The mother wept and the father scolded. All the relatives tried to persuade her. But Bhanumati refused to oblige. That very day she shifted full-time to the sadanam. Her friends hailed her as a brave martyr. They embraced and kissed her and shouted in joy. They swore they would suffer everything for her sake. Unable to bear the joy, Bhanumati wept.

After many days she is said to have told Radha, "If only I had died on that unforgettable night . . . O! how lucky I would have been!"

I have often reflected on this. Was Bhanu's act a sacrifice? Was it wise? The biggest things to be sacrificed on the altar of duty are the tender feelings of a person. Did she pluck out all her feelings and put them on the block? On close scrutiny, Bhanu was like any other woman. There was no hatred of the world in those eyes. No roughness in her behaviour. But when she set out in her armour of action she had an indifferent, serene discipline. The

Women's Association could not function indoors. In their efforts to destroy the indoor prisons, they had to come out and mingle with men of all ages and types. They needed to oppose them, argue with them and, sometimes, even beg for their cooperation. On this dangerous battlefield, one had to be most cautious. Bhanu had realised this. Whenever she faced the external world, she combined in herself the seriousness of a school mistress and the abilities of a housewife. Any one who saw that lovely young lady in a white cotton dress with no ornaments, would feel respect for her.

But she was not a sanyasini.

In maintaining hostel discipline, Bhanumati Amma was particular about one thing. No girl of lax morals would be admitted there. No one should talk of love or tender emotions. The discipline was that of a nunnery. I had wondered how a tender, sentimental poet like Radha could live there. "Beauty and poetry, poetry and beauty"—there was no life for Radha without these. It was impossible to see her without a song on her lips. She fluttered about in the kitchen, bathroom or workshop humming love-songs of the poet Changampuzha, and Bhanumati used to scold her. Yet Radha was her dearest friend. Bhanumati Amma was incomplete without her.

I used to look on with interest at the friendship between these two women, entirely different in character. Bhanumati was never a close friend. But many of her dear friends were my friends too. All the women's associations of the time were centred around the sadanam. I think Bhanumati Amma had some contempt for me, for I was a family-centred woman with children and problems. According to her, it was woman's gravest mistake to give more importance to family than to society. For her it was the greatest curse. May be. I did not contest this. Compared to Bhanumati Amma, her sacrifice and her services, I was, indeed, quite inferior.

Because of domestic commitments and pressures, I could not go to the sadanam for some time. But I garnered some information form Radha's letters and from others too.

The destiny of all social movements is more or less alike. The first stage reflects extreme zeal. Then there is a somnolent, drowsy stage as the heat and spirits subside.

As long as the basic problems remain, the movement may

not die out. Yet it is often difficult to survive this second, depressing stage. There were minor disturbances at the sadanam. Other parties arrayed against it. Radha wrote: "They spread canards even about our sister Bhanu. And some of our own colleagues believe the stories too. Any one but her would have given up by now."

Radha's words could not be taken at face value. She was a type which suspected even trivial things. But when I met Bhanumati Amma next, there was no self-confidence in her eyes. She told me that the sadanam would be shifted out of the city into the country. It would lessen expenses and give more freedom for women to move about. Quite unusually, she embraced and fondled my little child with great affection. Till then I had never seen her fondling a child.

Time passed. Since I was laid up with a serious ailment, I was cut off from the events in the world outside. Some reflections stirred like shadows. Some whispers would be heard like echoes. Nothing was clear. Nothing would penetrate. I was not surprised to learn that Bhanumati had retired to a famous ashram for women in another state. Such a great initiator could not have been confined to a little village. Her name, to be inscribed in history, must rise to full glory.

Again, days went by. I met Radha, quite unexpectedly, on a train journey. She did not recognise me. I too would not have recognised her. She was so thin. There was no more poetry in her eyes. No smile on her lips. No enthusiasm or humming of songs. Altogether, she looked like a mature housewife weighed down by problems. When she lifted her eyes from the newspaper she was reading and looked around, she saw me staring at her. Doubts, memories, recognition—different emotions flashed across her face. She rushed to me, laughing happily, and embraced me: "O my sister . . . sister . . . my . . ."

She rested her head on my shoulder and sat a while as if tired of the surge of emotions. Her eyes filled with tears and I could hear her heartbeats.

"Oh Sister, you have changed so much. So much. None but me would have recognised you."

"I know," said I in a broken voice. "All of us have changed, Radha . . . you . . . I . . . every one of us. The world belongs to changes. But it doesn't matter. It is enough if there is at least one thing in the mind that remains unchanged."

Radha's story was just an ordinary one. She went back to her house after the sadanam was disbanded. She married, became the mother of three children and later a teacher in a primary school. Her job, her deliveries and domesticity took their toll on her health and poetic pursuits. But she looked happy. When the talk drifted to the sadanam, Radha said, "O Sister, I'm not sorry about what happened to Bhanu chechi, it's a shame . . . A shame for all of us."

I was puzzled. "What's so shameful about it? She is in the Mahila Ashram . . . Did she join some revolutionary party now?"

Radha hung her head and said with pain in her heart: "Revolutionary party, indeed! That would have been a much better outcome, sister. None of us expected this of Bhanu chechi . . . She, who would not allow us even to laugh or sing or recite poetry.. She believed love was suicidal for women . . . And, finally, she of all people . . .!" Radha did not complete her sentence.

My curiosity overcame my patience. I asked, "What happened, finally? Did Bhanumati marry?"

"She didn't get married . . . But . . ." and Radha whispered in my ears as if imparting a gret secret, "but . . . she gave birth to a child."

In a moment everything fell into place, though not in any cogent order. When Bhanumati was leaving for a new destination, Radha had gone to the station to see her off. Quite by chance, they met a colleague who too was travelling to the same city. Bhanu was very pleased. Her services had won national recognition. Only such persons could be appointed to such high posts. She was a woman from Kerala rising up to join the ranks of national figures. Yet she was humble. Before leaving, she promised to return soon and rejuvenate the sadanam. Yet both of them burst into tears at the time of parting.

Radha was surprised at the tone of disappointment in the first letter Bhanumati wrote after joining the ashram. Bhanu had travelled long distances earlier, in connection with the business of the sadanam. But this particular journey seemed to have depressed her. She seemed sick in mind and body. Probably because the food did not agree with her, she seemed to be suffering from intermittent vomitings. "Radha, womankind is cursed," Bhanumati continued in her writing. "How weak they are. How unlucky too! One wrong deed, the weakness of one moment, is enough to completely destroy the hopes and ideas of a lifetime. It might destroy everything good about you. Yet, doing one wrong deed to correct another is quite a grave mistake, no?"

The sentences seemed to contain latent meanings. Radha became worried, Bhanu chechi would never talk like this. It was not her style to put on a tone of depression. She had been a nightmare at the sadanam because of her unemotional, unrelenting morality. She cared only for strengths and never for weaknesses. Was it the same Bhanu chechi who wrote thus? Did it reflect her violent new surroundings?

She became eager to be near Bhanu chechi and started scouting for a job in the same city. She wrote to all the friends she could think of. She sent applications to all the posts advertised in the papers. After seven or eight months of hard work, she finally got an interview call. From the railway station she headed straight to the ashram. She had much difficulty in finding the place. And what she heard was . . . that Bhanumati Amma had left it two months earlier. The middle-aged foreign woman, with a wry face, said with a contemptuous laugh:

"She is terribly ill. We do not accommodate such people in the ashram. Try the hospital or the orphanage; you may find her there."

Radha told me: "I have never felt such terrible mental agony as at that moment. I was bursting within to reach Bhanu *chechi*. My dear sister. My friend. My goddess. I was ready even to die for her sake . . ."

After a brief silence, she continued: "And then . . . then . . . I searched and searched and found her. An emaciated woman sitting in the hospital veranda, leaning against a pillar, with a tiny baby in her hands. It was not Bhanumati Amma. It was not our older sister whom we all worshipped. She was no better than the thousands of girls in my country . . . The ideal idol collapsed and was broken.

"I returned home by the next train and very soon got married."

The train had almost reached the station where Radha had to get down. We did not speak much again. Did we not have anything to say? Nothing to think, either? I had never regarded

Bhanumati Amma as a goddess above all imperfections. None amongst us is a goddess. Can't we remove this contempt towards human emotion? Can't we correct ourselves?

Hugging Bhanumati Amma (and many such fellow-women), let me exhort: "My dearest friend and sister, come back. Why do you hide your face for an unintentional slip? We who fight to destroy wrongs must learn to forgive and absolve. (Or, who are we to judge what is right and what is wrong?) Won't you forgive yourself? Won't you come back to the bright field of action? Let us come together once again, on the path to a glorious new dawn.

"And, then, let us inscribe the name for the generations to come—that unforgettable name. These papers are just for that. The pen of couse, is with you."

(Translated by B. Chandrika)

TREES FOR SHADE

K. Saraswathy Amma

Pushing open the imposing gates of the convent, the saffron-clad man walked in.

It took a long walk along the broad path to the buildings which lay deep inside the compound. In fact they came into view only when one had covered half the distance up the path. But walking in the cool, pleasant shade of the trees lining the path, refreshed and relaxed the mind.

The trees had been planted meticulously and systematically. Those near the gate had a lush growth of leaves on their branches. Wayfarers could rest in their shade for some time before resuming their journey. Further up the path were the rows of *anjilis*. If a herd of hungry, marauding children sneaked in to pick the fallen *anjili* nuts, not a soul in the convent would notice it. The fruit-bearing trees which benefited only the owners of the property became visible only as one approached the buildings. The path which started from the wide-open spaces of selfless service became narrower and narrower till it terminated at the dead-end of selfish gain.

He stepped into the veranda gently. There was no sign of any of the inmates. All the doors which opened into the veranda were closed. The faint notes of a piano were heard from the parlour. A soft, balmy voice sang a hymn in English.

Generally he liked to listen to music. They sang bhajans at the ashram every day. But then, *Tulsidas Ramayan* and the works of Jayadeva were not in English. He had no ear for Western music, which was just a cacophony of hisses, grunts and squeaks to him.

But this song had something enchanting about it. Its tune passed through his heart and reverberated deep in his soul. It gave him the sensation of a drop of sorrow swelling up as it rolled down the slopes of his mind, of rowing towards the horizon alone, in a boat, on the vast expanse of the ocean.

He felt the serene flow of music resurrecting a remembrance lost and dead. But he could not identify it. His mind refused to work on it. There was something odd about it—like being reminded of a red rose on seeing a pure white lily.

The music stopped. A nun opened one of the doors and came out into the veranda. She led the visitor into the parlour. "Please sit down," she said. "I'll send Mother in a minute."

The nun went out through a door at the back. He glanced idly around the room. It looked like a small museum. It appeared that the nuns had developed craftwork into a cottage industry. Anything from eggshells to bus-tickets had been turned into attractive little artefacts with the simplest of techniques and colours. Even the birds which fell dead in the grounds of the convent were not spared. On the branches of a planted tree sat kingfishers, weaver-birds and parrots. It was incredible that art should manifest itself in such colourful, vibrant forms amidst the cloistered lives of the convent, that the hands that rolled the beads of rosaries could also fabricate materials for teaching science and geography.

He wondered why he had not noticed any of these the last time he came here. But he remembered well the circumstances in which he had visited the convent then. He had not been in a mood to appreciate the nuns' handiwork. His mind had been completely occupied by the suffering of the helpless people. When the scourge of the epidemic grew into catastrophic proportions, when the bhajans in the ashram were drowned in the heart-rending cries of the afflicted, the inmates of the ashram realized that human beings needed their attention more than God. But they were not equal to the task. The might of the adversary required a more formidable force.

That was how he had come to the convent for the first time. The nuns might have been taken aback by the sight of a man who wore no cassock. But he had been too preoccupied to think about such things. The Mother grasped the purpose of his visit as soon as he began telling her about it. Her offer of help came immediately. She undertook the responsibility of looking after half of the affected area. She promised to put in all resources at her command to tackle the situation.

It didn't take long for him to gauge the extent of her

magnanimity, and the efficiency of the nuns. The people who lived around the convent had already had a taste of it. The area of their operation widened quickly. The quantity of relief materials and manpower that poured in immediately was remarkable. Too preoccupied with tackling the situation in the area which fell under the ashram's responsibility, he had little time to inquire about what Mother and her team of nuns were doing. But news about it reached his ears unsolicited. There was even a school of thought that held that it was the confidence and skills of Mother—or perhaps her mere presence which inspired love and compassion—that made the epidemic retreat. She must be an exceptionally gifted woman. Perhaps she too had a hand in creating the pieces that adorned the parlour.

He had got up to have a closer look at the pieces when Mother came in. "I am sorry to have kept you waiting," she said. "I was a little busy. Please sit down."

He wondered whether it was the same person he had seen the last time he had come here. If he remembered right, she had worn a mournful expression on her face then. But today she was cheerful and pleasant. There was nothing surprising in the way people glorified her. Her eyes brimmed with compassion. A mere look of hers was enough to inspire love and confidence in anyone.

"I am leaving this place," he said, "but don't think I have come to bid farewell to you. I felt it would be rude of me not to express my gratitude to you for responding whole-heartedly to my appeal the last time I came here."

"Why should you be grateful to me?" she thought of asking, but did not. She too had been moved by the suffering of the afflicted people. Though well aware that the need of the hour was organised, voluntary service, she had been regretting her inability to get down to work on her own free will, when he had approached her with an appeal for help. The convent and the ashram were galvanized into united action, which broke all barriers of creed and dogma. Soon after that, government assistance, cutting through red-tape, had poured in. Due to the combined efforts, peace and comfort had returned—not just to the affected population, but to his troubled heart as well. It was not a personal triumph; he rejoiced in it as the head of the ashram. Instead of the perturbation he had seen on her face during the last visit, he saw a radiating tranquillity now.

Taking in her thoughtful countenance, he said, "I had no alternative but to bother you with an appeal for help. I believe service to human beings is a more rewarding exercise than devotion to God."

She smiled. He continued: "It is not devotion that drives me, but plain altruism. I must confess I have still not attained that philosophical state of mind in which one regards material sorrows as trivial distractions."

"There are not many who have reached that state," she broke her silence. "Since it is difficult to change people's outlook, our efforts should be directed towards understanding their problems and trying to solve them."

"I have known what it is to love and lose one's object of love. I was not just making an academic observation," he said, his voice taking on a mournful note. "That is why it is impossible for me to watch dispassionately when it happens to others."

"It is this weakness of yours that we call compassion," she said, her voice gentle and soft. "Of course, essentially, it is a kind of selfishness. But it is a blessing that one can forget one's grief in contemplating another's—it is a blessing, too, for those whose sorrows are thus lightened."

They were silent for some time, withdrawn into themselves like introverts. He felt a nagging pain at the remembrance of the personal loss which he had just mentioned. She realized that though she had always known what human suffering was, she had never felt it deep in her heart.

The notes of the piano rose from the parlour. It was the same song again. He woke up from his reveries and listened. "The song sounds very familiar," he said after listening to it for some time. "But I can't recollect a word of it. Would I be too inquisitive if I asked you to assist my memory?"

"Not at all. In fact, it is quite well known," she explained. "Lead kindly light'. It is a hymn beloved to all of us here—more so to me."

He closed his eyes and leaned back in the chair. He now knew which chord of his memory the song had struck. The picture of a young woman sitting before a painting of Christ and singing the song with a distressed heart flashed through his mind. The picture triggered a flood of recollections and several scenes from the past were re-enacted before his mind's eye.

In a remote village in the countryside, two large houses stood facing each other across the road. The picture of Lord Krishna playing the flute would greet your eyes from the wall as you stepped into the veranda of one of the houses. In the veranda of the other, it was a crucifix that caught your attention. Both the families were endowed with a largeness of wealth and children. The eldest in one of the families was a boy, in the other, a girl. There was no match for Lilykutty in making flower carpets during Onam. When it came to decorating Christmas trees, nobody could beat Madhusoodanan. Lily had this strange habit of taking the candles which were to be lighted before the Sacred Heart to the prayer room in Madhu's house and setting them up on the *nilavilakku*[1]. Madhu took a fancy for lighting the incense sticks stocked in the prayer room before the image of the Virgin Mary. The two families celebrated Onam and Christmas with equal fervour and gaiety. They all had their Christmas dinners at Lily's house and their Onam lunches at Madhu's house. Madhu's sisters often complained that their father loved Lilykutty more than his own daughters. Madhu wondered, with growing uneasiness, whether his father could retain the same affection for Lily if she became his daughter-in-law. The thought had occurred to Lily too, and it frightened her. But they saw no way out. Neither of them dared to discuss it with anybody, not even to drop a hint about it. Lily knelt before the crucifix and prayed to the Lord to shed some light in her dark soul.

What a long time had passed since he had heard Lily sing the hymn in her tearful voice!

Closing his eyes, he said to himself, aloud: "I used to hear this hymn sung. This and another about all life being a dream. It was years ago, ages ago."

"When you were fond of walking around in tweed suits, wasn't it?"

Why was she trying to tease him? But her teasing voice was more familiar to him than the song. "Lilykutty!" he murmured. He opened his eyes and stared at her in amazement.

"I am Philomena Benedecta Beatrice. There is nobody here who answers to the name Lilykutty."

---

[1] Nilavilakku - a traditional bronze lamp

He was unruffled by her taunting remarks. He gazed intently at her and said slowly: "I didn't have the faintest hope of meeting you ever again. I used to talk about human bonds forged in previous births, didn't I? Here we meet, as if in another life."

She suppressed a smile. "But Christians don't believe in reincarnation."

"I never believed in God. Lilykutty made me lose my faith in human beings too."

"Why blame it on poor Lilykutty who was foolish enough to spurn the proposal of Paulose, the handsome young man? She rejected Paulose's offer of marriage to elope with poor Jesus."

"Jesus?"

"What a poor memory you have! Don't you remember Jesus Christ for whom you used to light candles at Lilykutty's house?"

"And Paulose?"

"You don't know Paulose either?"

"How would I? I have never gone in search of rich and handsome young men."

"The story would be incomplete if I don't say that none of them came in search of me either. He was a friend of Georgekutty's. Georgekutty was trying to persuade me to marry Paulose. I hope you remember Georgekutty, Lily's young brother."

He gave her a sharp, piercing look, as if to ask her how she could dare to think he would ever forget Georgekutty. After a long pause he said: "I hope you realize at last how reckless you were. Couldn't you have waited a little?"

"What a stupid thing to hear from a man who knew Lily since she was in her swaddling clothes! Don't you know it was not in her nature to wait for anything? Madhu declared he couldn't live without Lily. It was certain they couldn't get married with their parents' consent. Eloping was the only way out. She was ready for that too. But what happened in the end?

"We could have worked like everybody else," she continued spiritedly. "We were well educated, weren't we? Either of us could have got a job in a school or college. Or we could have engaged tuition classes. But it requires a man with courage and confidence to do it. What is the use of raving about love? One should be prepared to give up some comforts and luxuries, tweed suits not excepted."

"And silk saris."

"Yes, Lilykutty wears nothing but silk," she said sarcastically. "Nuns prefer silk!"

He glanced at her habit. The soft, fragile body, which used to look so becoming in smooth, colourful dresses, had forced itself to be wrapped in dark, coarse cloth. She could see from his expression how pained he was at the change.

"But he was a worthless idler. A spineless coward who loved to mope and cry."

"It is a long time since I heard sobriquets applied to me!" She smiled. "But you used to be thrilled on hearing them if they were honourable titles! I have an idea you still relish them."

"Do you think I would have tolerated anybody calling me names if I didn't like it? It is a pleasure to hear them from such a bright, smart woman."

"But the smart woman had to wait for you to come here today with the apparent purpose of expressing your gratitude."

"Forget today," he looked pleadingly at her. "I was talking about that distant yesterday in the past. Couldn't you realize that the worthless idler ran away only because he felt he wouldn't be able to take a decision if he lived near you any more? Didn't he promise you he would come back as soon as he found a way out? But what a cruel decision you took without breathing a word to him!"

"How funny you are! Is it cruel to become a nun?"

"Isn't it? You shattered two hearts in the process."

"Two hearts! I would be much obliged if you would be kind enough to bridle your heart and use your head for a moment," she said, a grave expression coming to her face.

"Think of the hundred of lives the two shattered hearts were able to save during the last two months. Try to convince yourself that your Lilykutty died young."

"No, I can't!" he looked agonizingly at her. "It is better to think I lost her."

"She was lost to everybody. But there was only Madhu to grieve over her."

"Yes, of course. The worthless young idler was too full of tears like a mawkish woman, anyway."

"That counts him out too, perhaps. The loss of a daughter would not have plunged her parents into sorrow. They had other daughters too. But if Lilykutty had married the man she liked, it would have brought disgrace to the family as well. It is good that everything happened as it did. Perhaps love is a sin. That is why we have to conceal it."

"If concealing makes a thing a sin, our bodies must be the greatest sins."

"Now you know why we conceal as much of it as we can!" she smiled playfully. "As for the Hindu *sanyasis*, who find nothing sinful in the body, the movement is in the other direction—towards complete nudity, *digambaratva!* That perhaps accounts for the relinquishing of the tweed suits. Or is there a tweed suit under the saffron shawl? How *this* sanyasi restrains himself when he passes the hundreds of cloth stores in the city displaying tweed suits is more than I can imagine!"

"One has to play up to the role one has taken. I have a suspicion too. What about the temptation to make a carpet of flowers in the yard of the convent when the children in the neighbourhood usher in Onam with their songs?"

"That reminds me. I think I can expect to find a fully decorated Christmas tree at the ashram on Christmas Eve."

"Oh!" he exclaimed suddenly with a rueful look at her head. "How could you bring yourself to have that beautiful, curly hair cut short?"

"Suppose I ask you the same question?"

"I have an answer ready for that," he said, rubbing his tonsured skull. "The most beautiful object I cherished in my life was lost to me for ever. I no longer wished to possess anything beautiful. When I shaved off my hair, I felt I had taken my revenge on Lilykutty."

"Not on Lilykutty."

"Huh?"

"On the menace of baldness."

He could not help smiling at her remark. The menace of baldness was one of her favourite phrases for teasing him when she was in the mood for it. How well she remembered everything! "You used to say that beautiful hair was God's way of compensating for an empty upper-storey. I no longer felt any need for the compensation."

"Very thoughtful of you to give it up early. Attack it before it attacks you—a brilliant strategy. The little girl who used to sit in Madhu's father's lap for hours, wouldn't be ignorant of the origin and evolution of the bald pate. It would have been a quirk of fate if the son hadn't inherited the father's bald pate."

"But Lilykutty was spared the humiliation of having a baldhead for a husband."

"And the mortification of watching a son turning into a baldhead."

They were silent for some time. Her words sent his heart flying up into the air, the attempts of his saffron robes to contain it going awry, into an imaginary world of conjugal bliss. As the kite fluttered in the wind, its string suddenly snapped. Abruptly, he said, "Madhu had five sisters. If he had done anything rash, his sisters would never have been properly married off. His selfishness would have been their doom."

"What about Lilykutty? She too had her sisters to think about."

"Yes, hers was the worst predicament," he admitted. "For a man there are some allowances. But for a woman, to elope would be to create an upheaval in the family and leave destruction in its wake. How could you have been so bold as to volunteer to elope when you knew this well?"

"It was agonising to watch you becoming so worked up. I had to do something. Remember, I never forced you to take a decision, though I was ready to come with you. I was really happy when you didn't. There was another thing that worried me. Our parents were so trustful of us. How could I have looked them in the face if I had conspired with you? I was tormented by the thought that I would be deceiving them. That is why I didn't write to you even once."

"My grouse is not that you never wrote love-letters," he explained hastily. "But you could have let me know before deciding to become a nun."

"Why?" Her voice became soft and pleasant again. "Lilykutty had placed a suggestion before Madhu. He rejected it and ran away without suggesting anything himself. Soon after that, Paulose appeared on the scene. How long could she put off her parents? How could she allow her life to be wasted away when she knew quite well that her man was capable of unending deliberations and procrastinations?"

"I was ready to wait till my next birth."

"Such infinite patience is natural for those who believe in

reincarnation." She gave him a teasing smile. "For them Time stretches infinitely, through hundreds and thousands of births and deaths. A lifetime is a mere drop in the ocean to them. Perhaps that is what makes them so docile and indecisive. But for me, time was too precious to be wasted. I had only one life to live."

"But haven't you been wasting your time since then?"

"Certainly not. I don't waste my time strutting about in garish clothes and exchanging gossip. I don't have a minute to waste. When the epidemic raged, the better-off families left for safer places. There were only a few castaways like me to look after the poor people."

"That was not a bad investment," he said, half in jest. "There are folks who are willing to swear that you are nothing less than an *avatar*?"

"*Avatars* are the exclusive property of your religion. I would prefer to be canonized."

"Being canonized as a saint certainly makes up for not being solemnized as a bride."

"But you forget. We nuns are the brides of the Lord!" She paused. "You might be wondering how Lilykutty spent her time waiting. She was making preparations for eloping with Madhu the moment he came back with such an intention. She had been picking up a good bit of cooking. So that her glutton of a lover did not starve. Now the skill has come in handy. Not for a single household, but for scores of hungry families."

"The news did reach me too. While we barely managed to give them *kanji*, you were serving them a variety of delicacies. Does it mean, all in all, that you don't regret what you have done?"

"What is there to regret about giving those poor, helpless people something good to eat?"

"What a magnificent pretense of innocence! I want to know whether you regretted eloping with Jesus Christ."

"I think it spared me the humiliation of regretting what I shouldn't have done. Regret is something you feel when your selfishness hurts others."

"Was that why you chose not to have a life of your own and

---

[2] Avatar - Incarnation

to merely exist in a no-man's land where there is no happiness of grief—shattering another man's life in the process?"

"You mean to say you had no sense of happiness or grief when you came here the last time in a panic? You may ask those people, whose case you came to plead, whether I have done anything to be sorry for."

"I am glad about it. I would have regretted it if you had turned into a misanthrope, hating everybody and envying other people's happiness. If you would hold Lilykutty responsible for making you what you are, she is only delighted to own up to what she did. Her heart leaps up when she hears his virtues being recounted."

"Does it? What about the spineless coward who loved to mope and cry?"

"The voice of the people should have precedence over the mutterings of the lone dissenter. What she heard from them nearly brought back the dead Lilykutty to life. She rejoiced in the application of those skills which would have been wasted in the confines of the home."

"But didn't I tell you a moment ago why I was willing to sacrifice everything for a group of people with whom I have nothing in common?"

"You did. But to love, to sacrifice, without attachment is the greatest of human achievements. In the last fifteen years I too have learned to love without attachments."

"I was really not so lucky. If I had been, I too would have kept up pretenses."

The allegation brought a smile to her lips. "Perhaps that was the best course of action. What a lot of time we have wasted talking of old might-have-beens. My fellow inmates must be puzzled at my talking to a visitor for so long, though they are too timid to ask me anything."

"What! You mean to say they are spineless cowards like Madhu?"

"It is the way of the world that the husband's parents stand in awe of the daughter-in-law who brings in a large dowry. Apart from the princely sum I donated, I brought a whole waggon-load of vessels to the convent. They still send me money from home when I ask for some. Do you have any idea of the sum I spent on food, clothes and medicine for the victims of the epidemic? The money was mine. But the convent cornered all the glory."

"Just like it happens in a typical middle-class household."

"Not exactly. Here everything goes to the extremes. There is more kindness and generosity. But there is also more gossip, more cattiness and more spying on one another. I suppose it is inevitable when the many wives of a man compete for his attention!" Though she smiled, a grave expression came to her face. "I don't blame them. Most of them are here because their parents thought it fit to offer them to the convent—like lambs to a sacrifice. But their instincts pull them the other way. I think most of them would have ended up as Communists if they had had the pluck to choose what they liked."

He sighed. "How can a woman suppress her motherly instincts?"

"You needn't have any apprehensions about that. Our society sees to it that at least the motherly instincts of nuns are not starved to death. Our orphanage has never been able to accommodate all the children brought to it. Never mind if some of them have been plucked from the tree of sin. A tree that bears fruit has always been considered superior to a tree that only gives shade."

"I don't like to bore you any more," he got up from the chair. "Just one last question before I go. Did you recognize me the last time I came here?"

"Since I had learned from Georgekutty that you had become an ascetic, I just wondered—in fact I was almost sure." She got up and accompanied him as he walked out. "But I didn't wish to confirm it."

"It was Georgekutty who wrote to me that you had taken orders. I resigned my job at the college where I had been teaching for some time and flew home. I wished to visit you at the convent. But the wishes of spineless cowards come to nothing."

"That was fortunate. Poor Lilykutty would not have been able to stand the sight of Madhu's tearful face. At the convent, nuns are allowed to relinquish orders if they wish, during the first three years. Try to imagine what would have happened if I had thrown off my black robes and come with you!"

"Everything would have gone back to square one. Frantic searches for suitable bridegrooms for the young sisters, fretful thoughts, fervent renderings of 'Lead kindly light . . ."

"How the song soothed me! It gave me the strength to take a firm decision. The decision did not bring any harm to anybody. It brought peace and happiness to everyone."

"Here we go again, arguing about happiness and peace for everyone!" he interrupted her. "There is no time for that now."

They gazed at each other in silence for some time. A naughty little girl frolicked before his mind's eye. Oh! All that sweetness and charm lay dead in that head, now shrouded by a black veil. It was his fault that religion had strangled Lilykutty to death. Nobody could bring her back to life now.

He turned as he descended the steps to the yard. "Please convey my deep sense of gratitude, in the name of the ashram, to everybody here. Goodbye."

(Translated by K. M. Sherrif)

MARINE DRIVE

Madhavikkutty (Kamala Das)

This story has mainly two characters—Anasuya and her lover, the Bison. Its theme is the love that grows between the two. Even after love has almost totally gone out of their relationship, the bond remains strong. For, a deep and spiritual relationship usually develops between the hunter and his prey, between the murderer and the one about to be murdered. The story can be begun at any point.

The time when the Bison, conquering the peaks of political power, wielding the deadly weapons of threat, bribery and extortion, and enthroning himself as the uncrowned king of the great city, revels away the evenings with seductive women and accepts with bowed head, bouquets and garlands and flattery at public meetings during the day; the time when he reigns supreme, prosperous and at pace with himself—let me begin the story here. Or let me begin at the moment when Anasuya, a follower of the religion of love, viewing life as a festival of poetry, strolls along the beach for physical exercise, and sees for the first time the one tattooed on the forehead—the Bison.

Most of those who go for a stroll quite early in the morning along the concrete-paved beach at Marine Drive in Bombay are celebrated millionaires. And one thing that millionaires earn, along with their wealth, is enmity. Therefore, with the passage of time, they come to fear their own shadows. Each of them believes that his greatest enemy is the dark shadow that comes creeping up from behind. To escape from the clutches of these shadows they present the beggars on the beach with coins, donate money to charitable institutions, build holy temples and renovate dilapidated ones.

Only a pale light cast by the street bulbs and, occasionally, by the moon, can be seen on that beach between five and five forty-five. The street lights will go out exactly at 5:45. After that you'll have to walk in pitch darkness for five or ten minutes. Reaching the foot of the street bridge set up at the beginning of Chowpatty, these millionaires will hold their breath. Are there enemies in the dark? Will all the poor of the world attack us? The rich man fears only the poor.

At the time of high tide, large waves resembling kraits will come dashing against the stone wall, and he will wake up and remove the rheum from his eyes with his fingers stumps. Then he will chant the name of Rama in a gruff voice till the sky lights up.

It is at this time, when you can hardly recognise a face a yard away, that the rich ones will come out for a stroll in their *dhotis*, white pyjamas and muslin *kurtas*. They are shy by nature. They feel that since they have spent a lifetime in the hard, devoted pursuit of wealth, they are deprived of certain other achievements. Therefore, it is only with a bit of inferiority complex and with heads bowed down that they can move through this great world inhabited by the wise ones and philosophers and poets and artists.

One morning, around a quarter past six, when Anasuya's stroll was almost over, the hero—the millionaire of millionaires, the king of kings, the Bison—crossed the street and came to the beach. He was wearing a Davangore dhoti, a white khadi kurta and a light blue Jawahar jacket. A distinctive aroma of imported perfume emanated from him. Their eyes locked for a moment. A wild and primordial hunger burst into flames in those four eyes. Anasuya then realised that it was a case of 'saw and knew'. Quickly getting into her old blue car, she drove back home.

Libertines and pleasure-seekers have a congenital gift of recognising the members of their private group. The faraway look in their eyes may mislead others. But members of their own group will never take it seriously. They know that they are a queer lot. They build houses near the sea or the river. They sip slowly and will relish the sweet essence of every moment. What flows through their veins is a mixture of blood and liquor. They sincerely believe that they are gods. Like gods they can flare up, be propitiated, revel and enjoy.

The hero, like Ravana, had ten faces. By the time she got closer to the face 'Peace' after passing through 'Lust', 'Rage', 'Horror', and so on, she would be exhausted. "I can't live without you," she would say. And the Bison would tell her, "Don't be a slave to emotions, Anasuya."

Yet, she felt his fingers suddenly turning merciful on her cheeks at moments of slipping into sleep. In that semi-conscious state she also heard him softly whispering her pet name.

Anasuya knew that it was not possible to bind him down with love and a regimen of sex. Because he was the chief 'Black Face'[1] on the primitive stage of politics. And the underworld emperor of *asuras*. For the rich and seductive prostitutes, he was the apple of their eye. Anasuya felt an indefinable gratification when she nestled him in her arms for an hour each, on two or three days a week. Even in that posture phones rang and doorbells clanged. Anasuya felt that her lover was a stone statue set up on an important street. Also that they were copulating on a stage, bathed in light in full view of all. She later realised how true that thought was. Movie cameras hidden among the books in the almirah immortalised every one of their movements. He showed that strange film to a bosom friend of his. And he told her: "He's someone very important for me. Why can't you please him as well?"

That day she went back home in haste, even without a goodbye. She was not prepared to stoop to that level. She woundered whether she too was eventually turning into a chaste woman.

Yet she went back to him.

"You can't live without me," he said with a smile. She nodded, touching his burned cheeks.

"Why do you invite all those Communists and journalists to your house?" he asked her once. "I don't trust their kind."

Anasuya got restless when the Communist activist who used to visit her and play the fiddle in her veranda on some evenings was found dead by the police behind a temple.

"Poor chap!" she murmured.

"You're the poorest one!" said her lover.

On his return from a foreign tour she could detect some changes in his behaviour. She realised that the final scene she had been expecting with fear was quite close to her. His eyes came to

---

[1] Black Face - Karivesham; the make up of a typical villainous character in Kathakali.

have a vacant look even while he was resting in her arms. Moreover, their eyes did not meet, like in the old days, while she was getting dressed or brushing her hair. She did not ask him about the reason for such a change. She had never asked the reason why he got close to her and why she was chosen as his beloved, had she? So, fixing forever in her memory that look and that stance that reminded one of a horned buffalo, she collapsed in a heap at his feet and hugged those knees. She could not utter aloud his pet name that lay dozing in every breath she took.

"Get up, Anasuya, it's late. I have to attend a meeting at 5:30," he said. Then he sprayed his white khadi coat liberally with the cologne he had brought from America.

Every two or three years he would consult his doctor in America with the idea of regaining his health. He had told her, not once but many times, that he was trying to avert an untimely death. Every time she heard those words she found it hard to suppress her laughter, knowing as she did that though his body was that of an exercise-loving youth he was in fact close to seventy years of age. She knew that he would lose the peace of mind he was experiencing in her proximity if she even once hinted at his old age or his weaknesses. For the very backbone of that man who was dreaded by all in that city was his supreme self-confidence. If that was shaken, those brawny legs would stagger, that heavy neck would droop, the guffaws capable of bringing the roof down would come to an end, and he would cease to be a king, cease to be a lion, cease to be Bhagwan Sri Krishna the eternal lover . . . So, removing with the caressing strokes of her slender fingers those little aches of his soul, she was transformed into mother, beloved and devotee.

But after his foreign trip, he was a changed man. Anasuya realised that all the appetites which she had sung to sleep were now awake. The honeymoon was over. One evening she went to his house earlier than usual. Rain throbbed on the city's forehead like a dull headache. The poisonous exaltation of the sea chased her. At the gate Anasuya watched a woman coming out of the house. She saw the sweat on her face and the cosmetics mixed with the sweat. There flowed, either from her hair or from her clothes, the aroma of some steam-baked sweetmeat. Anasuya's mind suddenly became restless.

"Master is resting," the manservant told her at the door.

In the bedroom he smiled at her, lying on his side on the cot.

"You're too early today, Anasuya," he said. She sat on the cot. He was sweating profusely even in that power-cooled bedroom. She wondered whether the flowers in the pots on the table had also acquired the smell of that sweat. Do flowers too smell like a man's sweat?

"What's up, my darling?" she asked.

"I'm not at all well. I have a pain on the back of my neck," he said.

She discovered red lipstick marks at two places on his *kurta*. But she did not ask him anything about it.

"Never try to change me and make me a different man," he used to tell her.

She closed her eyes to his deceits and stratagems. She started changing. She began to believe that hypocrisy was an integral part of politics and trade and romance.

"We fear nothing," he said. "We fear none."

She too repeated those words, pressing her face against his chest, "We fear none."

Once, while she was pouring him tea, the manservant knocked at the door.

"Who's it?" he asked with resentment.

"Sita Devi's come," he said.

"Damn it!" He rose in anger and went out of the room.

Anasuya stepping out onto the veranda, viewed the street and the sea lying spread out beyond it. She heard his rebukes from some room within. Then the grievances and sobs of a woman.

"You'll regret it if you're a nuisance again," he said finally.

Anasuya suddenly returned to the room. Her heart beat faster. Who was Sita Devi?

Later he reluctantly told her that story. He had been putting up his mistress Sita Devi, a former film star, in a house he had constructed for her, for the last six years. On obtaining evidence that she was just a prostitute he had turned her out.

"This is the worst of all humiliations," he said.

"How did you know she was a prostitute?" asked Anasuya.

"Don't ask unnecessary questions, Anasuya," he said. "Don't poke your nose into all these things."

On reading in a newspaper three days later that Sita Devi,

a former film star, had committed suicide in a small hotel in Colaba, Anasuya went weak all over. Her phone rang six times that day. But she didn't respond. He came to her with a bouquet at five thirty in the evening. White roses.

"White roses symbolise innocence," he said. "I've never seen anyone as innocent as you."

Anasuya sobbed, burying her face in his chest.

"Never forsake me," she said.

"How can I forsake you?" he asked, smiling.

In the early days many people had told Anasuya stories about him doing the rounds in the city. They told her that he had certified his eldest daughter as mad and put her in a mental home when she fell in love with a Communist leader; that he had taken his typist to Poona when she got pregnant and had killed her, pushing her out of the car down a deep ravine; that a well-known journalist investigating the inside stories of certain smugglers had been killed by his thugs, and so on. Later Anasuya tried to avoid everyone. She was gradually getting distanced from all. And soon she was convinced that she was all alone with him on the stage.

It was then that she became pregnant.

"You were trying to trap me?" asked the Bison. "You too have the characteristic feminine cunning?"

Eventually he told her firmly:

"This should be aborted. Or else I won't have any relations whatever with you from now on. You know, don't you? That I'm not an ordinary man. I have an important position in this nation's public life. You should remember that!"

The day she came back from the hospital he presented her with a diamond necklace.

"This pallor, in fact, adds to your beauty," he said, kissing her. But her health deteriorated. She withered like a rose plant affected by canker. The melody of her embraces got fainter and fainter. And the flames of her hunger grew paler.

"What's happened to you? You're behaving like an old woman these days!" he said. Then he threw away a Bhagwati idol placed in a corner of her room. "This excessive devotion has made you useless," he muttered.

Anasuya jumped to her feet.

"You monster, get out!" she cried. Her voice went rough

with rage. "I don't want to see you again."

He went out, slamming the door shut. Sobbing, Anasuya kissed the fallen Bhagwati idol. "O my Mother! Save me!" she whispered.

Around one o'clock that night loud knocks on the door woke her up. When she opened the door, a gentleman dressed in western style and a white-clad man who was often seen hanging around the Taj Mahal Hotel entered in a hurry.

"Who are you?" Anasuya asked.

"What's your rate?" the man in the suit asked her. She realised that his eyes were assessing her anatomy.

"You're mistaken," she said. "This is no such place."

"No, memsahib!" said the pimp. "We're not mistaken. Somebody gave us the name and address."

After shutting them out she lay awake till morning. Then she slept for some minutes. She dreamed of a garden with fragrant flowers in full bloom and a venomous snake at large in it. The snake looked at her once and smiled. Could snakes laugh? She stood watching with wonder, that smile, and soon the snake turned into a bison. Later it was transformed into Ravana lying sleepless on his finely decorated bed.

Next day she enclosed the diamond necklace presented to her and an amount of one thousand rupees in a big envelope and had them delivered at his house along with a letter:

"I'm sending a small amount as a token of gratitude for your services. Goodbye!"

Wouldn't that Bison bellow on knowing that she had imagined him a mere male prostitute? She visualised the scene and laughed.

After two days Anasuya kept strolling up and down along Marine Drive at dusk with a handsome study-mate. The Bison was standing at the open window in the veranda. She sat on a bench, leaning against her companion's shoulder. She cracked jokes and laughed aloud. The window in the veranda slammed shut.

Next morning when the street lights went out at five forty-five, Anasuya had reached the starting point of Chowpatty. At the foot of the street bridge two hands held her mouth shut. She had expected it. So she didn't try to escape. She realised that, bound and blindfolded, she was being taken somewhere in a car.

About half an hour later she opened her eyes in a bedroom decorated in a special way. Her lover the Bison was lying there on a bed.

"Your story comes to an end today," he said.

She nodded. She looked with affection at his glistening eyes and the divine symbol tattooed on his forehead.

"First come and lie down here," he said.

Then he told her that, exactly one hour later, her killers would come pushing the door open, that she would be knifed to death and liquified with acid in the bathroom tub, and finally, turned into a sort of dirty liquid. She would flow down from the tub through innumerable pipes into the city sewers.

"My Anasuya, the sweetest one in the world, you too are coming to an end today," he whispered in her ear.

Later, she gently kissed the Bison who was greatly tired. At the moment of slipping into sleep he said, pressing his face against her bosom, "Anasuya, I love you truly!"

"I know it, darling," she said.

She thus understood that though life had an end, love did not necessarily have to end.

(Translated by C. K. Mohamed Ummer)

INSIDE EVERY WOMAN WRITER

Sarah Joseph

After a series of verbal duels I decide to leave. I pack up my clothes, books and writing materials. I send a telegram to Aunt Mable telling her of my arrival. On my way back from the telegraph office I ring up Purushothaman and tell him that I have sent a telegram to Aunt Mable and that I am leaving by the evening train.

"You have no such aunt. Don't kick up trouble again."

Purushothaman repeats himself.

"Wait till I come home."

"Where are you calling from?"

I realise that he is slamming down the receiver with uncontrollable anger. His tactics. To prevent me from going over to Aunt Mable. This has happened earlier. But now I've got to go.

Yesterday I was in deep thought about my new work. I was lying on a grass mat in the corridor. I wanted to write a novel based on a very serious theme. There were vague shadows in the mysterious corner of the corridor. They made me feel uneasy. Then I came to realise the movement of the walls. The walls of the corridor shook and moved. Before I could even start worrying, the walls crept toward me and crushed me. Air and light were shut out of the corridor. Unable to breathe, I beat my limbs in vain against the walls which looked possessed and were crushing me.

One day I went out. When I came back and tried to open the door, the iron grilles bent and turned like molten wax and crushed me. Another day the vessels piled up under the water tap for washing suddenly stood up and began to speak. They gave birth to stinking heaps of rubbish and defiantly moved round the kitchen and the dining room. I staggered and fell, vomiting even the intestines, like a character in an absurd play.

I can't stand it. It's terrible. I need peace and quiet.

Aunt Mable's house has no walls. It is built of thin, beautiful, mysterious screens. It has no grilles or bolts. Only nerves. And throbbing veins and arteries.

Its backdrop is an infinitely vast and open seascape. There I have a room of my own—with three windows that open out to the horizon—where I can read and write. Aunt Mable never spreads dirty linen over my thoughts. She never puts a grinding stone on the ideas that take shape in my mind.

These days I live exclusively in my writing. Engaged in my writing with a heavy heart, I speak and do things like a machine. When it becomes impossible for me to bear the weight of the outside world as well, I stagger and fall. These are the days when I wish I could somehow curl up. If I can curl up in the primordial darkness and silence of my mother's womb, I can bring out my words in great secrecy. What I need is a labour room. A labour room which has nothing to do with the outside world.

Purushothaman would order that I need not write anything different, that I continue writing the same old stuff. Till now I have been writing a lot about love. Using the Radha-Krishna love as my key image, I have found the pain of parting and the spirit of sacrifice burning through my veins like an intoxication. It's I who found out that one could dedicate one's unrealised love and lust to Krishna. And I have developed it to a brilliant chemistry which can make one feel that illusion is reality.

Yet my works were rejected by the male writers whenever they assembled for serious literary discussions. They screamed that when the world was hungry, love was an extra expenditure. I am extremely sad that I created only women characters who made flower offerings at the same feet, who kept shedding tears endlessly, and who went on sobbing, sitting behind bolted doors with their heads bent low. Now my realities require a revelation. It is time for revelations of my experience of love as a lump of phlegm spat onto my face, and of motherhood as an iron chain crushing my neck.

I need time. And peace. In the brief intervals of relief when I fall into the easy-chair in the veranda to remember something good, Purushothaman's undergarments piled up in the bedroom come flying at me. One on top of the other, they fall on my face, my neck, my chest, smothering me with their unbearable stench.

A sword of humiliation drives into my heart. I must go. Before Purushothaman arrives I must get ready and stand at the threshold with my baggage.

He will definitely ask me about the children. I must convince him that I have already recognised more veiled aggression than helplessness in that question. Nothing would be beautiful as in the past. He must realise it.

At Aunt Mable's house I don't rule out the possibility of my getting occasionally worried about my children. As the evening dies out and darkness begins to fall on the sea, my life—my spirit—will wander over the waters like an orphaned lullaby. And my heart will feel the immense sorrow of my separation from my children. Yet I realise that I have to recreate myself through a separation, a departure.

I don't know if the moving walls will hunt Purushothaman instead of me. But, after all, he has more powerful muscles and, as he claims, "something more" in his skull—more than what I have. He can use it and try not to be rendered helpless.

The money for my journey is still a problem for me. I don't intend merely to travel to Aunt Mable's house. As I sit beside the window from where I can see the world's sights and travel quite freely without even bothering about a destination, the air I breathe will give shape to my work.

I don't know if Aunt Mable can do something about the money. I should find out how she meets her daily expenses and how she manages to maintain, quite prettily, her beautiful house and garden. On some days she doesn't cook food. Then she suggests that I go out and have my food. The free, solitary stroll through the seashore is very pleasant. I walk with my eyes and ears kept fully open. I love those evening strolls when I roam my favourite streets, seeing and hearing everything, and returning with a little packet of food for Aunt Mable. My brain would move with profound thoughts and I would respectfully carry these movements in my heart and feel proud of them. For that very reason, my head would be held high.

It is possible that in the city where Aunt Mable lives there are meetings of contemporary writers. I could never take part in writers' discussions till the end because the *panchaloha*[1] ring I

---

[1] Panchaloha : An alloy of five metals

wore on my ankle had sunk into my flesh. My mother had got this ring specially made for me when I was born. Later, as I grew and the ring didn't, it was enveloped by my flesh. The *panchaloha* ring screamed and ran helter-skelter and then laid eggs in my flesh, giving birth to a wilderness of little rings, which, declaring their existence aloud, would start running about and push me into the burning pit of unbearable pain.

Often, in the evening, I see a couple of poet-friends sitting on the railings on the bridge across the river, engaged in endless literary discussions. Behind their arms they have grown wonderful wings! Golden wings! They indulge in literary discussions with these wings fully spread out against the wind blowing in from the river. Struck by the magical light of dusk these golden wings would glitter! A fantastic sight! There would always be an audience for these poets.

I often wished I could join the audience while going to the vegetable mart or on my way back from the clinic where I took my children to be examined by the doctor. The poets spoke, wearing long and loose garments and flowing beards which ideally matched their wings. One must develop a proper attitude towards problems, they said. Open discussions such as this can profoundly alter one's perceptions of life.

I wished to stay there for a long time and listen to their conversation. And they reminded me of the late hour by looking at the withering vegetables, or at the child about to start crying, or at the darkening evening. Or they shook and stretched their wings and told me quite formally that they would lead me back to my house. Never did they continue their discussion from where they had left off.

When I invited them home, they came and sat in the veranda and talked to Purushothaman while I had to spend all the time in the kitchen preparing food and tea for them. By the time I removed the dishes after food, tidied up the room and came out, arranging in my mind whatever I wanted to tell them, they had done with the evening. They yawned, thanked me for the good food and flew away, beating their coloured wings.

I would certainly be able to take part in the writers' meetings in the city where Aunt Mable lives. Perhaps I wouldn't be able to say anything, but my mind would absorb everything, like sun-baked desert absorbs rain. It's a shame to be kept off from recognition in the name of a tender skin and plump body. Since my mind can take in anything, keeping off for the sake of skin care should not be repeated. And to give expression to my anger I need a better method than smashing teacups.

The very fact that Purushothaman would not be with me means my thought processes would not be hindered or broken. Whenever he accompanied me to literary discussions, he would keep glancing at his watch every now and then, start yawning by six o' clock, and nudge and prod me to leave without being seen. At Aunt Mable's place the first thing she asked me would be about my performance in the debate. Then I could lie back in my bed with a mind fully awake. Or perhaps, I could stay there listening to the roar of the sea and thinking deeply about my work.

I am packing my things up in this cloth bag. I wish I had a friend who could help me with the money.

It was my friend Jayadevan who advised me to go to Aunt Mable's house to write a book. Our thoughts and feelings were complementary in nature. And they attained perfection through the discussion we had after reading or writing something together. His seething brain would achieve a brilliant expansiveness and depth on the days that I spent with him.

Aunt Mable's quiet and beautiful house was an arbour ideally suited for the flowering of love. But I didn't consider it necessary to fall in love with Jayadevan. He too said one shouldn't insist on every relationship to end in love. What grew between us was a friendship of unconditional joy. Laughing, bickering and singing aloud, we recovered our lost childhood and presented it before Aunt Mable! Whenever I talked to Purushothaman about this quiet and pleasant friendship, he would explode!

Lie! Which Aunt Mable? Which Jayadevan? Don't be crazy—go away!

Purushothaman's stratagem to unleash the winds of madness in my brain! Now that I have recognised it and decided to expose it, I can go.

I should be at the threshold, ready for the journey, before Purushothaman arrives. I shouldn't have second thoughts and get inside again to discuss the problem. When all his tactics fail, Purushothaman will come out with the big romantic lie that without me life is impossible.

I sling my bag across my shoulder and pick up whatever money I have with me.

Before I reach the threshold Purushothaman comes running in.

"Started again?" he asks, panting. I keep staring at him mockingly.

Purushothaman, with sympathy, tries to take away the bag from my shoulder. I shake him off and with one big leap reach the threshold.

"I'm off to Aunt Mable's . . ."

"Who the hell is this Aunt Mable?" he shouts. I cross the threshold and walk out. Let him continue to use his tactics.

At the gate I stop and look back. Purushothaman is standing at the doorstep, lost in thought. Somebody has punished him. Who and why—let him find out for himself. I'm quite helpless there.

Now I walk with an absolutely free movement of my limbs. My hands touch the horizon and come back. A winged wind stirs free the strands of my hair and the folds of my clothes. My hair unlooses itself, soars and touches the sky, and my skirt whirls round in a wide, wide circle and covers the earth.

(Translated by V. C. Harris)

SERPENTS OF THE HOLY MOUND
Manasi

Ammini Amma was at her daily prayers. Ever since the molehills had come up on the earth, dank with the holy water and holy leaves of *tulasi* and *vilwa* offered before the faded picture of Shiva, Ammini Amma was expecting it to happen any moment. So, having ritually offered the palmful of water, she smiled as she caressed the serpent, bright like a gold wire, when it affectionately nestled itself in her lap.

"You and your pranks! I have only one request to you. Don't give me another life; and don't bother my children. Now drink this milk. My long prayers in ritual wet clothes and my prolonged sweeping and swabbing chores at the manor-house have given me this nagging pain in my waist. Let me see if my change of clothes is dry. You finish your milk."

When she came back after changing her wet, meagre garment, the snake had vanished. She put back the pooja-tray, collected her dry towel from the line and slinging it across her shoulders, went out on her daily routine.

On the porch of his shop sat Raman Nair, huddled up with the lingering sleep of a cool dawn.

"You must be returning from the temple," Raman Nair smiled as he lit his beedi. "For us the day is yet to start."

"No, I am on my way. In fact I am late. The lady at the manor-house will be angry. She is another one with little faith. She doesn't believe me when I tell her of Shiva revealing himself in the guise of a snake. I need a measure of rice, a little camphor and three joss-sticks; make it a loan."

"Thankamani must be at home."

"I dedicated her to Shiva long ago. She is no good for the toil at the manor-house. To think that I cast out an offspring when he was still all innocence!"

"You better hurry up."

Raman Nair gave her the packet and went inside. He was the first one to know of Unnikuttan's death in the lorry accident. Pilgrims returning from Palani had brought the news. It seems Ammini Amma had beaten Unnikuttan when he wouldn't stop crying for food. She had also told him, it seems, to go and get some money from the one who sired him. His father had died eleven years ago. So, Unnikuttan ran away from home. Three months later, the letter and money reached Ammini Amma. The first thing she did was to buy a lamp for Shiva. Then she thatched her house and framed an old photograph of Unnikuttan in the company of the scions of the manor-house. The women of the village, when their paths crossed Ammini Amma's, enquired after Unnikuttan with a new-found respect. Nani of the carpenter's family was the first one to offer a four-anna bit to the deity of the mole-hill in Ammini Amma's house.

That was when the letters and money from Unnikuttan ceased.

Ammini Amma's first reaction was that there was black magic behind it, black magic by the mother of some nubile girl.

Raman Nair gave his word to seek out the truth, while his eyes sought the lush black hair and the slim waist of Thankamani.

However, Krishnankutty, Unnikuttan's comrade in cattle-herding, was more forthright. Leaping off the buffalo he was riding, he confronted her.

"Why don't you ask that Shiva of yours whom you feed day in and day out, to prompt Unnikuttan to send a letter at least?"

"Sure enough. What do you take Shiva to be? Our servant?"

Ammini Amma bound her hair, wiped her perspiring neck and chest, and smiled.

In the grey of twilight the flame of her lamp gleamed. She looked steadily at the top of the mole-hill, filled with the smoke from the camphor. From the joss-sticks and through the flowers of worship. The mole-hill was a minor one when Unnikuttan had left.

"Go ahead and test. Salvation is never offered on a gold platter. I know it. But I don't turn back at failures. Yet, it is fourteen months now since Unnikuttan left. And I am not getting any younger. He would have been a support to me. It was yesterday, on my way to the bathing-ghat, that Cousin Madu stopped me. She said: 'Faith is fine. But are our girls destined to be no more than housemaids and sweepers? Thankamani is no child now.' I did not say anything, just hummed significantly.

"'Where are you running away?' Cousin Madu stopped me even as she was drying her hair. 'She may still be a child for you. But to others she is a woman all right.'

"Why do those others keep ogling at her?" I was provoked. "Are girls so scarce in this land?

"'I'm not the aunt of all of them. Thankamani happens to be my brother Appu's daughter.'

"Your brother! Your brother Appu! Twenty years after his death, now you remember his daughter? Listen, you won't get her for your profession. I dedicated her to Shiva long ago.'

"'A curse on your God!'

"Very much in her wet clothes, Madu charged ahead. 'Where were your gods when that slip of a boy of yours was crushed under the lorry?'"

Ammini Amma kept staring at the fuming joss-stick. The women around had pulled Madu away. No one till then had told Ammini Amma what the pilgrims from Palani had told Raman Nair. People around were in awe of the snakes of the mole-hill that was evolving in the shape of Shiva's coiffure in Ammini Amma's house. They feared their power. Shocked at Madu's words, they vowed offerings in their minds. Ammini Amma, ever busy with her drudgery at the manor-house, was unaware of the indifference of Raman Nair towards her borrowing of the pooja-materials or deification of the mole-hill by the neighbourhood women after they had heard of Unnikuttan's death.

It was the same when Ammini Amma mourned for full fourteen days the death of her husband. He had died after two years of marriage and two children. She had stopped crying and got up with a start only when the emissary of the matriarch of the manor-house had come to inform her that the portico and the yard in front of the big house were covered with dust and littered with the mess of fourteen days. Ammini Amma's worship of Shiva had started much earlier; perhaps in her previous birth. In a fit of anger her husband threw out the Shiva into a dark corner and since then that had remained Shiva's abode. In the new awareness of her loneliness after the emissary had come, she installed the idol of Shiva properly. On her tattered thatched mat, she laid Thankamani in front of the idol.

"Here is my daughter. Accept her or reject her, as you please."

She closed the door and came out. Unnikuttan was left with carpenter Raman's mother. By and by, his cries became distant. That was the day she sat in front of the mole-hill which had grown—to protect Thankamani as it were. Ammini Amma sat there saying nothing, seeking nothing.

"It's in vain," said Ammini Amma glancing at the smoke springing out of the diverse outlets of the mole-hill, and its miasma : "You cannot escape my eyes. If you have accepted Unnikuttan I have no complaints. In any case he was a good boy. He hurt nobody. If he is not accepted by you, who else will be? As for Thankamani, she has ever been dedicated to you. That leaves me out, the only one."

Ammini Amma stopped in her path. It was a sudden shock. "Don't you know me?"

"Sure, I do."

Without taking her eyes off the peacock feather on the crown, Ammini Amma hastily pulled down the towel from her shoulder, in deference.

"And so?"

"I am a subject of Shiva. Besides, I was preoccupied."

"So what?"

"Divided loyalty? If it angers Shiva . . ."

"And if I promise you salvation?"

"There you go! Still your old naughty self. Aren't you?"

Ammini Amma drew a handful of *kunni* seeds from the plant nearby and handed them over to Krishna with a smile : "This is not a formality of reverence. Haven't you told mankind, ever and always, that you like good deeds?

"Still, you saw me so close, and yet . . ."

"All right, you tell me one good deed of yours."

Ammini Amma was petrified. She could not remember a single good deed of her own. Confused and in haste, she said, as it she had just discovered it:

"The drudgery of the manor-house."

"Well, that's one to start with." Krishna said thoughtfully, playing with his *Kaustubha*[1]. But you know the conditions. Seven

---

[1] Kaustubha - A jewel

seas, seven continents, seven mountains . . . Beyond them and far away . . . to cross these hurdles, the drudgery of the manor-house may prove inadequate."

"Well," without permitting Krishna to have his say, she picked up a handful of the sacred rice and scaffered it at his feet, wet in the water over which he was standing. She bowed down to him.

"Well," she continued, "I don't seek salvation. I don't seek anything. Just tell me about Unnikuttan. Where is he?"

The reply came suddenly, like the thunder of the clouds, in a disembodied voice : "Strength lies in the basic awareness of what can be desired. Therefore, you wait."

As expected, Krishna had vanished. Out there in the distance, in the ripples of the river, gleamed a peepul leaf. She filled her cupped palm with the clear water of the river—as clear as tears —and poured it reverentially into the river itself, all the while keeping Krishna in her mind. She had planned to ask Shiva when he would appear in the form of a snake. But the *maya*, the universal *maya*, came in between and cast a sense of guilt. Patting her starved stomach, she continued on her path.

"I haven't gone past even a corner of one sea, leave alone the seven seas, the seven continents and the seven mountains." Ammini Amma decided that she should start on her penances. The fact of meeting Krishna at the river-side, she kept to herself. People had laughed when she told them of the footprints of Shiva on the damp floor of her house, of the coming up of the mole-hill like Shiva's coiffure in her room of worship, and of the serpents, playful in her lap as on the neck of Shiva. Deep inside her heart, she prayed to Shiva to bestow the gift of perception on everyone. Ultimately, even Thankamani was convinced when, on an abundant moonlit night filled with the aroma of nocturnal flowers, Shiva woke her up in her sleep and escorted her out.

"That wasn't quite right," was Raman Nair's view, when, graciously he poured down the camphor and the rice into her extended *mundu* : "Going to a man outside the caste—to a carpenter—when we are very much here. That was unfair."

With a shy glance at the bark-raiment she had bought from the tribals at the village fair, Thankamani turned back. What struck Raman Nair, blinding his eyes momentarily, was the hair coming down to her heels; the brilliance of the jewel of the serpents in their hoods. With a scream Raman Nair closed his dazzled eyes. The tale of his declining eyesight permeated the village like the steamy discomfort of an orphaned pregnancy. The women in the village turned nervous about Thankamani's chastity. They avoided the pathways frequented by her. Only the prostitutes sought her blessings, touching her feet and the raiment of bark.

Therefore, no one was surprised that Thankamani's son was born with three eyes. It was once again carpenter Raman who came to Thankamani's aid as she lay writhing in the agonies of confinement. Ammini Amma thought it incredible that the birth of a son of Mahesha, one of the triumvirates, should need the agency of a hospital doctor. The day Shiva vanished, bidding farewell to Thankamani, she was sitting under a spreading tree in the shrine of the serpents and looking at the many mole-hills around. As her long loose hair swayed and even as her shrieks rose to a crescendo, there stood carpenter Raman, calm, leaning against the trunk of that tree. He knew everything; he internalised everything. Unable to believe what she saw, carpenter Raman's mother threw down the bundle of firewood she was carrying and dragged him into the house. She was afraid of Shiva's wrath descending on the wedding of Raman, which was to take place ten days hence.

It was for the same reason that carpenter Raman's wife dissuaded him from his walk of expiation at the head of the stretcher that carried the sobbing Thankamani to the hospital. But Raman's wife, who stood like a live ember against the window grill, did not know that Raman was fulfilling the promise he had made to Shiva in the shrine of the serpents at midnight in that moon-washed night. Remembering the jewel that had affected Raman Nair's sight, carpenter Raman lifted up Thankamani's hair lest it should get soiled as it ripped down from the stretche The first time Raman had seen Thankamani lying entwined with a serpent was when he had come to the porch of her house to steal a couple of clothes drying on the line. He had caught a glimpse of her through the window. Raman was still steeped in the horrible fascination of that scene as he walked ahead of the stretcher like a sleepwalker.

Yes it was Ammini Amma who, without the support of either Thankamani or Shiva, had covered the triple-eyed one in a tiger-skin bought from the market, nurtured him and put him to sleep with her lullaby. Thankamani was all indifference. After her delivery she stood gazing out through the bars of the window. She saw the young wife of carpenter Raman sweeping the yard. She looked smart with her kumkum and her hair bound in a bun. Thanakamani ignored the carpenter who was cleaning his teeth and stood watching his wife. Thankamani was perhaps looking beyond him. The plateful of hot *kanji* which her mother had kept on the window-sill remained untouched. The mouth of the triple-eyed one went dry without ever knowing the moisture of mother's milk.

"The lady of the manor-house enquired after you yesterday also," Ammini Amma told Thankamani while trying to put to sleep the triple-eyed one in her lap.

"The matriarch there was asking me if Thankamani could take over. The triple-eyed one has to be fed thrice a day. Don't you think that Shiva, up above, will be watching you at your constant stand at the window?"

"If he has to be fed three times a day take him to that fellow who sired him, you old hag," Thankamani screamed. "You could ask your coiffured one which female has charmed him away now."

Saying this, Thankamani swept down, picked up the camphor and the joss-sticks and threw them into the kitchen fire. Ammini Amma tried to stop her. But the fire burned brighter.

Laying the triple-eyed one on the ground, Ammini Amma had tried to salvage the burning joss-sticks.

"How many seas have we crossed?" Lying by the side of Ammini Amma and hugging her, the triple-eyed one would query: "If you cross all the seven seas, Grandma, will you be able to see my Uncle Unni?"

"No, one has to cross seven mountains and seven continents."

"By then you will be very old, Grandma."

"Yes. Perhaps I may not reach there."

"And then?"

"I don't know. But Shiva will be gracious. There should be an end to trials also.

"I have never slipped up on my penances or on the austerities. Neither have I deviated from the path of serpents, but for that one instance when I asked Shri Krishna about Unnikuttan". Ammini

Amma would then hold the sleepy, triple-eyed one in a close embrace.

Thankamani had ignored him for months. Watching the wife of carpenter Raman through the window, day in and day out without respite, she withered like the worn-out wooden grill. She did not budge from the window even for the two months that carpenter Raman's wife was away at her mother's for her confinement.

The day he knew about it, carpenter Raman decided to quit the village. Thankamani, who met him on the way, had exploded. "The father who fled the day the bastard was born! Ask him where he's going to sow his wild oats next." It seems she had pushed the triple-eyed one who was holding Ammini Amma's hand. Before the jewel in Thankamani's hair could bedazzle him, he fled without looking back even once. He stopped only when he reached home and then he fell down in a fit of fever. That was how Raman died on the day he wanted to quit the village, ill with high fever. Raman's wife hollered and beat her breast. Thankamani took a good look at her, bound her hair, washed her face, adjusted her dress and stood in front of her mirror.

"A kumkum on your forehead will complete the new glow on your face," said cousin Madu as she came avisiting and took a good look at Thankamani. Madu spat out the juice of the paan and surveyed Thankamani. " Frankly, you don't look your age at all." Without turning her face from the mirror, Thankamani shot a glance at Madu. Then she dipped her finger in the sandalwood paste kept ready for the puja, and made a fine dot on her forehead.

"Now if you redden your lips with the paan . . ." Cousin Madu pushed the box of paan towards Thankamani, ignoring the presence of Ammini Amma.

Afterwards, some time after the funeral rites of carpenter Raman were over, after the excitement of the temple festival, when the barren earth was drenched and soaked with the onset of rains, there came the change of heart in Thankamani. Those who heard of it could not believe it. She abandoned the mole-hills, the snakes and the triple-eyed one, who were defences for her. Emphasising her eyes, putting the dot on her forehead, she walked into the shop of Krishna Iyer and bought gold-bordered, fine clothes. She herself revealed to him the matter of her marriage to Shri Krishna.

"Then let Shri Krishna buy the clothes for you. Why do you bother me?"

People were shocked to see Krishna Iyer's shop tremble as if in an earthquake. A contrite Krishna Iyer gave away the clothes to Thankamani. Wearing those clothes Thankamni averred: "Those who want to meet me may henceforth come to the temple at Guruvayoor." And like lightning, she vanished into the sky.

Ammini Amma knew of it on her way back from the manorhouse. Raman Nair told her. Ammini Amma sat down on the portico of Raman Nair's shop, drinking the glass of water he had offered. She said : "It is all a *maya*. But those who twisted my daughter's mind also will have to account for their action, when Chitragupta confronts them. Yesterday she came at me in a rage, when I asked her why the sacred lamp was not lit at dusk. I did miss a heartbeat. But in no way have I or my daughter hurt anybody. Perhaps my sufferings are to continue. The evil deeds of my past life may still be visiting me."

Raman Nair kept his head down. All that he said was, he had lent some rice and camphor to the triple-eyed one.

It was when Ammini Amma was watching the mole-hill with the triple-eyed one close by, that it happened. From the dark recesses of the mole-hill, there emerged a gold thread. As expected, Ammini Amma stopped her prayers. Softly, without breaking the sleep of the divine, Ammini Amma got up.

The triple-eyed one said:

"You forgot to say the prayers for Uncle." Without taking her eyes off the gold thread, Ammini Amma hummed in reply.

"I shouldn't have enquired about Unnikuttan of the seer. Perhaps he was annoyed. His subdued posture with hood down could be deceptive. Trivial knowledge is the source of all sorrow."

Full of repentence and fear, Ammini Amma stood there and joined her palms in reverence. Ignorance, after all, is a result of age. She knew all this, yet she couldn't resist the temptation when she saw the seer at his profession of peering into the future. In spite of herself she enquired after Unnikuttan. She had not had food for three days. She was exhausted physically and mentally. That was why, losing all her reserve, she asked him the whereabouts of her son. She told the seer: "If necessary I will take on one more life and propitiate Shiva with daily austerities." The wise one replied, "But Ammini, you have not escaped the *maya* yet."

The gold thread writhed once, lifted up the hood and stared at Ammini Amma. Ammini Amma hugged the triple-eyed one closer to her. Without taking her eyes off the hood, she said, "The boy has gone without food, the last three days."

Like a feather reaching high, the gold thread emerged from the mole-hill, razed the mole-hill to the ground and flew towards Ammini Amma. Ammini Amma became aware of a consoling cool, rising in front of her eyes still enmeshed in the maya. Suddenly she could perceive everything. In that state of perception she listened to the cries of the triple-eyed one with compassion. Later it became awkward when she could see clearly the treasures hidden at the bottom of the bathing pond and the piece of the yellow silk swaying on top of the peepul tree. Under her penetrating gaze, even married couples felt denuded openly. So people dodged Ammini Amma's path. The most embarrassed were the couples in love, adulterous men and common thieves. Since most of the village folk came under these categories, the majority in the village avoided Ammini Amma. Thus, in a most unexpected manner, Ammini Amma became the enemy of the people. Dr Krishna Kumar of the local hospital, who had earlier helped to abort an indiscretion of a woman of the manor-house, sent back Ammini Amma telling her that medicines were out of stock. As she sat on the porch of the hospital, tired and holding the hand of the triple-eyed one, the villagers looked at her with awe.

It seems she had asked the doctor whether Sukumari of the manor-house was all right now. "Since I no longer work at the manor-house I knew of Sukumari's case from the serpents."

Krishna Kumar who had faith only in reason, science and man, looked deep into Ammini Amma's eyes. "My child, mine is a case of a few hours more. I have come a long way. Now let life choose its own path. Unnatural death keeps out salvation. Then I may not meet Unnikuttan there either. Do you know of anything that will reduce this pain of mine? I know only too well that the leftover life has to be lived . . . *maya* . . .".

It was these words of hers that prompted Krishna Kumar, even in that midnight, to let her lie on the outskirts of the nursing home. A life which could claim rights over snakes and peacock

"Perhaps to heaven or to Mount Kailash, I wouldn't know," Raman Nair replied dreamlily without taking his eyes off the fast vanishing strands of gold. Cleaning the snotty nose of the triple-eyed one with his own *mundu*, he held the boy closer and said: "One would know only when one goes over there. Come on, child. Nothing registers when seen through eyes screened by *maya*."

(Translated by T. M. P. Nedungadi)

CHAMUNDI'S PIT

P. Vatsala

Parameswaran married Rukmini to have an assistant in his catering business. His job was to serve rice and curry to the pilgrims who visited the Krishna temple. That was his livelihood, his only mode of earning. Parameswaran took payment in money for the sacred service of giving meals to the people who visited the Krishna temple, situated in the midst of the mountain ranges, for worship, death rites, naming ceremonies and marriages. He earned just enough to make do. There was enough to thatch the roof of his house and buy two sets of clothes to wear. What was the point in wishing for more? Parameswaran did not know any other work.

When the road and the bus service were extended to the temple, the number of pilgrims also increased. He needed someone to assist him. A woman seemed to be the ideal solution. She could do the grinding and cooking. She could clear the remains of the food and clean the surroundings: a place where many people came and went. So he married Rukmini, who was from a distant village, and brought her to his dwelling place. In Parameswaran's eyes, her beauty and education were not important. All that mattered was the great deal of discipline she brought into every aspect of his life. They could now give the pilgrims breakfast as well as lunch. She had the knowhow and the skill to make some simple things for breakfast and dinner.

What then was the hitch in such a carefree life ? What did she lack? This was something Parameshwaran could never fathom.

The last of the guests finished his dinner and climbed the steps leading to the lodge. Rukmini put out the lamp and closed the door. She sat down in the kitchen and prepared to have her dinner. There was some rice in the basket. She glanced at the wilted plantain leaf and hoped that no one else would come. The

kept quiet.

"Please bring another plate. This rice is too much for me."

Without a word, she washed another plate and brought it to him. Then she withdrew from the front veranda. She was afraid he might demand some curry. Lowering the wick of the lamp, she stood in a corner of the kitchen. It was a dark corner from where neither of them could see the other.

He ate silently. There was not even a pappad to fry. She was unhappy. Usually she kept a stock of salted and dried beans and bitter gourd, and pappad made of jackfruit, for serving her special guests. She had even planted many vegetables near the kitchen courtyard for this purpose. The summer licked off everything. When the mountains burnt and the forest streams died with their throats parched, she was surrounded by a veritable desert. The rain seemed to be far away, somewhere beyond the mountains. There was not even a hint of a slight breeze that could grasp the rain clouds by the hand and lead them here.

She heard the guest get up after his meal.

She shivered. Where would she get him water to wash his hands?

The pots, pans and vessels in the kitchen were all empty and upturned. There was some boiled water kept aside for drinking. She poured a glass and brought it to him.

As he washed his hands, the guest looked at her face sideways.

She said softly : "The water is finished."

He gave her an astonished look.

"A scarcity of water in this place?" But then he sighed, looking at the garlands of red fire on the horizon.

Later, she decided not to have supper.

She put the pots and pans in order. As she was closing the door, the guest said, heaving his bag onto his shoulders, "I am going to the lodge to sleep. Where can I go to bathe in the morning?"

In the dark she pointed to the distant bathing ghat.

"You have to walk quite far. There is water only in the Chamundi pit. It is actually a deep pond."

As he climbed the stone steps and disappeared into the courtyard of the temple, Rukmini stared at the steep walls that loomed in front of her like Fate. Those walls carved out from rock; below, a piece of raised ground like a prison. No one, not even a stray breeze, had paused to look at her little thatched hut.

It was past midnight. When the hearth cooled, perhaps her husband would come down the steps of the lodge. Perhaps he wouldn't.

Closing the doors from the outside, she spread a mat in the front veranda. The mat smelt of wild turmeric, from the unknown guest.

She tossed and turned, not able to sleep. Her young son, who woke up from his sleep, came to her, mumbling something. He stretched out beside her. She knew that he was perspiring. She picked up the arecanut-spathe fan and fanned him to sleep.

Somewhere, far away, barren thunder trembled. The leaves in the higher branches of the trees in the courtyard rustled. Then she slept. The noise of a footfall woke her.

It was not yet dawn. High above, one or two birds chirped. She opened and closed her eyes, and then began to search for something near her.

A torch shone."What have you lost?" said a voice from the courtyard. In the light which tore the heart of darkness, she turned her gaze to the mat once again.

Nothing. Just emptiness. Bitterly, she remembered that her son was just a dream. A wasted shoot growing on a branch stuck in dry soil. Even before it could see the daylight, it had withered away.

She tried to forget her dream and smile.

The guest murmured, "I am going in search of a drop of cool water." He sought her eyes questioningly.

She folded the mat and joined him.

(Translated by Vasanthi Sankaranarayanan)

green[3] and smokes. I seat a little coconut-baby on my waist and, wearing a towel like a half-saree, became a wife and a mother. And in our baby house hanging on top of the sky, far, far from this world, an unearthly radiance spreads.

Amdist this great journey, I once followed a middle-aged man and reached the front of his house. As the footsteps disappeared inside, somebody slammed the door on my dazed face. I turned back, hiding my embarrassment in a thin smile.

Anyhow, after Mridula talked to me, I could no longer follow anyone's footsteps on my way from the hostel to the office. On the contrary, I went past them in great determination and hurry. The moment I reached the office and collapsed in my seat, sweating and panting, I began to burn, burn from tip to toe. And in this burning, I heard the thunderbolt of a change. I jabbed violently, vengefully, at the typewriter keys.

All of a sudden, Mridula got married. She came back to the office after a month's leave. Her eyes were full of sleepless nights. Her lips weary of the fullness of joy. And her curves enveloped in an idle indolence. At times her right breast jumped out from behind her saree and, in the temptation of a newly acquired fullness, trapped the eyes of both men and women. Then I felt increasingly ashamed of my own flat and insignificant chest. And I began to take special care in packing it up in a heavy cotton saree so that nobody would notice it.

I was relieved to find Mridula refusing to speak much to anyone. But, after four or five days, words came out of her mouth like a character who happens to bump into the stage. And a host of words came roaring, roaring. And they went round me, pecking and tearing at me. Mridula had uprooted her father-idol and installed the husband there—seeing which, I smiled bitterly. The intensity of his love for her, and their bedroom secrets, singed me. And thus, in my nights, the spring of sleep withdrew into the depths. As soon as I closed my eyes, a loveless drunkard of a husband with swollen eyes and sticky words of abuse came crashing in on me from the invisible plains of the future. Every morning the weight, the burden, on my chest kept increasing. As last I decided to consult a doctor, a specialist.

---

[3] Communist green - A kind of weed, so called in Kerala, probably because it spreads very fast!

The doctor was a black bull. His round eyes, narrow forehead and bushy hair reminded me of a bison. By the time I began to subject him to a close scrutiny, he had pressed his steth firmlly against my chest. I took a few deep breaths. The examination over, his head began to swing like a pendulum. Then, issuing a groan and a h'mm, he spoke in an uncharacteristic bird-voice: In place of the heart you have a rock. And it's growing harder.

I couldn't get shocked. I had begun to forget how to get shocked. He continued staring at my dry, shrivelled breasts: the last drops of tenderness in you are drying up.

As I came out of the clinic unmoved, I realized that this was an appendix to the scripture. Out in the scorching sun, I raised my face to the sky. What do you intend to build on this rock? In reply, a darkness filled my eyes.

(Translated by V. C. Harris)

GUADALAJARA : A THOTTEKKADAN MEMOIR

K. P. Nirmal Kumar

When commercial banks in the joint sector opened their special branches for foreign exchange transactions on Mahatma Gandhi Road, Mattancherry's monopoly in maritime trade was shaken to its foundations. The stockbrokers of Banerjee Road, who could not acquiesce in acts of cruelty to animals, spread the word that the Mother Goddess of Pazhayanoor had submitted to Father Ernakulam. As the Foreign Exchange Superintendents made a beeline for the Speed Post counters with bills of loading and marine insurance policies tucked under their arm, the wholesale merchants of Broadway exchanged bewildered looks. On the streets of Mattancherry, where the sheen of foreign trade was fast wearing off, packets of raw *pappadam* were offered at throw-away prices. Even the students in the evening batch of the MBA course at the Cochin University had to admit that an efficient, but not necessarily ethical, mercantile banking system designed to cater to martitime trade had arrived in Ernakulam from across the backwaters. For the pedestrians of Ernakulam who generally carried boiled tapioca and bouncing cheques, it was an agonizing sight to watch the exporters, who claimed to work miracles in foreign markets, thronging the overseas branches which lined the road from Madhava Pharmacy to Medical Trust, documentary credit in hand, in quest of packing credit.

The overseas branches wallowed in opulence. But the clerks espoused egalitarian ideals. Though lacking in mutual understanding, they were energetic and industrious. The chamber of commerce showered its blessings on their untiring efforts to satisfy their increasing appetite for precious foreign exchange. The multi-storied buildings on MG Road symbolised the achievements of the maritime mercantile credit system. Mattancherry resigned itself to small-time trading in spices.

Living in Guadalajara on the Periyar, Gautham Adhikari

plinth area of two thousand square feet, to multinational drug companies, and went down to live in the serene landscape of Thottekkattu-kara. These poor rich men who fled their homes under persecution from high-brow intellectuals, soon passed through the stage of total indifference into one of passive cooperation in Thottekkadan society. Evincing no interest in surgery or extra-marital relationships, they spent their last days fishing in the Periyar and reading *Sahitya Varaphalam*[3].

Gautham Adhikari too worked in the joint sector which was making concerted efforts towards registering high profits. On the top floor of the multi-storeyed building on Shanmukham Road which housed one of the banks which handled maritime mercantile credit, Adhikari was in charge of one of the several windows which had binoculars affixed to them. He gazed with bated breath at the sailing ships loaded with merchandise till they disappeared beyond the horizon (which was the word for 'west' among the *feringhis* of Pachalam). When pirates appeared in the darkened backwaters after sundown, Adhikari handed over the observation duties to Portuguese marines and returned to Gudalajara. As an expert in foreign trade, he was disturbed over the disarrayed state of the balance of payments. Thilothama braced herself to face another night of sexual assault.

Where the waters of the Kothayar ended their meandering journey across the black Thottekkadan rocks and fell into the Periyar as a torrent, on the flat, wet rocks on which the sexual exploits of the patriarchs of Central Kerala were etched, the physicians of Palarivattom, the retired medical college dons who came in search of lost values, had their scrub-and-bath. Lying on the ample hips of the rocks for a long time, allowing the arms of the water to embrace them, the eco-friendly physicians returned with wild images of sexuality crowding their minds. The waterfall quickened fiercely as it took in the enamouring smell of the toilet soaps they had left behind. Suburban ladies sat cross-legged and played on their veenas. The movement of hill-products down the Periyar slackened.

When Thilothama woke up in the middle of the night and opened a window, she saw reptiles creeping ashore from the

---

[3] Sahitya Varaphalam - A column in the weekly, *Kalakaumudi*, by M.Krishnan Nair, the renowned literary columnist.

exuberant Periyar and prowling around Guadalajara's nursery of medicinal herbs. She closed the window, flung herself on her bed, lay face-down and drowned her disgrace in tears. Gautham Adhikari, who had once described her as a mysterious goldmine of sexuality, lay on his bed at the other end of the room, fondling his sexual fantasies. When the hot springs of fantasy burst through the statutes of foreign trade and burned his thighs, he turned over and went to sleep.

There were some generals, who, free from the threat of war, dared to fish in the river. The members of the 'Save Periyar Action Group' were moved to tears by their territorial disputes. The stockbrokers of Banerjee Road, who had come down for their brief holidays, accompanied the generals. The holidays of the stockbrokers lasted till the fixed deposits of the generals matured. Despite their expertise in investments, the stockbrokers did not know swimming, and therefore spent their evenings entertaining the generals by snapping up fish from the river, with their teeth, like kingfishers. Thus the bathing sports of the Periyar too were not free from the odour of fixed deposits,

Thilothama cultivated her medicinal herbs in the Periyar Valley Estate behind Guadalajara, where silt deposits from time immemorial had enriched the soil. Gautham Adhikari's colleagues liked the way the terraced farm was designed. But Thottekkatukara was no longer the cradle of an organic civilization. There was a sizable middle class, their rustic innocence violated by neo-literacy, who owned a formidable collection of books. Their huge libraries were the envy of the citizens of North Paravoor. There was even graffiti on the walls. Free sex was not in vogue.

Was there anything enduring behind the frail facade of the Periyar? Jnana Sambandham, who crossed the Marthandom bridge in his parcel service truck, inquired in a gesture of fraternity. The manager of the General Insurance Branch gave him a fitting reply—See you, Jnana Sambandham—bade farewell to him and drove off. Where are the ships loaded with spices bound for, the pedestrians wondered. To the fathomless oceans, perhaps. And the parcel service trucks? To the Supreme Truth with their burdened hearts. The clerks who worked in public sector undertakings nursed their scars—relics of punitive branding incurred by disobeying orders—sang their mournful ditties and walked north across the bridge. The thin, lubricated condoms they threw away after use piled up on the steps of the bathing spots on the river. The members of the 'Save Periyar Action Group' were scandalised.

There was a time when Guadalajara throbbed with the wild, virile rhythms of love-making. On the clear, calm waters of the Periyar, ships laden with spices moved gently downstream into the ocean. There was no love or intimacy in the entwining bodies, only the trading of sensuality. And the trepidations of sexual assault. Like the ill-tempered son of a plutocrat, Gautham Adhikari abused his partner in bed.

The commercial life of Greater Cochin owed not a little to the glamour of Periyar. When the last of the ships disappeared from view, the sad-eyed retail merchants of Thottekkattu-kara were thrilled at the sight of the employees of commercial banks alighting from a train near Marthandom bridge and pouring into the by-lanes, discussing the exchange rates of dollar and pound sterling in excited voices. They took their refreshments, changed into bathing costumes and went down to the river along the path which ran behind Guadalajara. Their boss, who was no older than them, was having a leisurely bath in this private bathing spot. Thilothama stood dutifully beside her husband. When the generals returning with their catch of fish, crowding the narrow path, came into view, the bank employees forgot all about the rivalry between the public sector and the private sector and dashed towards the waterfall. There they hailed Eternity in ringing voices.

The shepherds regretted that the banks of the Periyar, for all its scenic beauty, lacked security, and the bank employees talked and sang in loud voices to ward off the hordes of sea-lions which infested the river. A bunch of representatives of multi-national drug companies was perplexed by all the group-bathing and fishing. About half a dozen MNC reps confronted the bank employees as they returned up the path in their wet clothes. The rep of Fortune 500 did most of the talking. The drug-peddlers were having their first encounter with such a patently international school of thought outside of medical stores. "Commercial banking to me has a subtle multinational identity," their spokesman muttered. Reproaching his friends in strong terms, he left for Ernakulam.

Thilothama, who had once been described by her husband

as a rich encyclopaedia of sex, did not challenge Gautham Adhikari when he began sleeping in his separate bed. The bedroom had alienated them from each other so much. Gautham Adhikari quickly became intimate with his mysterious sexual fantasies. He found his orgasm in the wild inexorable rhythms of fantasy. Sex with Thilothama was impossible without long foreplay. It disgusted him. In spite of this, there were several nights on which he got up from his bed and curled up in hers like a scared pet dog. When the women in his fantasies walked out on him, Thilothma conscientiously sent him to sleep by engineering non-coital orgasms. The sobs of several unsatiated women rent the air. Even in the pitch darkness, Thilothama sensed the presence of Adhikari's female acquaintances who had been ruthlessly abused in bed.

K. P. Nirmal Kumar, a writer from Ernakulam, often grumbled that Thilothama belonged to the Indo-European group, a branch of the Caucasian race. Nirmal Kumar, who was also a bank employee, alleged that the inhabitants of the city, who were Dravidians, were motivated by racial prejudice in casting aspersions on her married life.

The Citizens: Mr. Nirmal Kumar, as we are aware, Thilothama had been your colleague for some time. Do you mean to say you did not notice any significant hint being dropped during the course of their day-to-day interactions? Or do you mean to say you did?

Nirmal Kumar: Thilothama would have been pained even to learn that listeners were making such conjectures based on the possibility of such allusions being present in their conversation over and above the literal meaning that was intended to be communicated. (In a distressed voice) Thilothama was composed and unruffled even in the middle of a hectic day's work. Only her fingers moved. The Chamber of Commerce learned about her ever-alert mind from her eyes. But her eyes never pried into anything. Thilothama's banking career was a study in aesthetics.

The Citizens: But we fail to understand it. Sacrificing the position of a Grade I Officer for the sake of domestic peace!

Nirmal Kumar: May the sanctity of underclothes and domestic peace never be violated!

The Citizens: If you don't mind, could you tell us whether Thilothama still goes about dressed up.

Nirmal Kumar: It is nearly a year since I last saw her. Make-up suited her, for she was pure-blooded. Even the Portuguese marines who patrol the backwaters of Cochin will testify to the grace that flows from her face when she applies lipstick. When we tucked into our spicy non-vegetarian lunch, Thilothama appeased her hunger with tomato soup.

The Citizens: Purity of blood, besides purity of language!

Nirmal Kumar: Having grown up in cantonments till she completed her plus two, Thilothama does have her limitations with language. She speaks a mixture of the rustic dialects of Chelakkara and Chottanikkara.

The Citizens: (Bursting into tears) May she always up hold our cultural values. We beg your pardon, brother, for we have another question for you. What about Thilothama's sensitivity?

Nirmal Kumar: We, her old colleagues, would like to believe it is as alive as ever. But, as you know, her sterility is a fact, though a testicular biopsy showed the complete absence of sperms in Gautham Adhikari.

Thilothama never showed any interest in the articles her father-in-law, Dr Budhiraja wrote, or in finding out where he got them published. In her eyes, he had the image of a rural patriarch who always spoke in a booming voice. He held sway over the whole Guadalajara, except his son's bedroom. Dr Budhiraja was able to claim his domestic needs unabashedly with no more effort than a little haggling. Thilothama yielded to him at the dining-table and in the presence of poetry on his table in quick succession, which made any emotional attachment impossible. Journalists were free to be at home in Guadalajara. Budhiraja, who reviewed Malayalam poetry and held a Ph.D. from an American university; Gautham Adhikari, a Management graduate who dabbled in Forex transactions; Thilothama who spoke English with a convent accent—it was a rare combustion which reporters who prepared feature articles could not afford to miss.

But Thilothama soon became familiar with another side of Budhiraja's character, which the various facsimile dailies had no inkling of. The old, fleshy body often turned and tossed in bed. His wife had left him long ago. Though everybody knew the reason and her whereabouts, nobody did anything. His daughter-in-law's flowing nighties excited him. He pictured her going into the bathroom after being cheated of her motherhood by spermless ejaculations; saw her walking gently across the lawn to the river in the evenings. The old widower—not yet assaulted by debilitating diabetes—longed to possess her warm body. After hoodwinking the reporters on his sixtieth birthday, with the remark that he was "blessed to be basking in Thilothama's filial affections", he bemoaned his inability to have a look at Thilothama's supine figure on the bed, through the keyhole. "Thilothama, why do you disrupt the paradigms of my loins ruthlessly?" he lamented.

Thilothama ran down the black rocks of Thottekkattu-kara, the pride of the Western Ghats, into the torrent that emptied itself into the Periyar. It was dusk. Her body was splattered with blood. There were tears in her eyes. A Portuguese sailor pulled her up from the water and held her tightly to his trembling body. The hawkers on Marthandom bridge showered their curses on him. Delirious with lust, the sailor Bartholomew clasped Thilothama in a crushing embrace. A group of sea-lions which swam across the ship's wake cried, "Thilothama, no! Don't submit yourself to him!" But Bartholomew, who knew black magic, muttered something under his breath and the sea-lions fled. Gautham Adhikari, dressed impeccably, the letters of credit held high in his hands to avoid wetting, ran towards the river. The biosphere of the steep Thottekkadan hills suddenly exploded. "Thilothama, the essence of all precious stones! Thilothama, you who gathered unto yourself all that is alluring to the senses from everything that lives on earth, to become the embodiment of sensuality! Your prayers have set my spermduct right. The number of sperms and their movement are adequate now. Look! I throw away these letters of credit which promise precious foreign exchange, into the river. Come, we have the house to ourselves. Father will be staying at VJT Hall for some more days. Come!'" Gautham Adhikari beseeched her. But Bartholomew's hands tightened around her waist. Thilothama gazed at the sailor, her eyes reflecting the familiarity of ages. "Bartholomew!" she uttered the name, softly, affectionately. The laboratory technicians who were taking the sperm count pulled Gautham Adhikari ashore and carried him to Guadalajara. The ship disappeared from view.

(Translated by K. M. Sherrif)

THE TWELFTH HOUR
V. P. Sivakumar

That day also he got down from the bus and walked home. Like on all other days, that day also he reflected that he should resume the discontinued badminton games from the next day itself and increase the Provident Fund deposit by ten rupees from the next salary on. He was beginning to get alarmed about all his days ending like this. All his attempts at giving life a slightly different turn by going on an excursion, having an occasional drink and attending a poetry recital were all in vain. He walked towards 'sweet home'. The flame of the day had become extinct in his body. Night approached like a sigh. He did not mistrust the night even though he sensed that something fatal was lurking in it. Even otherwise, what else did he have to repose his faith in?

He reached the front of the house. He stood bewildered, seeing there an unbelievable patch of moonlight. What could it portend? His senses became sharp like that of a keen-witted wild animal. Suddenly, he noticed a neon lamp that had not been there till the previous day, burning on the street-light post. His mind relaxed. It was only a trivial novelty. He opened the gate. Stood still there for a moment to listen to the nursery rhyme his son was singing. He did not like to express his love, not to his son, not to anybody for that matter. It was a song about a Christian called Solomon Grundy. He listened to the song. What a horrible song! Slight and unceremonious like the life of Solomon Grundy, its connotations that oozed like a poisonous effluent seeped down into his mind as a creed, as the tragedy of faith, and purely as a sense of the tragic.

Reunion. "Father!" Son and daughter exclaimed together. They frisked about. His wife went inside and came back with an envelope: "Start immediately". A telegram from his native place. She stood mute, waiting. He sat on the cot. We shall go immediately. He was growing strong inwardly. This was the only gain from his staggering over so many years: the ability to creep through any hardship. He rose and went to the toilet. Washed his hands, legs and face and combed his hair. Then, look at that: he felt like going to the toilet once more. He decided against it. In truth, it was just an apprehension. However, the pain in the lower abdomen also remained a truth. Two truths? That was not right. There Would be only one truth ever. What did the psychologist know? Nevertheless, he went again to the toilet and resolved that it should not be repeated.

He could set out on the journey only after the children were asleep. Or else, they would weep and call him from behind. His fear of their calling from behind was not on account of a faith in astrology. The reverberations of those tender voices would haunt him throughout the journey. A person like him could get out only after herding all human relationships inside the gate and bolting it. The sob heard at the penultimate moment was sufficient to upset the mental balance of one with weak nerves. If they were put to sleep soon enough, he could take the Fast Passenger bus at eight-thirty. The son raised a lot of doubts as usual, snuggling close to him. He did not lose his temper. He did not like to make the children weep when he set out on a journey. He wished to travel seeing their smiling faces as in the latest photographs. The daughter, lying to his left, asked, "Father, will you die?" He made a guttural noise in the affirmative. "Mother, too?" He affirmed again. "Elder brother and I, too?" A lump got stuck in his throat. No, they will not die, he yearned earnestly to believe. But, as often happened, his tongue betrayed him: "You will die." That was cruel. "Only this house will remain then?" The daughter was really smart. She seemed to think about many things. He stroked her hair, and caught a wilted jasmine in his fist . . . A house in the center of an empty compound, in which everything has withered away! A horrendous whiteness of barrenness! The unsatisfied lives of you and me will hover for ever among the crystalline suns that wobble around inside mirages . . . He would usually kiss his son before he slept. Now, he was already asleep. Whenever he thought about his son he would see his old age and death. His son doing funeral obsequies for him with trembling hands. He disengaged his son's hand from him. Those were the hands that would lift him up like a saving grace when he stood alone in the midst of the startling bluish darkness in the netherworld, where thunder claps boomed all around. He kissed his son's eyes. A causeless sob rose inside him. Then he got up without shaking the cot. The neon light that came in through the window hovered in that room like a dream. He whispered: wake up with a smile tomorrow, as a rebirth, full of innocence like a flower . . .

He turned energetic like a leopard-cub, thinking about the busy schedule ahead of him for the rest of the night. Hurried through dinner. Drank a lot of water. And tasted a little of the 'burfi' brought from the family next-door. Packed the bag with necessary things including cigarettes and matches. Took leave and left hurriedly. Stopped under the new neon lamp, to glance at his watch. Eight thirty—Oh! No need to hurry now. Can take any bus and go. He slowed down. Before reaching the bus station, he heard a bus departing.

This was his usual experience. Precisely because of this, he would only walk, even to places two or three miles away. But that day the place he had to reach was far, far away. He had to get into a bus. He leaned lazily against the shutters of a shop. The streets were turning empty. A dog came near, observed him keenly and turned away. Three persons passed on a bicycle. Only a drunkard who had forgotten about the journey home, hung around the bus station lazily, and then fell asleep right there. He considered having a drink before getting into the bus. He would sleep comfortably in the bus. No. If Mother died at that exact moment, it would remain an unhealing wound. The only intoxication derived from the entirety of life was when each calamity was experienced in its whole intensity. He stared at his watch. Ten o'clock. Feeling bold that nobody would notice him, he spread his handkerchief on the floor and sat on it. A bus roared in. He rushed out and signalled it to stop. The conductor regarded him from head to toe and rang a double-bell. He did not feel anger or disappointment. All that time it was the night that resounded in him. Such a journey was something new to him. He was used to travelling only after reserving the ticket in advance. However, he waited now, generously resolving 'come what may.' The Electricity Board employee in khaki uniform arrived on a bicycle, got down briskly, and rushed past after pulling out the fuse, dropping a curtain of darkness.

He opened his eyes wide into the darkness. He felt relieved. The wrinkles on his face straightened out. His mind that had dozed off in the intensity of light, stretched and rose. The relief of that moment touched somewhere upon the delicate wall of the mind. He got up. Placing his foot upon a high stone and craning his neck, he looked to the far end of the road. Hoping to have a cup of tea, he walked, marking the fragment of light seen somewhere far off. The vapours that rose from the molten road, and the chill that descended from above, met in him. When he had walked some distance, he reached a spot where a country orchestra was practicing. They sat motionless like ghosts around a dim light around which winged termites were flying about. He walked in short steps like a circus clown. Then, when the flame of the sound grew thin, his mind was inflamed momentarily by the small breasts of a half-naked woman he saw in a shadow through a roadside window. A long line of women he had looked at with desire, formed in his mind. Finally it ended in a pale face with big eyes. He had forgotten about the bus, when he called out for a tea and waited. The glass of tea landed in front of him with a thud. He tasted it. The tongue was scalded. Once or twice, he blew on the tea to cool it down. He did not drink it.

Suddenly he heard a roar from the road. He rushed ahead with his bag. A bus that was running out of time. Nobody had told him that there was such a bus. He howled at the bus like a mad man. Brakes were slammed on. He jumped in. The bus roared on.

The conductor said it was the very first trip of a service started along a new route from a remote Malabar village to South Travancore. An experimental route. It might become permanent if there were enough passengers. At that time, the bus was only half full. Some of them had already gone to sleep. He sat in a seat near the driver. That way he could get a little warmth from the heat of the engine. The draught of wind was less there. He guessed that the driver was a native of Thiruvalla, listening to the sort of talk he resorted to, putting his head out when he had to apply the brake to avoid a group of cattle meant for slaughter. Buying a ticket and putting the change given by the conductor in his pocket without counting it, he reclined on the seat and looked out.

Imperious night. It had subjugated the mountains and the wide expanse of paddy fields. The road appeared as a bridge of thread. He thought he heard from somewhere the ancient rolling of a drum, as the bus rounded a bend. The bus rumbled forward. He leaned back clutching the bag between his thighs. Light appeared before him now and then, like an unsolicited boon. Whenever people appeared on the road, the driver let out at least one word of abuse. He felt respect towards the driver for his macho, adventurous gestures. The driver turned the steering-wheel lightly, stroking his upturned mustache. Once, he lit a beedi, removing both his hands from the steering-wheel while the bus was running. The bus stopped in front of a Pentecostal convention center. "I am to Thiruvalla, please," a pastor clad like a navy man, jumped into the bus. He smiled looking at everybody in the bus. An ordinary person who had none of the pretensions of a pastor. A simpleton who had come after praying for what he thought best. His mind fluttered. How far away from him was even a prayer! No ... The pastor started singing psalms all alone, from the back seat. Worldly events lead fast to the hour of darkness of the earth and to the end of time! Time was coming to an end! You should not perish with the world! ... A group of college students who were going for a football match opened their eyes from slumber and began to repeat the psalms. In a strange background in which devotion, frivolity and derision mixed together, the vehicle flew forward, piercing the night. The driver also seemed to have been carried away, because the speed of the bus had gone up greatly. He felt immensely happy. He felt then what he had felt when he went up high on a swing, as high as a tree, in childhood. It was the thrill of terror. Although beautiful, it was dangerous, like lightning. Many times during his lifetime, it had peeped through the cracks of his mind, like a naughty child, but never had he experienced it so distinctly and intensely. It burned upwards from his navel. The bus fell into deep pot-holes, bounced up and flew ahead. He prayed: let this feeling not leave me, no matter what I lose. Lives depended on him. Where would they go? The wife is a person who had never demanded attention for herself. She lay upon the earth with pricked-up ears like a sacrificial victim before ghastly life. In whose lap would the sleeping offspring seek refuge the next day? He had begun realising then. While the howling of the wind remained an indistinguishable boom, in the hilarity budding from the excessive speed, he forgot everything, noting the bus rounding a bend. If it swung a foot to the left, it would plummet down a precipice. What else was there but a road, in between sleep and death, two deaths, or a birth and a death? Outside, hills like gigantic statues sleeping on their backs. The pastor was silent. Leaning his head on the shoulders of a child, he slept like a child. All were asleep. Midnight. He cursed his fellow travellers who were sitting and sleeping as if stacked in the belly of a python. Why are you not awake to share this hilarity of mine? He yearned to wake up somebody and shout, "Look". He forgot himself. A mother lying somewhere, nearing her death, entered into him. She dissolved into the universe, as the tragedy of being oppressed in life and rising to immortality after death. The bus shook frighteningly. He was comforted that there was a road below. He felt as if the bus had run over a human being. A primordial laughter exploded in him. With a thrill it spread over his body on which the rose-water of many springtimes had fallen. His impression that he was the tragic hero who falls dead in the very first act left him. He realised that he also had a moment of stupendous satiety.

The visions of the nature he saw were steeped in fantasy. All reasonings of the eye were uprooted by them. Darkness stood away from that midnight alone. The big hills, pointing towards some as yet unravelled saga of the origin of the universe. Where was the light from? He did not understand anything. It might be another world. There was no source for the shadow and the light he saw there. He experienced something beyond the three dimensions . . . No. That is my world, surely my world, only. Only that at times it changes forms like a *yakshi*. Although she may exhibit cruelty in weak moments when she cannot suffer or forgive any longer, she is compassionate, she is all-enduring, who is the earth. It is there, somewhere inside the dark shadows, that my mother, my wife and children are lying asleep . . . He did not realise then the speed with which the bus was racing. His mind was empty. The bus did not appear to be moving. No sounds were heard. The wind had sunk down to the depths of some strange experience. He leaned back and sat still, lest he should move. He beseeched that he might not be set free from this stillness. Life so far had been for this . . . His heart thumped. He opened his eyes as one who had got the gift of sight for the first time. It was at the driver that he looked first. The driver did not blink his eyes. He sat like an iron statue, his eyes protruding. He was not turning the wheel. The bus was racing along. Black blood was oozing out through the corner of his mouth. It wets my feet, he said to himself. The bus was racing along. The driver was dead. With that sight, a prayer wheel turned in his mind. He retrieved his presence of mind. For the first time, he concluded that it was only a beginning. His mind was at the same lofty level. He did not at all see the bus. The prayer wheel turned once more. How many names! How many generations flash and fade in it, he wondered. Nothing stands stable! From somewhere among them, he saw his mother's hands calloused with love, stretched towards him. Excitedly, he also stretched his hands, but they moved away. He waited for them to come near him once more, completing the cycle. He suddenly recognised his son's voice. He pricked up his ears. That call went far down, like the pathetic scream rising from a bus falling into a gorge. He was alone again. No grief. Then he was alone in his world. And a hapless mind that came flying through time and space. He closed his eyes. The final moment. A slight movement somewhere in his mind. More movements, Something woke up there. A sob in a voice like bursting bubbles. Gradually it became a piercing wail. It rose and rushed upwards as the hard voice full of the strength of love. That was a wail for humaneness; the wrath of helplessness: a lone and grave protest that rose against death in a solitary human being. That voice reached his lips. But, without forming into words, it stood startled, seeing the outside world. Tears welled up in his eyes.

Suddenly it happened. With a hideous noise the bus plunged headlong into a canyon. The moment arrived when all the sleeping people startled awake as a single body, opened their eyes towards death and closed them again instantly. Fate simply deceived them without giving them time even for a serious meditation on life. None of those who travelled in that bus survived. That man who had set out on that journey just to have a last glimpse of his mother also died. However, that death was not unforeseen as other deaths. It was very logical. It was a natural death. The moment the bus plunged into the gorge, his dress was smeared with a little faeces and urine like on a corpse lowered from a scaffold. One or two drops of semen that had been ejaculated in a final ecstasy. On each half of the head that had cracked open, vertically rested two halves of a smile as if proclaiming, "Look, here was one who was awaiting death throughout life."

(Translated by A. J. Thomas)

BLUE PENCIL
N. S. Madhavan

The view from Chulliat's office window looked onto a road which that night wore a different look. At ten in the night the traffic was already taking a curtain call. The light of roadside sodium lamps looked more zestful than usual; laced with an unearthly sheen, it reminded Chulliat of his childhood evenings, especially at that yellow hour when shadows lengthened to ten feet.

Chulliat gave up the window to rest his pipe on the table. Though long put out, he had been persisting at it, sucking absently. Its hard tip was lactating the viscously bitter saliva of fever. Whenever history was at a fork Chulliat always felt a fever coming on. On the night of 14 August, 1947, when the Union Jack came down for the last time, it was malaria. Gandhi died with the thin red line in the thermometer touching 103.

"Mullik, I am done for the day. A touch of, ah well, more than a touch of fever," Chulliat spoke into the intercom.

"Then the editorial?" Mullik asked.

"Editorial? I thought it was Viswanathan's job."

"But, today?"

"Viswanathan is fine," Chulliat raised his voice in feverish impatience.

"All of us at the desk were wondering about a front page, signed edit by you."

"God's sake, no. By Viswanathan, at the usual place."

Mullik put the phone down and looked vacantly at the sub-editors seated around his half-moon table. All evening they sat there, like a frieze of a moving trail of refugees with their heads down. Not all of them. Zuhra stuck to the computer on her table.

"I can't believe my ears," Mullik addressed no one in particular. "K. K. Chulliat's got to go home. Fever."

"Today?" Chitra Ramakrishnan asked.

"Yes, today," Mullik said.

"What's the fuss about today? A couple of domes came crashing down in Ayodhya," said Abhijit Sanyal, the oldest hand among the subs, "that's all today is to Chulliat." He checked himself when he heard a sharp pitter-patter over a computer keyboard; Zuhra was punching it like an old typewriter.

"Tortoise," Vijayan said lazily. "Tortoise?" asked Chitra Ramakrishnan, a fresh recruit, yet to be initiated into the newsroom argot.

"Believe me, no one here has seen Chulliat's body. He sticks out his bald head through his cabin door. That's it, like a tortoise," explained Nakul Kelker.

News Editor Mullik picked up the phone: "Viswanathan, the Chief is asking you to go ahead with the edit." Mullik then proceeded to put on Chulliat's Oxford accent: "And yes, no need to get emotional. Mark it with a gentle beat of considered opinion. And, do not write today is the darkest day in Indian history."

Mullik put the phone down and almost immediately Vijayan asked: "What made Tortoise say a thing like that?"

"Tomorrow you will read this line in every paper," Mullik said.

"Must be a rub-off from his Oxford days—Tortoise's ability to preempt a cliche," Nakul said admiringly.

"Shh... Tortoise," Vijayan cautioned when Chulliat showed his head through the door. He and Nakul kept their eyes down, reading patterns in scattered bits of newsprint on the floor. Chitra cupped her mouth to suppress a giggle. Abhijit looked at Chulliat, his eyes cold.

"Mullick, get on with the lead story. I'll see it before I go," said Chulliat and quickly withdrew his head. He homed straight on to his window. A couple of army trucks passed by, followed by a police jeep with an angry Shiva's third eye on its forehead. The road was emptying when a fire tender rushed past, its bells tolling in frenzy.

Chulliat breathed into his palm in an effort to measure his fever. He walked over to the bathroom and took out a couple of tablets from the cupboard. Standing near the pot to urinate, he could not help leaning against the wall; all of his seventy years chose to visit him in these vulnerable moments.

On his way back to the window Chulliat paused before the

computer. Alphabets were streaming in trickles. The cursor twinkled its green light, like an amorous firefly's bottom. He looked back as he felt another presence in the room. An office boy was stalking back after carefully placing the lead story's printout on the table. Chulliat went through it quickly.

"Get the car please, I am leaving," he spoke to his secretary through the intercom.

"Chulliat has flown," Mullik informed the sub-editors around his table.

"Anyone for tea?" Abhijit Sanyal asked. Vijayan, Nakul and Chitra got up immediately. Chitra went over to Zuhra and patted her shoulder: "Coming for a cup of tea?" Zuhra surprised them into silence by getting up. Suddenly finding himself alone, Mullik panicked. He hurried to the sports desk.

Abhijit and the others felt the layers of cold air thickening as they went down the stairs to the basement canteen. Tea stains and pockmarks left by stubbed-out cigarettes lay scattered over its grey cement floor; some stale samosas were pitifully stacked in the glass case. Four of them sat on the chairs around a portable steel table; Chitra drew in a chair and sat next to Zuhra. Abhijit knocked on the table with the pepper pot and soon Phool Chand came in.

"Phool Chand, five cups of tea, quickly," Abhijit said.

"No help today, sir, everyone has gone home to stock up on things."

"Why?" Chitra asked.

"If and when there is a curfew, it hits us the hardest."

"Then why didn't you go?" asked Chitra again.

"I borrowed some money and asked Mewaram of the Cash Section to get my stuff — twenty kilos of wheat flour and half a bag of potatoes. Where will you go for tea if I shut down? The roadside stalls are all closed."

Phool Chand went back to the kitchen. Soon the buzz of the paraffin stove pervaded the canteen. Abhijit ran his fingers nervously through his greying curly hair. He stared at Zuhra and asked: "Why are you so quiet today?" Zuhra raised her head and looked at Abhijit with uncompromising fierceness. Vijayan conjured up a smile and said: "When Phool Chand and his friends were scurrying about to buy groceries, know what Abhijit was up to? He scooted off to buy three bottles of rum. Suppose the shops are closed tomorrow?"

Chitra smiled charitably, Abhijit held the pepper pot in his hand and played with it. Then he spoke: "I am a midnight child. Like Rushdie, I was born in 1947 in Calcutta. A Nehruvian childhood, you know, not much religion, but plenty of reason. I got from my mother love for Rabeendra Sangeet. But some time in the sixties, Tagore gave way to the Beatles."

"The Beatles? Abhijit, you must be ancient," Chitra said. "For my generation, the Beatles is classical music."

"Chitra, before you were born, in Vietnam there was someone who answered to the name of Ho Chi Minh. Sartre held fort at Sorbonne. So did Tariq Ali in London. Here, in Bengal we had Charu Majumdar, Kanu Sanyal and Jangal Santhal. When I first met Charu Majumdar he was lying on a string bed, struggling to breathe from an oxygen cylinder. From there he baptised me. I was studying in IIT, at Kharagpur, near the forests of Bihar. So I didn't have to go far to ferret out class struggle. Oh yes, with the customary sling-bag over my shoulder. A season, a terrible season, of retaliation followed. Many disappeared. Those who surfaced feigned not to recognise you. Madness claimed some. I kept suicide and madness at bay with a bit of self-deception and er, an occasional drink did help. It all ended when I caught the Kalka Mail to leave Calcutta for Delhi."

"My childhood was less intricate," Nakul said, "in Bombay's Shivaji Park, we wanted to grow up to be Gavaskar."

All eyes were trained on Vijayan. He hung his head and said: "I have nothing to say. Remember those people who shut themselves up in an inn against the plague? Should we also tell stories like them—the Decameron tales?"

Chulliat lowered the car's window by a crack. At first he felt refreshed by the rush of cold wind; but soon he began to feel dizzy with the vicissitudes in temperature. He tapped the driver's shoulder: "Bahadur, you know Dr Iqbal's house? Take me there, I am not feeling good."

Iqbal always brought back to him the memories of the day Masood, Iqbal's father and Chulliat's friend from England days, first took him to meet his first-born. Chulliat found an embarrassed little boy lying under a small white tent; freshly circumcised.

Iqbal's house was dark from the outside. When Farah heard Chulliat opening the cast-iron gate, she came out and put on the portico light.

"Iqbal at home, dear?"

Farah went in without a word. Soon Iqbal came out in a light blue salwar suit—a true Pathan, in his father's mould.

"Iqbal, I feel feverish."

The thermometer, as usual, tasted of metal. Chulliat felt tired, deep inside his bones, when Iqbal relentlessly pumped air into the BP apparatus strapped around his arm. Iqbal went inside and came back with a syringe. At the moment the needle pierced, Chulliat could not help shutting his eyes.

"By tomorrow you'll be all right," said Iqbal. Then Farah and Iqbal relapsed into what Chulliat feared would be an eternal silence. He got up to leave.

"Thanks, Uncle," Farah said.

"For what?"

"You were our only Hindu friend who did not mention what happened today. We got a lot of calls. Some people even dropped in. Like death visits."

Chulliat turned around and looked into their eyes: "Children, when did I become a Hindu to you?"

The car was stuttering in wintry reluctance. Iqbal opened its door. Chulliat got in and hurriedly waved at the couple. "Bahadur," Chulliat told the driver, "back to the office."

The news room, shaken out of sleepiness, was getting ready for the final burst before bringing out the next day's edition. Mullik made several trips down to the press. The sub-editors, except for Zuhra, stood before the telex and fax machines, soaking in the last bits of news.

"Viswanathan did not pack much punch in his edit," Vijayan remarked.

"Tortoise wanted it this way. Remember, the gentle beat of considered opinion," Abhijit said.

"Tortoise must be sleeping by now," Chitra said.

"Mullik," suddenly Chulliat's voice boomed in the news room. Chitra could not believe her eyes that this pipe-smoking old man in a dark coloured suit, rapidly striding across the news room, was Chulliat himself. The first sight of the Chief Editor in the news room brought the sports editor and financial correspondent to their feet. The bleary-eyed cartoonist finally gave up his day's efforts to draw a congruous cartoon and ambled to Mullik's table, making his way through the crumpled balls of India-ink stained paper. Mullik gazed at Chulliat zooming in on his table. Zuhra did not move from her place. Downstairs, the machines of the press rumbled like the north-eastern monsoon over distant hills.

"Mullik, who did the headline for the lead story?" Chulliat put the printout he was holding on Mullik's table. Slowly, the subs started moving towards Mullik's table, but Zuhra remained where she was.

"Mullik, I am speaking to you. Who wrote the headline? If you choose to remain silent, I wish to tell you that he can quit this paper from now." Chulliat's lips betrayed an angry quiver. By then, all the employees in the news room, including Zuhra, were crowding around Mullik's table.

"Sir, I did," Zuhra said softly.

Chulliat drew deeply on his pipe. He gestured to Vijayan to pick up the printout from the table. Chulliat then walked to Zuhra and patted her on her head: "Dear, fetch me a pencil."

Mullik handed over a ball-point from the table. Chulliat addressed all of them: "When I started my career at the *Manchester Guardian*, my old Welsh editor used to say that blue pencils are an editor's weapons. Blue pencils are now extinct, but that shouldn't stop me from using this pen."

Chulliat leaned over the printout on the table and with the pen gripped like a chisel in his shaking hands, scored off the first two words of Zuhra's caption : 'Disputed structure destroyed.' Above these words he wrote in bold, each alphabet painfully undulating with tremors of Parkinsonism: 'Babri Masjid'.

Tears trickled down from Zuhra's large eyes, like sap from a freshly wounded tree. She looked at Chulliat and said: "Thank you, sir."

Chulliat walked back, bowing down to another lunar pull of fever. No one stirred in the news room till he went into his office and the door closed shut behind him.

(Translated by the author)

WE, THE SONS
C. V. Balakrishnan

We sat in the waiting-room awaiting our father's arrival.

As we had learned that the train was seventy minutes late, we could have taken a round of the city, eating ice-creams, glancing at cinema posters and observing the movement of the hands of the large tower-clock which kept time for the city. But we chose to remain glued to our seats in the waiting-room. *Chettan*'s[1] face was pale, I noticed. Perhaps my face was pale too!

Most of the occupants of the waiting-room were sleeping. Others were reading, gazing idly in front of them, or talking in low voices. The platform was bustling with commuters. Some of them peeped into the waiting-room, but seeing the seats occupied, withdrew immediately.

After some time *Chettan* said in a grumbling voice:

"I don't think *Achan*[2] will go back again."

Startled, I withdrew my gaze from the platform and stared at him. But strangely, from the expression on his face, it seemed *Chettan* had not uttered a word.

"What did you say?" I asked him, bewildered.

"Nothing," *Chettan* said without looking at me.

"But I heard you say something."

Chettan said nothing—as if he had not heard my question. But my perplexity deepened. I had distinctly heard him say that *Achan* would not go back again.

Or had I imagined it? Anyway, *Achan* was certainly not going back this time. Usually *Achan* went back when his leave was over. We spent our days in terror till he left. We couldn't step out of the house without his permission. We were wrenched from our friends, the river, the whistling bamboo bush, the tree, the

---

[1] *Chettan* - Elder brother
[2] *Achan* - Father

birds, the hills and the sky. All our laughing and bantering at home died away. We were encapsuled in our silence. Only *Achan's* voice was heard in the house. Everything was done as he wished them to be. In the morning, we were torn from our sleep by his terrifying voice. "What! Not up yet!" At night, when it was still not very late, *Achan* would say, "That is enough reading for today. Go to bed."

Suddenly throwing me into confusion, *Chettan* muttered again:

"Wait till he comes. Wait till *Achan* comes."

When I looked at his face, a nameless terror struck me.

Was it time for the train? Was it time for *Achan's* arrival? Would *Achan* come in the train?

The train was late by more than seventy minutes. By the time it arrived, the rush on the platform was unusually heavy. As the arrival of the train was announced over the loudspeakers, the occupants of the waiting-room rushed out. The sleepers woke up with a start. *Chettan* held my hand as we walked out into the platform.

As we reached the door, I couldn't help exclaiming, "Oh, God! What a crowd! How shall we ever find *Achan*?"

"Let us wait at the exit. That is the only way we can catch sight of him."

I nodded. We held hands and made our way through the crowd. There was a clamour of voices and noises from the platform. A man coming from the opposite direction ploughed through us, pushing us roughly to either side, and hurried away down the platform. We held hands again—more tightly this time—and walked towards the exit.

We heard the sound of the train in the distance. We tightened our grip on each other and increased our pace. We reached the exit where two ticket examiners stood waiting. We were sure we would be able to see *Achan* from where we stood.

At last the train arrived. We swept our eyes over the doors of the compartments to pick out *Achan* from the group of passengers getting ready to alight. The train ground to a halt. The passengers got down on the platform from the compartments. The commuters on the platform were jostling each other as they moved towards the doors. The porters were shouting. My heart thumped in fear.

Suddenly we saw *Achan* quite near us. *Chettan* saw him first.

Pressing my hand he said, "Look, there is *Achan*!" A porter with a large suitcase and a mattress balanced on his head was following *Achan*. We made our way through the crowd towards *Achan*. It was not the rush, but fear and a sense of doom that suffocated us. Though we called him loudly, *Achan* didn't hear us. As we reached him, wriggling through the crowd, *Achan* said gruffly:

"I thought you hadn't turned up. What were you doing all the time?"

Not daring to reply, we looked down meekly. Achan had two suitcases in his hands. He gave one to *Chettan* and one to me.

When *Achan* went to get a taxi, I whispered to *Chettan*, "He looks a bit run down, doesn't he?"

"You are just imagining it. He looks all right to me."

In the taxi, *Achan* sat in the front seat with the driver. Chettan and I sat in the back seat and gazed at the people and buildings on either side of the road which rushed past us. *Achan* spoke about various subjects with a mixture of annoyance and contempt. Soon we left the city behind us. I fell sleep. *Chettan* was still gazing out of the window. Suddenly *Achan* laughed loudly. I woke up with a start. *Chettan* looked sympathetically at me and smiled. I closed my eyes again. The cold wind, coming in through the windows, cut into my face.

I woke up when Chettan shook me. The taxi had come to a halt at the head of the narrow lane which led to our house. Lakshmi, who carried loads on her head, came running.

"I have been waiting for a long time," she said. "Thought I would have a chew of betel."

Achan placed the large trunk and the mattress on Lakshmi's head. *Chettan* and I took a suitcase each.

"Come," *Achan* said.

The suitcase was too heavy for me to hold. I shifted it to my left hand before I had walked a dozen steps.

Amma was standing under the large poovarasu tree, holding Kuttan at her waist. Radhika, Gopika and Sarika were standing beside her. Though they saw us, none of them moved.

"Is it too heavy, son?" Amma asked me.

"No," I said.

There was no need for *Chettan* and me to go to the railway

station, I thought. We could as well have waited on the road, at the head of the lane with Lakshmi. After all . . .

But I knew that I was not entitled to say a word. Everything was to be as *Achan* wished. There was nothing for us to do except carry out his wishes. When it was time for his evening walk, *Achan* would call *Chettan* and me. We had to dress immediately and go out with him. We followed him like two loyal servants. We remained silent all the way. But *Achan* never stopped talking. The essence of what he said was that we should strive, like him, to achieve success in life. We would listen attentively as he described how he had come up in life, fighting against odds. As *Achan* spoke, *Chettan* and I frequently looked at each other with frightened expressions. We followed him through the clusters of trees and overgrown grass.

The vacation ended in no time. I had to go back to my boarding school.

"Now I will be all alone," *Chettan* said sadly.

I didn't know how to console him. I suppressed a sob.

"But you'll be going to college, won't you?"

Chettan sighed. "But I have to come back home everyday."

"You had to be a day scholar because there was nobody else to look after everything in the house. Now *Achan* is here. Why don't you stay in the hostel?"

"I don't think *Achan* will let me stay in the hostel."

"Let us speak to Amma about it."

"That will make no difference." *Chettan* had no hopes about it.

He was right. *Achan* told *Chettan* categorically that he would remain a day scholar as he had been for the last three years. Gathering up courage, *Chettan* started saying something about wasting four hours each day travelling to the college and back. Achan jumped up from his seat angrily. His eyes were red and swollen. Perhaps he was drunk. Finally *Chettan* slunk away to his bedroom, nursing a smarting cheek. I followed him like a shadow. *Chettan* sat in a corner and moped.

I was at a loss for words to comfort him. I heard *Achan* speaking angrily to Amma. Some time later I heard soft steps behind me. Amma.

I went back to school on the last day of the vacation. *Chettan* stood on the road watching the bus drive away. I turned back to look at him. There was a drizzle. *Chettan* had no umbrella with him. He waved at me through the rain. I felt tears welling up in my eyes. I put out my hand through the window to wave back. When I withdrew my hand, there were raindrops all over it. I closed my eyes and leaned back on the seat. The rain thickened like sorrow.

I was among my classmates again. The dormitory, the skylight, the trees with bright red flowers and dark green leaves. The vast, grassy playground. The lab. The classroom at the end of the long corridor on the first floor. I followed Gomez, the peon, down the flight of stairs. Gomez did not know who was waiting for me below in the Headmistress's cabin. He only knew the visitor had come from home.

It was Achuthan Nair, our neighbour.

"Come with me, child. Your mother is ill."

When I reached home, Amma's pyre was burning itself out.

I asked the walls of my house, "Tell me, where is Amma?" The walls said nothing. I went into Amma's bedroom. The air was heavy with the smoke of incense sticks. I saw *Chettan* standing near the window. Sarika was sleeping on the floor. Kuttan sat in Radhika's lap. Gopika was staring vacantly at the wall.

Glancing at me *Chettan* said, "Amma has left us forever."

When I asked him where she had gone, Chettan looked at me helplessly and said, "I don't know."

I stood numb. I could see the smouldering pyre through the window. When I went to sleep, I saw Amma coming into the room, flames darting from her body. I woke up with a scream. *Chettan* asked me what had happened. I looked at the door and sobbed. The smell of mother's milk filled the room. I was trembling. *Chettan* drew me to him. I snuggled up to him.

Chettan said slowly, "*Achan* killed Amma. " I stared at him terrified. *Chettan's* tears fell on my cheeks.

"*Achan* never loved her, never spoke a word of comfort to her . . . I will confront *Achan* with it . . . some day."

"I think the two of us will have to settle scores . . ."

Suddenly we felt a strange presence in the room. We held our breath, startled. There was a sob, and a trembling voice said: "No, sons! . . . No!"

(Translated by K. M. Sherrif)

THE POSTMAN OF KALLERI
V. R. Sudheesh

Sivan Kutty, the postman, had to cross three rivers and two hills to reach Kalleri. Bounded by rivers in the north and the west, and by hills on the other sides, Kalleri lay sprawling like a crescent-moon—the late poet, beloved of the villagers, who was killed in a landslide, had immortalised Kalleri with this description. In the middle of the village *maidan* stood a *krishna* tree which bloomed in summer. When Sivan Kutty reached the village, the noon-sun would be blazing. Like the flowers on the tree, Sivan Kutty came only in summer with his bag of letters to convey love, regrets, fond prattlings, silly banter, and, of course, news. After delivering the letters Sivan Kutty also collected the letters dropped into the only post box in the village. When the sky started rumbling in the month of *Karkatakam*, Sivan Kutty's visits would cease. Only when the rain clouds departed and Kalleri donned its fresh sunshine would he come again. By then, the monsoon, which would have drowned the village in a spate of disasters, would also have turned Sivan Kutty into a distant memory. But the villagers' longing for Sivan Kutty's arrival, their frustration at having to wait so long for the next letter and the next summer, was nothing compared to the tribulations Saumini went through as she waited under the *ami* tree behind the mud-wall, her eyes fixed on the path which led to the *maidan*. When Sivan Kutty's umbrella, which had turned grey from years of exposure to the sun, appeared on top of the hill, Saumini's heart would be the first to leap up. Sivan Kutty, whom the villagers welcomed like an angel, was the prince of Saumini's dreams. After distributing the letters, Sivan Kutty would drink a glass of *nannari sherbeth*, to be followed by a lunch of rice and *kadali* plantains. He took his siesta under the banyan tree, and, when the cluster of evening-shadows criss-crossed the village, walked away and disappeared over the hills. All the while, Saumini, who stood rooted to the ground under the *ami* tree, did not take her eyes off him for a moment. Sometimes Sivan Kutty did throw her a tender glance which watered her sprouting desire.

Saumini was never found among the crowd which gathered under the *krishna* tree to receive letters from Sivan Kutty. She knew well there was nobody to send her letters. If only she had a letter coming to her, it would have given her a chance to speak to Sivan Kutty. Could Sivan Kutty read her mind as she stood behind the mud-wall under the *ami* tree and gazed at him fondly? As Saumini continued to wait under the *ami* tree for Sivan Kutty in the days that followed, hoping he would speak to her one day at last, the monsoon came with a rumble. The roaring rains chipped away the hillsides and the floods came sweeping down with a vengeance, licking up everything with its thousand tongues, in its ravaging spree. Disaster after disaster plunged the villagers into grief. Saumini, the few villagers who expected letters, and the summer sun which had gone into hiding, pined for Sivan Kutty.

On the three days a week on which Sivan Kutty arrived in Kalleri like a star of fortune, it was Major(retd.) Govinda Kurup who treated him to a glass of *nannari sherbeth* and a sumptuous lunch, complete with curry and fish with *kadali* plantains for dessert. Govinda Kurup's son was in the army. Kurup would get letters from him on all the three days. But Govinda Kurup would have given Sivan Kutty his *sherbeth* and lunch even if there were no letters for him. When the young sun donned its fresh, serene apparel and walked across the pathways of the village which had been laid waste by the demonaic dance of the *Thiruvathira nhattuvela*, a new luminiscence shone bright in the dark recesses of Govinda Kurup's mind. Now he would start getting his son's letters again! As Sivan Kutty reached the village, crossing rivers and hills, it was Saumini, as usual, who first spotted him. She suddenly had a strange wish. What if she could turn into a megaphone! The thought of announcing Sivan Kutty's arrival to the village with her voice, amplified a thousand times, thrilled her. Sivan Kutty walked in gently into the ken of the scores of weary-eyed villagers who had assembled under the *krishna* tree. He had put on weight. The long hair had been cut short and the sideburns had been broadened like a carpenter's chisels. Quite a dandy, Saumini thought as her eyes swept Sivan Kutty from head to foot.

There were a few new faces in the crowd under the tree. One of them was Kadeesumma, who was eager to hear from her daughter who had gone abroad after marriage. Another was Sreedharan Nambiar who wanted to know how his son, studying medicine in London, was doing.

Sivan Kutty had to disappoint everyone except Govinda Kurup and Kadeesumma. They too had no letters, only a telegram each. Slipping out of the circle of curious onlookers who wanted to know the contents of the telegram she had got, Kadeesumma pushed the telegram into Sivan Kutty's hands.

"Read it for me, son."

Meanwhile, Major Govinda Kurup had collapsed with a scream. Sivan Kutty ran his eyes over the message typed on the small sheet of blue paper. Appukkuttan was killed on the battlefield. Kadeesumma stared at Sivan Kutty in alarm.

"Son, read mine." There was a catch in Kadeesumma's voice.

Sivan Kutty shut his eyes tightly and stood paralysed for several moments. He was reluctant to announce yet another tragedy to the village. But when Kadeesumma insisted, he had to reveal it with trembling lips.

Amina was dead. Raped and murdered. Someone in the crowd caught Kadeesumma as she collapsed fainting. Not tarrying another moment, Sivan Kutty turned and walked away. For the first time since he began coming to Kalleri as a postman, Sivan Kutty returned with an agitated mind and an empty stomach. Saumini was still standing under the *ami* tree watching Sivan Kutty receding into the distance. It was only later the news of the tragedy reached her.

Soon, stars in mourning appeared in the sky over Kalleri to console two grief-stricken homes. In the yards of homes lit up by a weeping moon, cries of grief ebbed away as the night passed.

It would be Saturday, Saumini reckoned, when Sivan Kutty would come next. Before the sun spread its noon-veil over Kalleri, the crowd of villagers had assembled in the *maidan*. Major Govinda Kurup was not among them. Nor Kadeesumma. They had no need to wait for Sivan Kutty any more. Saudi Mohammed joined the crowd, grinning from ear to ear as he loudly announced his decision to treat Sivan Kutty to a glass of *sherbeth* and lunch henceforth, on all the days he came to Kalleri. Sivan Kutty brought letters and demand drafts from his son, Niyaz, who worked in Saudi Arabia. As soon as Sivan Kutty arrived, Mohammed shook his hand profusely and said:

"I will give you lunch from today whenever you come."

Sivan Kutty did not respond to this sudden burst of hospitality. He had brought only a single postal article today—a telegram for Saudi Mohammed. Niyaz was executed by decapitation in Saudi Arabia. Without a word, Sivan Kutty put the telegram into Mohammed's pocket, turned and walked away. He gave a pitiful glance to Saumini who was still gazing at him from under the *ami* tree. Saumini smiled. Sivan Kutty wanted to return the smile. But, afraid of his smile making a grotesque caricature of his face, he quickly averted his eyes, ascended the hill and disappeared from view.

At dusk, when Saumini sat in the veranda, she was tormented by distressing thoughts. Sivan Kutty, whom she had been worshipping secretly all these days, had on the last two visits turned into a messenger of death. How she longed for the sight of Sivan Kutty calling out the names one by one, distributing the letters, and taking his siesta under the tree after lunch. Sivan Kutty's way of smoking cigarettes amused her. He always blew out the smoke in rings. As she gazed at his retreating figure disappearing over the hill, she had often asked herself: when will he ever give me a letter? When will he ever utter a word to me?

Saumini lay awake the whole night with disquieting thoughts.

She prayed fervently for Sivan Kutty to bring glad tidings for the village on his next visit. But Saumini's hopes were shattered. On the following Saturday, Sivan Kutty did not bring demand drafts or money-orders or letters wishing the best of health and cheer to the addresses. Sivan Kutty did not even look at Saumini as she stood under the *ami* tree waiting. There was no bag on his shoulders. He walked up quietly, his arms swinging freely. He called only one name—Sreedharan Nambiar's. It was a telegram. The sight of the telegram was enough to send the whole crowd into panic. Ignoring their reaction, Sivan Kutty handed the telegram to Sreedharan Nambiar and walked away. The whole village was aghast when Sreedharan Nambiar let out a scream, pummelled his chest and ran home madly.

When the pyre of tears had burned itself out, one of the mourners who had gathered in Nambiar's yard whispered:

It was gas-poisoning.

Saumini was terrified as the visage of the village, which had always been cheerful and eagerly expectant on the days of Sivan Kutty's visit, now looked dark and foreboding. Sivan Kutty, the angel, had metamorphosised into Kalan, the god of Death. Locking up her affections for Sivan Kutty—which were as deep as the sea and as vast as the sky—in her heart, Saumini awaited Sivan Kutty's next visit.

There were only a handful of villagers in the *maidan* that day. They were the only ones who felt any need to wait for Sivan Kutty. Kesavan Vaidyar, who expected to hear from his son who had gone to Allahabad to attend an interview of the Service Selection Board, ran towards Sivan Kutty as soon as he saw him. Close on his heels was Anwar, who was a clerk in the Grameen Bank. He was awaiting a letter from his wife, Nadira, who lived in a distant village. Both received telegrams. Kesavan Vaidyar's telegram said:

Dileep killed communal riots.

The second message read:

Nadira child dead reason unknown.

Once again laments rose from the *maidan*. Saumini felt a scream shattering her throat. Sivan Kutty walked away without a word. Suddenly Saumini had a revelation. An inexplicable strength moved her. She ran after Sivan Kutty and caught up with him as he began ascending the hill.

"Postman," she called.

The sweet, melodious voice halted Sivan Kutty in his tracks. He turned and recognised the girl he always saw standing under the *ami* tree. It was the first time he had seen her so near. The words stuck in Saumini's throat. She trembled. Somehow, with a sob, she managed to say:

"Postman, please bring us some good news the next time."

Sivan Kutty was petrified. But Saumini was walking away without waiting for his reply. In the *maidan*, somebody was carrying away Anwar, who had fainted. There was no sign of Kesavan Vaidyar. When Saumini turned back to look, she found Sivan Kutty too turning back to look from the top of the hill before disappearing from view.

Saumini became a large teardrop in the river of tears that now flowed through the village, But she was still hopeful. She was certain that Sivan Kutty would, for once, bring letters which contained only small talk, and intimations of joy and hope, on his next visit. She could see Anwar's house in the distance, looking like a tombstone wet with dew.

After two days on which an eerie silence reigned in the village, it was time for Saumini to resume her wait under the *ami* tree. Her eyes were fixed on the summit of the hill, on which the summer sun was pouring its wrath, to pick out the grey umbrella when it appeared. The *maidan* was empty. Did it mean nobody expected to get letters any more? Had all the hopes and longings in the villagers' hearts died out? Saumini could not believe it.

Saddened by Saumini's fruitless wait, perhaps, the sun seemed to move faster away across the sky. When the evening shadows lengthened, there was still no sign of Sivan Kutty.

Finally the sun vanished behind the hill, sending Saumini into a fit of despair. But a faint hope stirred in her. There was the next day to look forward to. Saumini detested the minutes and hours which seemed to take her to the next day at a grovelling pace. Nobody came to the *krishna* tree till noon from the village. But the grey umbrella appeared promptly on the hill. Saumini's pulses quickened as she saw Sivan Kutty descending the hill. Saumini was frightened that Sivan Kutty, who had rolled up his trousers and was walking with a swagger, would turn back on seeing the *maidan* empty. The first thing Saumini did as soon as Sivan Kutty was near enough, was to ascertain whether he had the bag of letters in his hand. She saw with a start that he didn't.

Sivan Kutty stopped under the *krishna* tree and lit a cigarette. He was waiting. He had at least one message to be delivered. Suddenly Saumini saw a crowd of villagers advancing towards Sivan Kutty. She recognised Mangattu Parambil Sekharan Kutty. She could not make out what Sivan Kutty had handed to him—a telegram or a letter. Two women, one old and the other young, also received something from Sivan Kutty. Suddenly a chorus of wails rose from the *maidan*. Saumini felt dizzy. She leaned wearily against the trunk of the *ami* tree and shut her eyes tightly. A tumult, rising towards its crescendo, made her open her eyes. The whole village had emptied itself into the *maidan*. Sivan Kutty was running as fast as his legs could carry him. A hail of stones followed him. The villagers armed with sticks and chopping knives were gaining on him. Some of them stooped to pick up splinters of granite to hurl at Sivan Kutty. As he stumbled and fell, shielding his bleeding head with his hands, as the sticks rose in the air and descended on him, a scream which rose like the surge of the sea was stifled in Saumini's throat.

(Translated by K. M. Sherrif)

A PATH IN THE MOONSHINE

N. Prabhakaran

Moonlit nights are surely a reality even in these times. Scattering spangles of intoxication among the wakeful beings; some human beings filling themselves with it like the fabulous Chinese jars . . . No. In my case, nothing of the sort happened. I was in conversation with a friend, full of levity and with the equanimity of an ordinary human being. The place must have been the portico of his house.

This friend with a moon face and a handsome body was a TV repairer. Except for a clandestine infatuation with music, the other surgings of the soul were alien to him. Literature, the graphic arts, politics, etc., would never peep into his thinking. Though knowing full well that straight paths are seldom found in this world, he was never worried about it. He lived as though there was no one to spread thorns in his path. The flow of this faith enveloped all his actions like the morning sun. "A man full of grace," I used to call him inwardly.

It was an exceptionally moonlit night. Although out of context, I tend to remember something. It was not many days since I was elected to the District Council. I had just managed to scrape through with a margin of sixteen votes in a stiff contest. I was relieved, and he was jubilant that I won. We talked for a long time about many ordinary and trivial matters. All that time his sister was sitting next to us in a cane chair, reading a book of fiction.

My friend and I are aged around thirty-five. His sister is past thirty. She is the wife of a bank employee and the mother of two children. However, it was as a young girl in a light-coloured top garment and a white miniskirt with small saffron flowers printed on it, that I saw her now beside us. Her countenance, though grave, was serene and pretty. Once upon a time I had loved this girl furtively and had somehow managed to utter one or two words smacking of this love.

When the conversation between my friend and me reached a juncture where it remained sluggish, she stopped reading, stood up and started singing an ancient Chinese song in a most dulcet voice. That song was filled with the heartaches of a young woman called Linging who had loved a hunter named Wangchou, without his knowledge. When the song was over I stood up and congratulated her very formally. Then I told my friend and her together, "I am going now. See you two months later."

"Two months! It is good that one can forget a politician at least for two months a year," she said. I should have been pained. But it did not happen that way. I laughed aloud as if I had heard a joke. Then I got out and walked away.

I was to pass through an alley that was clean and tidy. High ranking officials and rich merchants resided on either side. While walking, I happened to think for a moment about that song. None of us knew the Chinese language. Then how could she sing that song? How did I grasp its meaning? How could I visualise, with the mind's eye, an orchard of the Fukian region while I was listening to that song? It is all so very strange. I can say for sure that I am not dreaming at all. It is not likely that such a logical strain can be there while dreaming.

I stood still for a moment with a firm resolve to get my doubts cleared. It was in a strange tremulousness of the soul that I moved forward after that. Walking some distance and turning a corner, I found that the path had become very narrow. The wall on the left had been pushed forward a little. It was only two or three days since the wall had been rebuilt. The cold smell of cement and mortar was still in the air. The plot beyond that wall belonged to Koneri Damu. It was Damu who had steered my election campaign. I had heard many things whispered against Damu who was a land broker. I was not at all interested in getting him as my Election Committee Chairman. But the party had decided it that way. Or it was thus that Damu made the party decide.

Someone would complain to me about the encroachment of the public pathway one of these days. It is certain that I would necessarily have to have a confrontation with Damu. If presented in a straightforward manner, Damu will scoff at the matter. Subtle manoeuvres should be set in motion. Similar incidents will occur again if he is not subdued in time. Damu, who was a nobody in the party and public life, had grown to be a power centre in front of one's very eyes. Many are approaching him for favours. A group of acolytes has formed around Damu. Student activists, youth leaders, and even leaders of teachers' organisations are busy imitating him. Grooming their hair Damu style, laughing like him, hawking and spitting noisily like him ... From now on, things cannot be allowed to go on this way. In my capacity as a Councillor, I can also do certain things. I can also look forward to the support of the idealists in the party.

Ruminating on many things in this strain and turning many corners I arrived in front of Kuppuswamy's ashram. This ashram is one of the cornerstones of civic life in my Division. It is rumoured that while Kuppuswamy was still alive, several shady incidents including prostitution and murder had taken place in this ashram. Now the head of this ashram is Yoginiamma who was one of Kuppuswamy's old handmaids. She may have a name of her own. But everyone calls her "Yoginiamma".

I had gone to the ashram to meet this woman along with Damu. I had wished to avoid such an audience with her. Damu had not budged. "You ask me whether you should meet her? Any doubts about that? There are three hundred and twenty-seven votes in that woman's hand. That is not a trifle as far as this Division is concerned. If you go and bow your head once before her, she will bless you. Just now they have a notion that we will win. The ashram's politics is to stand firm with the winners. If we do not meet them, they will act in a vengeful manner."

I do not know whether Yoginiamma helped us or not. Anyhow, she had treated us with great affection when we visited her. When that woman, clad in a saffron sari and reclining in an easy chair, had raised her withered hand above my head in benediction, I had felt a sensation of fear for some reason.

But now she is clad in gold-bordered long cloth and upper cloth and is strolling among the flowering plants in the garden in the courtyard of the ashram, with the sprightliness of a *Thiruvathira* dancer. The middle-aged man who is walking behind her, chewing something like a bun, is the ashram cook. That long-limbed man has now turned into a dwarf with a very long tail. I burst out laughing, noticing the tail trailing behind on the ground.

When I moved two or three steps forward after passing the

main gate of the ashram, another wondrous thing caught my eye. The wall of the ashram had grown across the path, and had touched the wall opposite, blocking the alley. "It is sheer roguery; I am not going to allow this at any rate," I must have said to myself. My body must have quivered all over and I must have gnashed my teeth and the blood must have rushed to my eyes. When I lifted my head suddenly and looked up, it was Piandre I saw sitting on the wall, wearing a sports blazer and cowboy hat and smoking his pipe serenely. Piandre, the agent of an arms manufacturing company in the States, is a well-known figure the world over. Although we had not met each other before, Piandre smiled at me as at a friend of long standing. For my part, I felt like talking to him about some profound topic. "Poetry is pain; it is an all-consuming thirst; it is a fire flower that blooms in the dark valleys of solitude," I said that much in one breath. Piandre nodded his head in agreement to all that. Then he proffered his hand in perfect amity. Hanging on to that sturdy hand, and lifted high in the air, I fell at the other side of the wall and was filled with glee beyond limits. Whose hand did I catch hold of? Who lifted me off the ground with a single hand? How did I merit such luck?

For what a length of time did I stand transfixed on the path beyond the ahsram, immersed in the headiness of blissful oblivion! The first thing that caught my eye after I resumed walking was an extensive coconut grove. Thousands of coconut palms laden with coconuts growing luxuriantly. At a single glance one can see that they are the high-yielding type. I somehow felt that I should get hold of that grove by any means. I should continue in politics for five or six years more. Then I should put an end to all that and come and stay here with my family. Money for the asking; serenity as much as you want; then the much celebrated existence in perpetual communion with nature. At last, here is a way to reach the fullness of life. For the time being some funds should be organised to make some token advance payment for this coconut grove. That is easily managed if Piandre would give a thought to it.

Koneri Damu himself should be the agent. There is not another man as experienced as Damu in land deals, to my knowledge. Let us forget for the time being that he had moved his wall far out into the public road. If there is any allegation rising against him in the party, that can be silenced in an appropriate manner. It is always better nowadays to be friendly with everyone. Even Gorbachev, who is so much more diligent and worldly-wise than I am, is thinking along these lines. Maturity and equanimity are important, above anything else. All the rest will automatically follow. I have learned some such things in the meanwhile. If I put my mind to it sufficiently, I can go forward with confidence. Yes, here I am, reaching the threshold of success in life. All circumstances are in my favour. Nothing is likely to go away. A careful step . . . just a single step!

Perhaps because of the inordinate excitement, both my eyes were shut tight all of a sudden. When I somehow forced them open, it was my friend's sister whom I saw right in front of me. She came running and caught hold of both my hands and She kissed all over them. Then, leaning on to my shoulder she told me, " You should not have forgotten me; you should not have hidden your love." Seeing her public exhibition of love or hearing her words, I am not sure which young men sitting on the platform under the banyan tree laughed aloud. "What a savage thing to do," their facial expression seemed to say. The group consisted of youths ranging from workers of a communal party having roots only in my Division, to some extremists. Their sarcasm was beyond the limits of my endurance. I was overwhelmed by an intense desire to save my face somehow. I was in a hurry to demonstrate that I had no part whatsoever in this love affair. "Hey! What nonsense is this!" I pushed her aside with a theatrical movement and surged forward. But I faltered in my very first step. I slipped and fell into a deep chasm.

I must have lain unconscious for quite some time. When I opened my eyes and looked around, it was a green grassy expanse that I saw. Her words had enveloped me like a mellow light and like the fragrant air from a distant valley.

I do not know when, but I saw a man dressed in a long, flowing Arabian gown and a gold-laced head-dress moving a little far off. There was a big watermelon in his hand. He was moving forward in a very leisurely manner, tossing the melon high in the air every now and then, and catching it in the palm of one hand. When I ran up and reached his side, he wheeled a round abruptly to face me. His hairless face, though pleasant, was quite pale. "Where are you going? Where are we?" I asked him in some perplexity.

"You started off from the world of the dead. Although you went astray in between, you are now back in the same world." Saying this much, he handed over the watermelon to me, walked away and disappeared from sight.

Again I was alone. The primordial sky and the boundless expanse of green, this watermelon and I. Enough, it is enough now. There is no meaning in my going any further with this story.

There is no golden seed or some other wonder in this watermelon in my hand. Only the red flesh and faintly sweet juice that quench thirst, revive and give one the joy of life for at least a little while. Only one thing I am able to say. It had grown hugging the earth, learning the secrets of the sweetness under the soil. I hope that there is at least one reader who has followed me all this way up. I give it to him.

(Translated by A. J. Thomas)

THE CRY OF THE EARTH
P. Surendran

This Bangarappa will never come back from the hill with the shaving knife. After shaving the head of the fallen one, this knife should be thrown into the temple pond. Drawing all sins through each strand of hair, let this shaving knife go straight to the bottom of the sacred pond.

No, this is not a barber's knife.

Before putting everything into the shoulder bag, Bangarappa took the knife in his hands again. "Let this be your last job," he said.

Suddenly a cry rises from some unfathomable depths: "Please don't shave off my hair. Our jasmine bush is covered with flowers. I want to wear jasmine in my hair and go for the fair in Thirthahalli."

The shaving knife, shuddering once, slashes the tip of his thumb. The smarting wound smothers him. In his brain, an opening of a third window, of a day dream. Then a country road.

On the road, a fast moving, decorated ox cart. In the cart, a bride and groom. On each side of the road, fields of sunflowers. A land of yellow radiance. The groom notices the sunflowers only when awakened by the sound of harsh whips falling on the back of the ox. A cloud had covered his eyes as he climbed into the cart. It was the luxurious hair of the bride that her sari failed to hide.

When the wind swept the veil off her head . . . a profusion of jasmines which reminded him of the white clouds that suddenly appear on top of dark hills.

How many flowers to adorn her hair? He asked the sunflowers. The yellow earth swung high and low without answering. And he hid his flustered face from them.

On their first night he murmured in her ear: All round the Karanji pond we should grow jasmine. Then, when the fog of strangeness left her, she hid his face in her hair and made him breathless.

She nursed her hair like hallowed grounds. When she gave the villagers their eyes of wonder, he too began to love her hair.

He bought expensive shell combs from the city along with his farm implements. Every day she oiled and combed her hair. Beautified it with flowers and changed it into a lovely maiden. After her bath when she stood in the sun, with her hair spread to dry, her dancing curls became his fields of millet.

When did the elephants come and trample that field?

When a strong arm stretched itself with a bunch of orange flowers, through the third window, seeing snakes come out of her hair, Bangarappa woke up in horror. He took the thumb out of his mouth to have a look. It was still bleeding.

How much of my blood did I drink? God . . . Bangarappa got up in search of herbs to press on the wound.

That night Bangarappa was in a chasm of horrors. A terrible night it was. A long line of people to be tonsured. As he stares at them bewildered, someone gives him a barber's knife. With a whimper he says, "I am not a barber."

Raucous laughter from the crowd, followed by an order from somewhere: From now on, this is your work. You should always be on this hill and you are not ever allowed to put this knife down. You may now begin your work.

After an arduous attempt at shaving the first head, he reaches the second one. By then the first head is full of newly sprouted hair.

Again the jeering of the crowd and a curse from hell: Barber, you shall never go down the hill again.

"I am no barber. I am a farmer. I want to go back to my land." Saying this, he wakes up perspiring profusely.

Listening to some night birds sing of the morn from a tamarind tree, he knows it all to be a dream. A little light dithers through the window. The undeciphered dream disturbs Bangarappa. Deciding that all will be revealed on top of the mountain, he gets up and wakes up Seethamma. His plan is to take the first bus to Veerambadi. To reach the top of the mountain before the heat begins to bounce.

When they reach the bus after a quick morning ablution, it is there, as if waiting just for the two of them. As they settle in, the bus starts. There are very few people in the bus. Bangarappa looks around to see if there is anyone to go up the mountain but finds none. Seethamma didn't sit near Bangarappa. She is in the front seat, all alone. Her red face disturb him. When the bus begins to move her hair falls between the seats, to the floor. When her hair touches his feet Bangarappa jumps up as if bitten by a snake. He is afraid to look at her hair. He retreats to another seat behind and opens the shutters. While looking at the fields covered with fog, the barber's knife runs amock through the hairs of his consciousness. When the knife scrapes over the infected scalp, chopped hair covered with scabs, pus and blood tumble down on him.

This is the pilgrimage of the sinner. After the tonsure, in the soil devoid of sin, seeds of millet should be sowed. In a kiosk of vines on a cold bed . . . he was afraid of the sin filling his heart. Right now his Seethamma is not his. All she is a defiled statue of a goddess. Till it is cleansed it should not be revered in the heart of its priest. He didn't embark on this mountain climbing, with the blind faith of washing all his sins off, with a mere tonsure.

Bangarappa had only seen the Patel's son putting flowers in Seethamma's hair. She said he forcibly put them in her hair and then ran off. "I did not stop for him. I have not sinned. Please don't shave my hair." When she cried that out even in her dream, Bangarappa could easily measure the depth of her sin. If a stranger touches her hair, she can redeem herself by shaving it off. Then if she takes a dip in the sacred pond, she can regain her purity. Never again should Seethamma's hair tempt anyone. All the jasmine in the garden should be uprooted and thrown away.

By the time the bus reached Veerambadi, the sun was bright. The mountain had fully emerged. Bangarappa looked carefully to see if anyone was walking up the path through the fields leading to the mountains. He was alone. A lonely climb is miserable. With someone to talk to, you don't feel the strain.

When you climb the mountain with a sinner, there is nothing but suffering. Seethamma was sobbing as she got down from the bus. Then on the way, often it turned loud and bitter. When they reached the highlands, Bangarappa said:

"This is sacred land. Don't desecrate it with your tears."

Only then did he remember the pot with no water in it. Beyond this place, water is available only on top of the mountain, after a steep climb.

"You stay here. I'll go get some holy water." Saying this, he parted the thick creepers and went in search of water. Bangarappa knew that one of the sacred waters of the seven rivers was somewhere in that plateau.

When he came back with the holy water, Seethama was still crying; it created an echo from the depths of the dense forest. The cry of the wilderness scared him. Seeing Bangarappa, Seethama fell at his feet.

"I do not want to climb the mountain. I have not sinned. You can kill me and throw me down somewhere in this forest. But don't shave me."

By now, Bangarappa had changed completely. He was like the priest with a sickle in his hand, ready to slaughter the sacrificial lamb.

He broke the branch of a tree. As it landed heavily on Seethama's back, a crow flying from somewhere landed on the pooja things. Then he took the scissors and the shaving knife. Seethamma's weary eyes turned to Bangarappa.

"We should climb down the mountain before evening." Bangarappa said.

Seethama sat on a stone, close to the pond, bending her head. Below her the sacred water was like a mirror. The scissors moved and the pond broke in waves. Seethamma closed her eyes. She crushed her lips between her teeth. They were bleeding.

She saw farms with arid fields being ploughed, and the skulls and bones that come out of the parting earth. The wind-swept trees, the oxen running in a frenzy, and then the fields were drowned in a flood of water.

Bangarappa's hands did not tremble. Right then, he didn't remember anything. Neither the carriage that ran amidst the blazing sunflower fields, nor the gardens of jasmine. Not even the tired, hot night when he slept with his face pressed against her cool hair. He was just a farmer clearing the ground before cultivation.

When the work of the scissors was done, Bangarappa took the knife in his hand. After sharpening it on a stone, he placed it on Seethamma's head. The knife moved, forming a crescent on the scalp. As it grew into a full moon, Bangarappa felt the shedding of sins.

The rhythm of the knife grew tight. It was sheer rapture for Bangarappa. Like the slow losing of strength in a blissful moment of surrender. After the tonsure, throwing the knife in the pond, Bangarappa sat rapped out.

When Seethamma sat at the pond with a parched throat, the crystal-clear water tempted her. But now when she opened her eyes after the tonsure, her thirst was gone.

In the mirror of the water, Seethamma saw her head. It became a white flower and grew as big as the pond. When that whiteness melted into nothingness, in the depths of the water, she saw the blue sky. As she looked on, a white crow appeared in that blue sky. The bird became two, four, five . . . and as they multiplied enough to fill the sky, with the innocence of a child, Seethamma walked into the pond. She cried out in anguish.

Amma . . . Goddess . . .

The sacred pond parted, revealing the emerald steps in front of her.

When everything was over, without even waking the waves, the exhausted Bangarappa's head was still resting between his knees.

Then, when he got up startled by the sound of something crashing, breaking the glassy layers of the sacred pond, a white crow flew up high, lamenting soulfully.

(*Translated by Elzy Zachariah Taramangalam*)

THE PSYCHOLOGY OF LEAN MEN AND WOMEN

Methil Radhakrishnan

If I could imagine, given the situation I was in, that I was a newspaper which had entered a locked-up house through the keyhole, I am also entitled to think that I am much better at analysing situations in minute detail than news reporters. This is a description of the totality of an individual's condition against the background of the totality of a given situation. (If you are familiar with the techniques of cinema, I would call it a montage.) If you are not convinced, consider the following facts. I am a newspaper boy. I deliver two dailies and a weekly magazine for the perusal of the occupants of this double-storeyed house with its walls painted yellow. The house had been locked up for the last five days. I was moving through the pitch darkness inside in the middle of the night. My objective in entering the house, by breaking open the back door effortlessly, was burglary! Now, consider the expression, "a newspaper which had entered the locked-up house through the keyhole". There is another useful aphorism: A news item is somebody else's secret; a house is one's own. Now, consider once more the expression, "a newspaper which had entered a locked-up . . ."

As I pushed open the unlocked door of the room and entered, I realized, even before I switched on the flashlight, that it was a woman's bedroom. Like a newspaper printing reports of events occurring at several different places on the same day, I inhaled the smells emanating from several different points of time: when she came out of the bathroom; when she took out a new dress from the chest and put it on; when she sprayed perfume all over her body; when she perspired again in the middle of her exertions. These smells of events which occurred at different points of time (if you haven't been able, yet, to make out the fact that it is a young woman's bedroom—the pitch darkness not withstanding—well, pleased to meet you, Mr Rishyashringan!) originated from *her*. Yes, undoubtedly. For I had, by now, swept the room with the beam of the flashlight in my hand. Then, making sure that all the windows were tightly shuttered to prevent the light in the room going out, I switched on the light in the room. I had recognized some of the dresses I found in the room. The sari which lay rolled up on the bed—large flowers in pastel colours—I was sure I had seen her wear it. I saw her sitting in the cane-chair in the veranda reading a book, probably a Robert Ludlum paperback, only on the days I delivered the papers late. But I certainly saw her at least once a month—when she paid me the monthly subscription and took the receipt from me. The receipt was made out in her name—Mrs Shobha Gopinath.

What possessed me immediately were, I suppose, the basic instincts. Though her soft voice and mild expressions had often generated in me respect and esteem for her, on that night, at that moment, I was swayed by the biological instincts of a young bachelor entering the bedroom of a young woman. The frenzied privacy of her body . . . the agitation it caused in me, as if she were actually present in the room . . . When I picked up the sari with both hands—as if her body was still wrapped in its folds—I was still in the grip of those primitive animal instincts. But there were other items of clothing under the sari: a bra, an underskirt and—reminding me of somebody's wisecrack, "seagulls are the bikinis of God"—a pair of the most intimate of human attire. The animal instincts now thronged my body and the air around. The sari would have caught fire in the static electricity generated when it brushed against my hands. I could have buried my face in those clothes and lost myself in a series of tantalising, even obscene, viciousness. But suddenly, I stood immobilised and embarrassed by a sudden realization of my condition and my mission. I asked myself: Ramachandra, what do you think you are doing? Talk about newspapers reading their readers!

I know what I am doing, repeating this to myself over and over again to expose myself, like removing the veil of a nun in public. I ascended and descended the stairs several times, opened and shut the doors over and over again and walked up and down the house for a long time. The cups and dishes in the kitchen, the toothbrushes and tongue-cleaners in the bathroom (they must have forgotten to take them when they left), the clothes hanging on the pegs on the wall, the pair of sandals on the floor, the letters lying scattered on the table ... I was carrying out a plan. If I was burgling the house, it was not a significant event. Suppose that I had turned to burglary because I could not subsist on the commission I got from selling elite, highbrow dailies and weeklies. This was a fact, a situation which could easily be accepted. It was fully supported by both sociology and statistics. But Ramachandra, that is not the problem. It is not that trivial.

The problem was something else (meanwhile I had returned to the woman's bedroom). Yes, this was the problem: This bra, these panties ... the whole room! This was somebody else's privacy. The privacy that could be obtained by shutting oneself off from the world's eyes, behind closed doors and shuttered windows, an identity detached from the multitude; the political freedom of the individual, which even a lifeless mirror can understand; the existence of separate houses, separate rooms in them, and separate closets, even in those countries which practice collective farming; your wife, if you have one, not being somebody else's wife as well—all these are the result of conventions which emerged from the recognition and approval of this privacy. We are, however, not concerned with the ethics of closets or the politics of private property, but with the underclothes of urbanity itself. Ramachandra, to put it in a nutshell, burglary is a kind of rape, not different from the act of breaking into the nakedness and privacy of a woman.

To make a long story short, I was compelled to leave without removing anything from the house. Embarrassed, at a loss as to which part of my body I should hide with my hand. I felt like one caught peeping into an occupied bathroom, like a man standing naked on a thoroughfare. It was at this point that I realized that the nakedness of the soul could be exposed as demeaningly as the nakedness of the body. I switched off the light in the room. I had begun to get the idea it was a spotlight turned on me and that I was confronted by a restive audience roaring obscenely, boos and catcalls raining on me like rotten eggs and tomatoes. Then, in the light of the flashlight (ha! that was my private light) I did something which may be construed as childish and inexplicable. I picked up a pencil and a piece of paper from the table and wrote in large letters on the centre of the paper:

"*Mappu*"[1]. In the morning when I had gone to the town to take the bundle of newspapers, my friend Verghese had given me a gift—a steel bracelet. I remembered it when my shirt-pocket, soaked in sweat, sagged with its weight. I took it out and kept it on the piece of paper. The word I had written on the paper was fully enclosed by the circle of the bracelet. It struck me that the bracelet was a magnifying glass as well as a paperweight. This action of mine, with the childish imagination behind it, made me very happy for some inexplicable reason. But I had the presence of mind to remember that the bracelet would function as a magnifying glass in the hands of a detective if his services were solicited. But it was also a paperweight! Reassured by its pressing down firmly on the piece of paper, dispelling all my anxieties, I stepped out of the house through the backdoor and closed it gently behind me.

I knew the household (the young woman, her mother and a boy who looked about seven years old) were to return the next morning. On the following day I had quite a few things to attend to. Besides two dailies, I had to deliver the weekly *Mandate Azhchappathippu*, collect the monthly subscription, and, finally, monitor any signs of the household having detected my attempted burglary and be prepared for their response to it. At first glance, there was no sign of alarm or consternation. Perhaps there was nothing unusual about it. Forgetting to put out the lights before locking the door in a hurry, leaving the windows open—these were quite normal slips for households setting out on a journey (as natural as leaving toothbrushes and tongue-cleaners in the bathroom). There would be a few surprises awaiting them on their return. Recriminations would follow. Finally, when it became clear that nothing untoward had happened, everything would fade away in the process of settling down again. I presumed that it had happened precisely that way here too. When I pressed the doorbell, it was not the old woman, or the boy, or the maid who opened the door. It was the young woman herself. That, too, after an interval of about three minutes. But she explained everything: They had just returned from the trip to Bangalore. Her mother and brother had gone to the temple. When she saw that I had also brought the bill along with the weekly and the dailies, she smiled

---

[1] Mappu - Pardon

vaguely. "Please give me five minutes," she pleaded apologetically. I noticed the exhaustion and drowsiness on her face. As her dishevelled clothes reminded me of the act of rape I had carried out the previous night, I hastily said (though I needed the money badly) "It's all right, I'll come later." "Please sit down," her voice was firm. She was visibly irritated by my deferential manner. The slightly raised voice suited her tall, lean, firm body!

When she disappeared into the house, I sank into a chair. I would have stood rooted to the ground if she hadn't asked me to sit down. Sitting on the chair, I reflected: I did have with me a comparative study of lean and fat people! Fat men and women are fond of gestures like shaking hands and hugging, which involve overt physical contact. Lean men and women are allergic to such gestures. It is a resistance that lies dormant in their bones. The maid brought a cup of tea on a saucer. What was I to read in the cup of tea, a hint of delay, or the threat of an interview? All right, it didn't matter. But what was the problem with lean folks? They are very stout about preserving their privacy. Ha! Ha! The young woman cut the flow of my thoughts as she came into the veranda. She had combed her hair and changed her clothes. Did the threat of an interview loom large before me? She held, between the fingers of her right hand, a few currency notes spread out like the cards of a card-sharper. Lowering herself onto the settee, she placed the notes on the table. I noticed it only when she withdrew her hand from the table and leaned back. She had kept a paperweight on the currency notes, a potential magnifying glass to magnify the signature of the Reserve Bank governor. Yes, my steel bracelet! While I was negotiating the precarious moments when the cup and saucer would have rattled in my hands, she said:

"I suppose this is your bracelet?"

"Yes."

"You can take it back."

I obeyed her, but not before asking, "How did you find out?" I knew the question was unnecessary as well as absurd. Even if she did not possess the intelligence I attributed to her, she would have come to the obvious conclusion by comparing the handwriting on the bill with my apology note of the previous night. More precisely—if you have not noticed it already—the first and last syllables of *'Mandate Azhchappathippu'*[2] joined in that order gives you the word, *mappu*! My question was like a seive fabricated with minute holes to collect myself as I shrunk into a worm or a speck of dust and threatened to slip through. In the last chapter of detective novels, the sleuth is entitled to a certain amount of exhilaration; the ecstasy of exposure and explanation. Why should I deny her that ecstasy? Perhaps she had read my thoughts. Ignoring my question, she remarked: "It's amazing that you secretly wished to be caught!" She then went on to narrate an incident involving a bracelet. Her husband, Gopinath, used to wear such a bracelet. Once when Shobha and Gopinath were returning after their shopping, there was another man in the lift with them—an old Sardarji. He asked Gopinath why he was wearing the bracelet. Controlling his annoyance, Gopinath indignantly asked the Sardarji what he meant by the question. The Sardarji apologized for his indiscretion. But he added: you shouldn't touch a cigarette with the hand that wears this bracelet. Gopinath did not smoke. Yet the Sardarji went on: don't smoke or drink with the hand . . . "But," I interrupted, "I didn't wear the bracelet. It was in my pocket." She stared at me for a moment, astonished. Then, she tossed back her hair and laughed. No, she was not amused by what I had done. She was reminded of her husband. Why did the Sardarji's curiosity annoy him? She stopped laughing and asked me: "How much do you know about me?"

That was quite unexpected. There was a certain discontinuity about it—like in the middle of a game of bridge, when one of the players suddenly starts picking and discarding cards as if he were playing Rummy. I peered into this discontinuity. That is the secret of womanhood. It is this discontinuity that we have in mind when we say that the moods and habits of a woman are subject to sudden changes—a respite, an interval which men invariably miss. There was a continuity in that interval, like the continuity of the land mass under the surface of the ocean. It was at this interval that I looked. Unable to decipher anything, I retreated to conversation. Pseudo-psychological formulas about lean and fat people apart, what did I really know about this young woman? I knew that it was less than two years since Shobha married Gopinath; that Gopinath owned a film distribution

---

[2] Azhchappathippu - Weekly magazine

company at Bangalore; that Shobha had returned from Bangalore about eight months back; that Gopinath had not visited her since; that it was only in the previous week that she had gone to Bangalore next; that the neighbours who had been busy with their conjectures and gossip, were now fed up with the subject; that Shobha's recent trip to Bangalore had revived their interest... All these were the headlines. I didn't attempt to read the details. From a long association with newspapers, it was natural for a person like me to think that nothing was news until it was published in the papers.

"Let me tell you the rest," she said. "I went to Bangalore to finalise the formalities of our divorce. Everything is over now. I have come back alone, legally separated. I am now an individual who is free to stand alone before the mirror. There are no strange shadows in my bedroom. The only shadow you will find is mine, apart from my body and my mind. I have often felt that a mirror represents the limits of our freedom—a mirror to show the wrinkles of only one face. It is like the insignificance and death of a single individual. That is the relationship between liberty and death. Life mixes up everybody. Death identifies one individual from all others. Like a man who picks out his girlfriend from a large crowd, your death and the mirror in your bedroom pick you out. But I didn't say—nor did you ask—why I left my husband. He didn't have that quality abundantly possessed by the man who broke into my house to burgle it, the quality of respecting other people's privacy! I cannot explain more. You are a bachelor."

I am on the road again, pedalling along on my bicycle. My movements resembled an acrobat's, for there was something stout perched on my back. Yes, the same reflection on fat and lean people. Well, to continue the train of thought... What was the first law governing lean people? They hate formal, overt physical contact. What was the second law governing lean people? They had an overwhelming desire for informal, covert physical contact. Those who violate the first law (her husband Gopinath, for example) necessarily violate the second too. This reflection about lean people amused me. Instead of asking me why I am amused, ask me why the tyres of my bicycle have flattened. Yes, the reason is that I am fat, and since I am fat, and since fat people like to shake hands and hug others, let me confess, at some juncture in our conversation, I longed to embrace her and kiss her passionately.

Yes, momentarily, I ardently desired to love her, to know her, to journey to the depth of her veins, to turn her inside out like a glove. But there was a risk involved. It was invasion of an individual's privacy! Her mind, in its moments of privacy, would have appropriated God, or even a whole mob. But, but . . . how terrified she must have been till a few days ago to look into the mirror. Was there the shadow of a stranger stalking her? However, my job was not to love her, but to bring her newspapers. Now consider, once more, the expression, "a newspaper which had entered a locked-up house through the keyhole"!

BRIEF NOTES ON AUTHORS

Vaikom Mohammed Basheer (1908-1994) Born at Thalayolapparambu. Left home while in the fifth form to take part in the Salt Satyagraha in Calicut. Worked as accountant, teacher, cook, *khalazi* in a ship, hotel worker, mill-labourer, magician's assistant, book-seller etc. Wandered in India and abroad. Spent time with Hindu and Sufi monks. Settled in Beypore after a belated marriage. Authored 32 works including *Balyakala Sakhi* (Childhood Friend) *Ntupuppakkoranendarnnu* (My Granddad Had an Elephant) *Sabdangal* (Voices), *Matilukal* (Walls) and *Pattummayude Adu* (Pattumma's Goat). Won several awards and honours including Sahitya Akademi award (1972) and fellowship, Padmasri (1982) honorary doctorate from Calicut University and the *tamrapatra* for freedom fighters from the Government of India.

Thakazhi Sivasankara Pillai (b.1912) Born at Thakazhi. Became a lawyer after passing pleadership examination in Ambalappuzha. *Thottiyude Makan* (Scavenger's Son, 1947) was his first important novel. He authored more than 25 novels including *Randitangazhi* (Two Measures of Paddy), *Chemmeen* (Shrimp) and *Kayar* (Coir). Awards and honours include Sahitya Akademi award and fellowship, Jnanpith Puraskar (1984) and Padmabhooshan (1985). Lives with his wife, Kaattha, in Thakazhi in Central Kerala.

Ponkunnam Varkey (b. 1910) Born at Edathwa. Was jailed for participation in the Travancore State Congress rebellion. Co-founder of National Book Stall in Kottayam. Suffered assaults verbal and physical, for having stood against the Church and the landlords. Was President of the Kerala Sahitya Akademi and the Writers' Co-operative Society in Kottayam. Works include *Sabdikkunna Kalappa* (The Whispering Plough), *Democracy, Aramam* (The Garden), Selected stories in 2 volumes, *Jetakkal* (The Victors). *Visarikku Kattu Venda* (The Fan Needs no Breeze (Plays) and *Ente Vazhithiruvu* (My Turning Point (Autobiography).

Uroob (P.C. Kuttikrishnan) (1915-1979). Born at Ponnani in Malabar. After education worked as Staff Artist in All India Radio, Calicut (1915-75); later became editor, first of *Kumkumam* and then of of *Malayala Manorama* weeklies. Authored eight novels including *Ummachu*,

Mindappennu (The Silent Girl) and *Sundarikalum Sundaranmarum* (The Beautiful and the Handsome), 21 collections of short stories, 4 plays, 3 books for children and 2 collections of essays.

P. Kesavadev (1904-1983) Born at Paravur. Studied upto third form. Communist ideologue and trade unionist. Was President of the Kerala Sahitya Akademi and the Writers' Co-operative Society. Won Kerala Sahitya Akademi award and the Soviet land award. Works include novels *Odayil Ninnu* (From the Gutter), *Ayalkkar* (Neighbours), *Nadi* (Actress) and *Swapnam* (The Dream), fifteen collections of short stories including two volumes of selected stories, plays and autobiographical writings.

Karoor Neelakanta Pillai (1898-1975) Born at Ettumanoor. Became a teacher after passing the seventh class from a vernacular school. Founder leader of the Writers' Co-operative in Kottayam as also its first Secretary (1945-65). Has authored 37 books, most of them collections of short stories. Won Kerala Sahitya Akademi award for the short story collection *Mothiram* (The Ring, 1968) and for children's literature (*Anakkaran*, The Mahout, 1959)

S.K. Pottekkatt (1913-1982) Full name, Sankarankutty Kunhiraman. Born at Putiyara, Calicut. Did various jobs in Bombay from 1939 to '44, with intervals of wandering all, over India. From 1949 his wanderlust grew more intense and took him to various places in the world especially those of anthropological interest. Became Member of Parliament (1962-67). Was President of the Writers' Co-operative and executive member of the Sahitya Akademi. Won Sahitya Akademi award and Jnanpith Puraskar (1981) for the novel *Oru Desathinte Katha* (The story of a Nation).

Kovilan (b.1923) pseudonym of V.V. Ayyappan. He quit the Sanskrit College, Pavaratty where he was a student, inspired by the Gandhian Movement (1942). Served the Royal Indian Navy (1943-46) and Army Signal Corps. (1948-68). Works include, besides short stories, novels *A Minus B*, *Tottangal*, *Himalayan*, *Bharatan* and *Tattakam* and two collections of essays. Has won Kerala Sahitya Akademi award for fiction.

T. Padmanabhan Born at Pallikkunnu near Kannur. Retired as Deputy General Manager from Fertilisers and Chemicals Travancore Ltd. Author of twelve collections of short stories including *Makhansinghinte Maranam* (The Death of Makhan Singh) *Sakshi* (The Witness), *Kalabhairavan* and *Patmanabhante Kathakal* (Padmanabhan's short stories) besides an autobiographical work *Ente Katha, Ente Jeevitam* (My Story, My Life). won Kerala Sahitya Akademi award for short story in 1973 (declined)

M.T. Vasudevan Nair (b.1934) Born at the Koodallur village. Works include novels like *Nalukettu*, *Kalam* (Time), *Asuravittu* (The Dragon Seed), *Manju* (The snow) and *Rantamoozham* (The Second Round) as well as several collections of short stories including *Iruttinte Atmavu* (The Soul of Darkness), *Nashtappetta Dinangal* (The Lost Days), *Bandhanam* (The Bondage) and *Vanaprastam*. Awards and honours include Kerala Sahitya Akademi award, Sahitya Akademi award, Vayalar award and Jnanpith Puraskar. Has also several award winning films and filmscripts to his credit.

M.P. Narayana Pillai (b.1939) Born at Pulluvazhi village. Educated in Muvattupuzha and Banares. Worked in the planning Commission, *Far East Economic Review* and Commerce Publications. Lives in Bombay. Popular economic columnist. His chief works are *Murukan enna Pambatti* (A Snakecharmer called Murukan), collected stories (2 volumes) and the novel *Parinamam* (Evolution) that won the Kerala Sahitya Akademi award (declined).

O.V.Vijayan (b.1931) Born in Palghat district. After a brief stint as a lecturer in English joined *Sankar's Weekly* as a cartoonist in 1958. Worked as cartoonist and columnist in *Patriot*, *Mainstream*, *The Illustrated Weekly of India*, *Mathrubhumi* and *Far East Economic Review*. Works include novels like *Khasakkinte Itihasam* (The Legends of Khasak*)*, *Dharmapuranam* (The Saga of Dharmapuri), *Gurusagaram*, *(The Infinity of Grace) Madhuram Gayati* and *Pravacakan* (The Prophet); collections of short stories like *Kadalteerattu* (On the Seashore), *Kattu Paranja Katha* (The Tale Told by the Wind) and four collections of articles. Several awards including Kerala Sahitya Akademi and Sahitya Akademi awards and Vayalar award.

Kakkanadan (b.1935) Pseudonym of George Varghese. After higher education, joined Karl Marx university in Germany for research, which however, was left incomplete. Worked in Delhi and then edited *Malayalanadu* weekly in Kollam. Novels include *Sakhi* (Witness), *Ezham Mudra* (The Seventh Seal), *Vasoori* (Small Pox) and *Ushnameghala* (The Tropics). Collected stories. Won Kerala Sahitya Akademi award for novel as well as short story.

M. Mukundan (b.1942) Born at Mayyazhi, an ex-French colony. Works at the French Embassy in Delhi. Works include novels like *Delhi, Mayyazhippuzhayude Teerangalil* (On the Banks of River Mayyazhi), *Deivattinite Vikritikal* (The Pranks of God), *Ee Lokam Athiloru Manushyan* (This world, A man in It) and *Adityanum Radhayum*, collections of short stories and on Modernism in art and literature. Awards and honours include M. P. Paul prize, Sahitya Akademi award and Kerala Sahitya Akademi awards.

Punathil Kunhabdulla (b.1940) Born at Onchiyam. Physician by profession. Works include novels like *Smarakasilakal* (The Tombstones), *Marunnu* (Medicine) and *Khaleefa* (The Caliph) and collections of short stories like *Katti* (The Knife), *Malamukalile Abdulla* (Abdulla of the Mountain Top). Awards include Kerala Sahitya Akademi award and Sahitya Akademi award.

Sethu Born at Chendamangalam. Graduated in science and worked in various parts of North India. Now with the State Bank of Tranvancore. Novels include *Pandavapuram, Niyogam* (The Mission) and *Kiratam* and collections of stories like *Dootu* (The Message) and *Guru*. Won the Kerala Sahitya Akademi award for novel.

P.Padmarajan (1954-1991) Born at Mutukulam in Alappuzha. Worked with All India Radio. Novels include *Nakshtrangale Kaval* (Guard us, Stars), *Vatakaykku Oru Hridayam* (A Heart for Rent), *Peruvazhiyambalam* and *Pratimayum Rajakumariyum* (The Statue and the Princess); collections of short stories like *Prahelika* (The Riddle), *Aparan* (The Other) and a collection of screenplays. Won Kerala Sahitya Akademi award for novel. Has won several awards for film scripts and direction.

Zachariah (b.1945) Born at Urulikkunnam in Meenachil. Worked as lecturer in English in Kanjirappally and Bangalore, as manager of a factory in Coimbatore, ran a publishing firm in Delhi, was with P.T.I., and is now with Asianet, a private television channel. His collections of short stories include *Kunnu* (The Hill), *Arkkariyam* (Who knows), *Nasraniyuvavum Govli Sastravum* (the Christian Youth and the Science of Omens), *Oridathu* (In Another Country), *Bhaskara Patelarum Ente Jeevitavum* (Bhaskara Patelar and My life) and *Salam, America*. Won Kerala Sahitya Akademi award for short stories and Kerala government's award for filmscript.

Anand (b.1936) Pseudonym of P. Sachidanandan. Was born at Irinjalakuda in Trichur district. Engineer by profession. Was in the Military Service in various places in India including Bombay, Gujarat ar W. Bengal; retired from Delhi as Director (P.P). Central Water Commission. Also a sculptor and poet. Novels include *Alkkoottam* (The Crowd), *Marana Certificate* (Death Certificate), *Abhayarthikal* (The Refugees) and *Marubhoomikal Undakunnatu* (How Deserts are Made), several collections of short stories including *Veedum Tadavum* (The House and the Prison), *Ira* (The Victim) and *Asantham* (The Disturbed) and contemplative works like *Jaivamanushyan* (The Organic Man). Won several awards including Kerala Sahitya Akademi award for fiction and non-fiction and Vayalar award.

C.V.Sreeraman (b.1933) Spent his childhood in Ceylon; worked in Andaman and Nicobar Islands. Now settled in Central Kerala as a practising advocate. Three stories have been turned into award-winning films. Several collections including *Vasthuhara* (Dispossessed), *Kshurasyadhara* and *Chidambaram*. Awards include Kerala Sahitya Akademi award.

Pattathuvila Karunakaran (1925-1987) Born at Kollam. Studied at Kollam, Madras and New York. After M.A. joined Piers Leslie Co. in Calicut; retired in 1982. Works include *Muni, Nattellikalude Jeevitam* (The Life of Vertebrates) and *Katha* (Collected Stories). Awards include Kerala Sahitya Akademi award.

M. Sukumaran (b. 1943) Born at Chittoor. After S.S.L.C. became a clerk in the Accountant General's Office in Trivandrum in 1963; dismissed in 1974 for trade union activities, ran a publishing house, now works in a printing press. Ten collections including *Marichittillattavarude Smarakangal* (The Monuments for the Living) and *Seshakriya* that won the State Film award for the best story. Awards include Kerala Sahitya Akademi.

N.P. Mohammed (b.1929) Born at Kundungal near Calicut. Worked in P.C.C society; now Resident Editor, *Kerala Kaumudi*, Calicut. Seventeen books including *Thoppiyum Thattavum* (The Cap and the Veil) *Presidentinte Adyatte Maranam* (The President's First Death) and the novel *Deivattinte Kannu* (God's Eye). Won Kerala Sahitya Akademi award and the Sahitya Akademi award.

U.A. Khader (b. 1933) Born in Burma to a Malayali father and a Burmese mother, brought up in Kerala. Studied in Badagara and Madras College of Arts. Worked in Kerala Govt. Health Dept. and A.I.R.; retired in 1990. Seven books including *Thrikkottur Peruma* (The Glories of Thrikkottur) that won the Kerala Sahitya Akademi award.

V.K.N. (b. 1932) V.K. Narayanan Kutty; born at Tiruvilwamala, worked in Malabar Dewaswom from 1951 to 1959 and as a journalist in Delhi from 1960 to 1967. Now settled in his native place. Satirist and scholar. His novel *Arohanam* (The Ascent) won Sahitya Akademi award. Other works include *Adhikaram* (Power) *Anantaram* (Afterwards) novel *Pitamahan* (Grandfather), *Syndicate* and about fifty stories.

Lalitambika Antarjanam (1909-1987) Born at Kottavattam in Travancore. Educated at home. Several collections of short stories. The novel *Agnisakshi* won her the Vayalar award, Odakkuzhal award and Sahitya Akademi award.

K. Saraswati Amma (1991-1975) Born at Kunnappuzha in Trivandrum. After graduation in 1941, worked as teacher for two years and then was in Kerala Government service. First story 'Seetabhavanam' published in *Mathrubhumi* in 1936. 12 volumes include *Pennbuddhi* (Feminine Wisdom), *Streejanmam* (Woman's Life), *Cholamarangal* (Trees for Shade) and *Purushanmarillatta Lokam* (A World Without Men).

Madhavikkutty (b. 1932) (Kamala Das) born in Punnayurkulam in Palghat. Daughter of the poet Balamani Amma. Writes short stories in Malayalam and poetry in English, lived mostly in Calcutta and Bombay. Now settled in Cochin. Several collections of short stories in Malayalam including *Tarisunilam* (The Wasteland), *Pakshiyude Manam* (The Smell of Birds) and *Chandanamarangal* (Sandalwood Trees) besides collected stories. Autobiographical writings: *Ente Katha* (My Story), *Balyakala Smaranakal* (Reminiscences of Childhood). Won Kerala Sahitya Akademi award for short story, Sahitya Akademi award for *Collected Poems* in English besides Kent Award and Asan World Prize for Poetry in English.

Sarah Joseph (b. 1948) Professor of Malayalam, feminist activist; directed the anti-dowry play *Stree* (Woman). Collections include *Papathara* (The Ground of Sin), *Kadinte Sangitam* (The Music of the Woods); and a collection of novellas, *Nanma Tinmakalude Vriksham* (The Tree of Good and Evil).

Manasi (b. 1948) Born at Tiruvilwamala. Discontinued education in chemical engineering. Settled in Mumbai. Two collections of short stories, *Idivalinte Tengal* (The Sob of Lightning) and *Manjile Pakshi* (The Bird in the Snow). Writes rarely.

P. Vatsala (B.1938) Born in Calicut. Headmistress of Govt. Training

School, Calicut. Was Member, S.P.C.S. Directorate and Kerala Sahitya Akademi. Works include *Nellu* (Paddy), *Nizhalurangunna Vazhikal* (Pathways Where Shadows Sleep), *Agneyam* (Of Fire) *Gautaman, Pembi, Trishnayude Pookkal* (Flowers of Desire) etc. Many works deal with tribal life in Wayanadu in North Kerala. Awards include Kerala Sahitya Akademi award.

Gracy Born at Maradi near Muvattupuzha. First story published in 1972. Works as a lecturer in a college in Aluva. Two collections of short stories: *Padi Irangippoya Parvati* (Parvati Who Left Her Home) and *Naraka Vatil* (The Door of Hell).

K.P. Nirmalkumar (b. 1941) Born at Chelakkara. Senior Manager in a public sector bank. First story published in 1968 in *Mathrubhoomi*. Collections include *Jalam* (water), *Oru Sangham Abhayarthikal* (A Band of Refugees) and *Krishnagandhakajwalakal* (Dark Sulphurous Flames). Won Kerala Sahitya Akademi Award in 1972. Recent stories are highly experimental.

V.P. Shivakumar (1947-1993) Born at Mavelikkara. Worked in various Govt. Colleges in Kerala until he died of cancer. Works include *Otta* (The Lone), *Marayogam* (The Village Council) and *Thiruvitamkoor Kathakal* (The Travancore Tales). Translated several modern European writers.

N.S. Madhavan (b.1948) Born at Ernakulam; studied in Ernakulam and Trivandrum. After M.A. in Economics, joined Indian Administrative Service; worked in Bihar and Kerala, now in Delhi. Won the first prize in *Mathrubhumi* short story contest. Two collections: *Choolaimettile Savangal* (the Corpses of Choolaimedu) and *Higuita*. Won V.P. Sivakumar memorial award and Odakkuzhal award.

C.V.Balakrishnan (b.1952) Born at Annur in Kannur. Began to write while still a student. Freelance journalist and filmscript writer. Three novels, including *Ayussinte Pustakam* (The Book of Life), four novellas and four collections of short stories including *Marukara* (The Other Shore).

V.R. Sudheesh (b. 1961) Educated at Talassery and Madras. M.A., M. Phil, teaches in a private centre. Five collections of short stories including *Deivattinu Oru Poovu* (A Flower for God), *Swatantryattinu Vayassakunnu* (Freedom Grows Old) and *Priyappetta Kathakal* (Dear Stories). Edited a collection of short stories on the themes of love and death, and one of love poetry in Malayalam.

N. Prabhakaran (b.1952) Born at Parassinikadavu in Kannur. Lecturer in Govt. Brennen College, Tellicherry. Three collections of short stories including *Ottayante Pappan* (The Lone Tusker's Mahout). Won first prize in *Mathrubhumi* short story contest; Kerala Sahitya Akademi award for the play *Pulijanmam* (The Tiger's Birth). Also writes articles.

P. Surendran (b. 1961) Born at Pappinissery in Eranad. Teaches in a High School. Won prize in *Mathrubhumi* short story Contest. Has made a study of Karnataka's *Devadasi* system with a scholarship from the Kerala Sahitya Akademi. Also writes on art. Three short story collections: *Piriyan Govani* (The Winding Stairs), *Bhoomiyude Nilavili* (The Scream of the Earth) and *Haritavidyalayam* (The Green School); two novels: *Mahayanam* (The Great Journey) and *Samoohyapatham* (Social Studies).

Methil Radhakrishnan Born at Pudiyankom in Palghat. M.A. from Sree Kerala Varma College; was a leftist activist in his youth; worked in All India Radio, Trichur; trained in computers. in U.K., headed the computer department in a Norwegian shipping company in Kuwait; has done research in entomology; writes articles and poems in English and Malayalam; has travelled widely. Two collections of stories including *Nayakanmar Savepetakangalil* (Heroes in Coffins), one collection of eco-political poems. *Bhoomiyeyum Maranatheyum Kurichu* (On Earth and Death).

K. Satchidanandan Born on 28 May 1946 in Central Kerala, India. Postgraduate in English Literature. Professor of English at Christ College in Kerala for 25 years. At present, secretary, Sahitya Akademi, New Delhi. Doctoral thesis on Post-Structuralist literary theory.

Authored 15 collections of poems in Malayalam besides an equal number of collections of translations from world poetry and Indian poetry, a collection of plays and fifteen collections of critical essays, seminar papers, talks and interviews. Edited three avant-garde magazines in Malayalam, three anthologies of modern Malayalam poetry and one anthology of English poetry. Took part in several national and international seminars.

Poems have been translated into all major Indian languages besides English, Russian, Latvian, Serbo-Croatian, Japanese, Vietnamese and Spanish. Anthologies in Hindi, Tamil, Kannada, Gujarati and English. Represented Indian poetry at 'Kavibharati' (Bhopal, 1987), 'National Poets' Meet' (Hyderabad, 1988), 'Kavita Asia' (Bhopal, 1988), 'Valmiki World Poetry Festival' (New Delhi, 1985), 'Sarajevo Poetry Days' (Yugoslavia, 1985), 'Festival of India' (Mosco-Riga, 1988) 'SAARC

Writers' Meet' (Calcutta, 1992), 'Festival of India in China' (Beijing, 1994) and 'North Eastern Zone Poets' Meet' (Shillong, 1994). Won Kerala Sahitya Akademi Award for essays (1984) and for poetry (1989), Sreekant Varma Fellowship for Poetry Translation (1989), The Best Public Observer Prize (IYA, 1986) and Oman Cultural Centre Award (1993).

Printed at : JK Offset Printers, 315, Jama Masjid, Delhi 110 006